Legal U.S. Immigration
Influences on Gender, Age, and Skill Composition

Michael J. Greenwood

and

John M. McDowell

1999

W.E. UPJOHN INSTITUTE for Employment Research
Kalamazoo, Michigan

Library of Congress Cataloging-in-Publication Data

Greenwood, Michael J.
    Legal U.S. Immigration : influences on gender, age, and skill
composition / Michael J. Greenwood and John M. McDowell
    p. cm.
    Includes bibliographical references and index.
    ISBN 9–88099–190–9 (alk. paper). — ISBN 0–88099–189–5 (cloth :
alk. paper)
    1. Immigrants—United States—Econometric models. 2. Human
Capital—United States. 3. United States—Emigration and immigration.
4. United States—Emigration and immigration—Government policy.
I. McDowell, John M.   Title.
JV6465.G74   1999
325.73—dc21   99–38679
                                                        CIP

The facts presented in this study and the observations and viewpoints expressed are
the sole responsibility of the authors. They do not necessarily represent positions of
the W.E. Upjohn Institute for Employment Research.

Cover designed by J.R. Underhill.
Index prepared by Nancy Humphreys.
Printed in the United States of America.

CONTENTS

List of Figures

List of Tables

Acknowledgments

We are indebted to the W.E. Upjohn Institute for Employment Research for providing the grant that allowed us to conduct the research reported here. Our project monitor, Timothy J. Bartik, was patient beyond the call as we struggled to develop and organize the massive data set that underlies our empirical work and to prepare the econometric software necessary to estimate the models. Donald M. Waldman actually wrote this software. Without his assistance we could not have used our preferred econometric technique.

Steven Zahniser provided research assistance throughout the study. His expertise in dealing with the huge Immigration and Naturalization Service Public Use Tapes and building data files therefrom was invaluable.

First Georgia Borgens, then Valerie Cook, and most recently Nancy Kovacic skillfully performed the word processing of the manuscript.

To all who supported our research, we are grateful.

The Authors

Michael J. Greenwood received his Ph.D. in economics from Northwestern University in 1967. He was Assistant and Associate Professor at Kansas State University from 1965 to 1973. During 1971–72, he was a Brookings Economic Policy Fellow in the Economic Development Administration, U.S. Department of Commerce. From 1973 to 1980, Greenwood was Associate Professor and Professor at Arizona State University. Since 1980, he has been Professor of Economics at the University of Colorado at Boulder, where he served as Director of the Center for Economic Analysis from 1981 to 1998. Between 1995 and 1997, he was co-director of the Economic and Social Impacts Group of the United States Commission for Immigration—Reform Mexico-United States Bi-National Migration Project. Greenwood has published numerous papers on both internal and international migration, and he is author of *Migration and Economic Growth in the United States* (Academic Press, 1981).

John M. McDowell received his Ph.D. in economics from the University of California, Los Angeles, in 1979. He has been at Arizona State University since 1978, receiving the rank of Professor in 1990. McDowell has published numerous articles, including many on international migration, in journals such as the *American Economic Review, The Review of Economics and Statistics, The RAND Journal of Economics, Contemporary Policy Issues, Journal of Regional Science, Public Choice, Journal of Economic Literature, Economica, Journal of Economic and Social Measurement, Economic Inquiry, Applied Economics,* Journal of the American Statistical Association, and *Regional Studies.*

1 Introduction

One of the least understood aspects of human migration is the composition of the migration flows. Numerous studies have described migrant composition in terms of measures such as age, education, occupation, income, employment status, gender, and more, but few studies have actually attempted to explain or model such aspects. Why do certain migration flows consist of relatively more men than women, relatively more young than old, or relatively more skilled than unskilled? We do not have good answers to such questions. The primary objective of this study is to model the gender, age, and skill composition of legal immigration to the United States.

For many years, immigration issues were not widely studied, presumably because immigration was not an important source of U.S. population growth, either absolutely or relatively. For example, the foreign-born population increased by about 283,000 during the 1920s and contributed only 1.7 percent of the incremental national population between 1920 and 1930. The Depression discouraged immigration during the 1930s, and World War II prevented immigration during the 1940s. During the 1950s and 1960s, the "baby boom," as it came to be called, attracted far more attention as a demographic phenomenon than immigration. What attention was directed at international migration issues by economists during this period was mainly by economic historians, who focused on the period of unrestricted flows, and by those interested in the "brain drain," who were concerned with the flow of high-level personnel from poor to rich countries (Greenwood 1983).

Immigration to the United States began to change dramatically with the U.S. immigration law enacted in 1965 that opened the door to immigration from Asia (which had virtually been banned since the 1880s). Because European countries were experiencing rapid economic growth in the 1960s, demand for entry from these countries was low, and immigration from the Americas (especially from Mexico) was becoming important.

These changes produced an immigration policy debate that became more heated during the 1970s and (especially) the 1980s, and immigration issues began to find their place in the mainstream literature of economics. The work of Barry Chiswick, who used census microdata to study the earnings assimilation of the foreign-born, was particularly noteworthy. George Borjas, who formed "synthetic" immigrant cohorts using 1970 and 1980 census microdata to also study earnings assimilation, further emphasized the importance of immigration in the economics profession. Today, immigration issues are widely studied and discussed in various social science disciplines.

ECONOMIC EFFECTS OF IMMIGRANTS

Do immigrant workers cause a reduction of domestic wage rates and displace domestic workers from jobs? This question has long been asked in the United States. The United States Immigration Commission, after meeting from 1907 to 1911, concluded that immigration was responsible for many of the poor working conditions then evident in the country. Bernard (1953, p. 57) felt that the Commission misrepresented the impacts of immigrant workers on domestic job opportunities:

> One of the most persistent and recurrent fallacies in popular thought is the notion that immigrants take away the jobs of native Americans. This rests on the misconception that only a fixed number of jobs exist in any economy and that any newcomer threatens the job of any old resident.

Bernard argued that immigrants as consumers cause an expansion of the market and encourage increased investment expenditures, thereby further contributing to increased aggregate demand. Moreover, immigrants contribute importantly to technological progress and entrepreneurial activity. Bernard is suggesting that immigration causes an outward shift of not only the labor supply schedule, but also the labor demand schedule, but he presents no reason why the demand shift should dominate the supply shift. If the supply shift dominated the demand shift, the consequence would be that wages would fall and indigenous workers would be displaced, though not to the extent that would have happened had no offsetting demand shift occurred.

Substantial quantitative evidence suggests that the position advocated by Bernard may have prevailed in the United States up to 1900 and perhaps even to 1920, during which time aggregate economies of scale probably existed. However, opposing evidence also exists; for example, Jerome (1926) showed that during the nineteenth century, immigration rose during expansionary periods and fell during contractionary periods, with the effect that immigration did not contribute to unemployment as much as would be the case if immigration were not so responsive to the domestic business cycle.

Spengler (1958), in a conceptual (rather than empirical) work, argued that the main economic consequences of immigration are derived from two demographic effects of immigration. 1) In the short run, immigration increases the rates of population and labor force growth, which in turns boost the rate of growth of output. 2) Immigration also changes a nation's age composition, favoring working ages and augmenting the nation's labor force, while reducing the dependency ratio (i.e., the ratio of the nonworking population to the total population). Spengler recognizes that this second effect is also short run, with the long-run effect dependent upon such factors as the size, sex composition, continuity, and precise temporal dimension of the flows.

Spengler (1956) also argued that the skill composition of immigration changed as the sources of U.S. immigrants shifted from western and northern Europe to southern and eastern Europe. The "first wave" of immigrants (see p. 37) had served as a catalyst in U.S. economic growth, since it included many innovators and entrepreneurs. He contends that the "second wave" of immigrants, on the other hand, originated primarily in relatively underdeveloped, agriculturally oriented economies, and those immigrants tended to be illiterate and lacking in occupational and industrial skills. However, with American industry becoming more mechanized at about the same time as their arrival, this wave of immigrants satisfied the growing demand for unskilled labor in the nation's cities. Thus, the "second wave" performed a more or less passive role in U.S. economic development.

In general, historical evidence suggests that the direct consequence of immigration was to affect adversely the wages and working conditions of less-skilled domestic workers. As Williamson (1982, p. 254) wrote, "surely, in the absence of mass migrations, the real wage would have risen faster and inequality trends would have been less pronounced." Indirectly, however, the effects of immigration may have been strongly positive. Economies of scale may have been increasing in the aggregate until the early years of the twentieth century, and immigration may have contributed to the faster achievement of these economies. Moreover, immigration's impacts on land and mineral development, as well as on capital accumulation and the general growth of markets, may well have been positive. Hill (1975), studying the period 1840–1880, concludes that the existence of a 10 percent economy of scale would cause observed immigration over the period to increase per capita income by 3.1 percent.

Finally, Williamson (1982) stressed the idea of the "absorptive capacity" of permanent immigrant settlement in the United States, referring to the effects of immigrants on the wages of domestic workers. If absorptive capacity is high, immigration will have little if any depressing effect on wages. Absorptive capacity is high if the native labor force has high supply elasticities (i.e., native secondary workers are crowded out of the labor force), if demand elasticities are high, and, in a dynamic model, if a high elasticity of response of land and capital with respect to immigration prevails. Quantitatively, the forces that presently underlie absorptive capacity may be considerably different than they were historically.

The debate today frequently focuses on illegal alien immigrants (although it could as well focus on less-skilled immigrants in general), and widespread disagreement exists about the effects of immigrants on native-born workers. Briggs (1975a, 1975b) has expressed what might be called the "replacement hypothesis," asserting that illegal aliens depress local wage levels and take jobs that would otherwise be held by native workers. Hartley (1972, p. 66) supports this view, arguing that illegal aliens "displace low income American workers, hampering unionizing efforts, encourage employers to disregard wage, hours, and working conditions statutes and generally depress the labor market."

Other writers have put forth what might be called the "segmentation hypothesis." Abrams and Abrams (1975), for example, have taken a position that the jobs filled by illegal aliens are not at the expense of native workers. They argue that the labor market is sufficiently segmented that American workers are insulated from direct employment effects caused by immigrants.[1] Piore (1979) has pressed this argument even further by arguing that one component of labor demand in advanced industrial societies is for jobs that are simply undesirable to the native labor force. As a consequence of this demand and the failure of the native labor force to meet the demand, a migrant labor market develops and thrives. Marshall (1986) has taken an intermediate position, arguing that while it would be unrealistic to argue that illegal immigrants do not displace any domestic workers, it would equally unrealistic to argue that the displacement is one for one. The "controversy therefore is over the extent of displacement not whether or not it occurs" (p. 26).

The most common approach to studying the economic consequences of immigration is the production-theory approach, which essentially asks whether immigrants and natives are complements or substitutes in production. The magnitudes of the wage and employment changes due to immigration depend upon the elasticities of labor demand and domestic labor supply, the magnitude of any immigration quota, and other assumptions. In general, the more inelastic the demand and supply relationships are, the greater will be the reduction of domestic wages due to a given number of immigrants. Moreover, the displacement effect will be greater the more elastic the domestic labor supply is and the less elastic the labor demand is.

One of the most troubling assumptions of the production-theory approach is that labor is homogeneous. Such an assumption rules out issues of the differing impact of immigration on various members of the native-born labor force. Borjas (1985 and 1987b) provided evidence that earlier immigrant cohorts generally do relatively better (in terms of earnings) than both natives and immigrants in more recent cohorts, thus suggesting that immigrant "quality" has been declining over time. While this evidence is inferential, Borjas (1992) and others (Smith 1991; LaLonde and Topel 1991b) also have noted a decline in observable skills, such as educational attainment, in more recent immigrant cohorts. If U.S. immigration is becoming more oriented toward less-skilled individuals, the most directly relevant demand and supply elasticities are those in the low-wage labor market. Furthermore, if the labor market is indeed nonhomogeneous, issues concerning the ease or difficulty of transferring skills internationally (as well as those associated with the economic adaptability of immigrants and their offspring in the receiving country) take on added importance.

Studies that take the production-theory approach often recognize that the short-term impacts of immigrants on native-born workers may differ from the long-term impacts. In the short run, physical capital is fixed and time is insufficient to accumulate additional human capital. In the long run, however, general capital accumulation and intersectoral shifts of capital may be induced by immigration, and the immigrants themselves may invest in human capital. The domestic groups with which the immigrants initially competed in the domestic labor market may therefore differ from those with which they later compete.

The short-term effects of immigration should be to increase the relative rates of return on factors of production that are complementary to the migrants' skills and resources and to decrease the rates of return of factors that are substitutable for those of the migrants. Thus, for example, if migrant labor can be substituted for native labor, the relative earnings of native owners of capital will rise, whereas native labor earnings will fall. A number of models assume three factors: capital and two classes of labor, skilled and unskilled. Considering the case of three factors of production and assuming a constant elasticity of substitution (CES) production function, Chiswick (1982) suggested that immigration of either type of labor will increase aggregate per capita income.[2] However, migration results in a decrease in the marginal product of native workers who possess the same type of labor skill as immigrants and results in an increase in the marginal product of both capital and the other type of labor. Thus, if immigrants are assumed to be less skilled than the average native worker, immigration will increase the average earnings of skilled workers and owners of capital and decrease the average earnings of low-skilled native-born workers.

The increase in the wage differential between skilled and unskilled workers that results from the inflow of unskilled migrants will set in motion another set of adjustments. Members of the indigenous population who were at the margin between whether to invest in more human capital are now more likely to make such investments. As this skill adjustment occurs, the wages of unskilled workers will rise relative to those of skilled workers. Over time immigrants will also adjust the level of their skills. Consequently, the initial impacts of the immigrants may differ considerably from the ultimate impacts.

EMPIRICAL MEASURES OF THE EFFECTS OF IMMIGRATION

Aggregate Effects

A few studies have attempted to simulate the effects of immigration on native-born workers by using relevant demand and supply estimates. For instance, Johnson (1979) argued that because estimates of the elasticity of supply of low-skilled labor are close to zero, employment among low-skilled native workers will fall only slightly due to immigration, but these estimates imply a strong negative impact on their earnings. In a later paper, Johnson (1980) postulates that in many industries domestic wages are inflexible downward in the short run. Consequently, immigrants who find jobs do so at the expense of the employment of native-born workers. The rate of labor market displacement depends on the magnitude of various parameters. Using a plausible range of these parameters, Johnson (1980, p. 335) suggested "a labor market displacement effect that is only around 10 percent."

Using cross-sectional data for 1970, Grossman (1982) estimated a translog production function to determine the substitutability between capital, employed native workers, employed second-generation native workers, and employed foreign-born workers. Based on measures derived from factor-share equations estimated for 19 standard metropolitan statistical areas (SMSAs) for 1969, she concluded that "both second generation workers and foreign workers are substitutes for native workers, but second generation workers are much more highly substitutable for natives than are foreign-born workers. In-migrants substitute for second generation workers more easily than for native workers" (p. 599).

Considering the effect of a 10 percent increase in the number of legal U.S. immigrants and assuming that the wage rates of native workers are downwardly rigid (as they might be in the short run), she concludes that native employment would fall by only 0.8 percent and wages of the foreign-born would fall by 2.2 percent. In the long run, however, if all wages were flexible, native workers would suffer about a 1.0 percent decrease in wages, second-generation workers a 0.8 percent decrease, and foreign-born workers a 2.3 percent decrease, but the price of capital would rise by 4.2 percent. Thus, Grossman (1982, p. 602) concludes that "large inflows of immigrants . . . do not pose serious economic threats to natives, although the effects are not negligible."[3] These findings are consistent with Borjas's (1986a) conclusion that during the 1970s, male immigrants failed to affect the earnings of black men but had a small negative influence on the earnings of native white men.

Grossman's empirical results are now widely accepted, but her estimates must be interpreted with caution.[4] Using a production-theory approach but with a special form of the normalized quadratic functional form, Greenwood, Hunt, and Kohli (1996) found that, in the short run, an exogenous increase in the number of (recent) immigrants causes the employment of native workers to fall, but the effect is quantitatively small. This decrease in employment of native workers contributes to a short-run decline in gross domestic product, but this decline is also quantitatively small. Because the rental price of capital rises, owners of capital are better off. In the long run, the wages of native workers fall only slightly. However, the wages of recent immigrants fall considerably. The wage of nonrecent immigrants rises, which suggests that recent immigrants are more like native workers than nonrecent immigrants.[5]

Given the differences in underlying methodologies and data sets examined and Borjas's inclusion of controls for the skill levels of individuals, the similarity of the findings of Borjas (1986a), Grossman (1982), and Greenwood, Hunt, and Kohli (1996)—that immigrants have had a very small (negative) impact on the earnings of the native-born population—is of considerable interest. Indeed, a recent study by the National Research Council (1997, p. 5–23) concluded that "the weight of the empirical evidence suggests that the impact of immigration on the wages of competing native-born workers is small—possibly reducing them by only 1 or 2 percent." These findings, however, imply nothing about how quickly the economy adjusts to an exogenous change in labor supply. Even though the resulting change in wages may be small, adjustment costs may be large.[6]

Moreover, in each study, different immigrant groups are aggregated into a single homogeneous population. Several important issues are raised by this approach. First, since existing evidence illustrates that immigrants of different racial and ethnic background differ in terms of the characteristics they possess upon arrival in the United States, one may question whether immigration's impacts on native workers differ by race and/or ethnic origin. Furthermore, the various analyses deal primarily with the impact of legal immigrants on broadly defined classes of native workers. Therefore, their conclusions may be questioned, because more finely defined subclasses of workers may have impacts that are unidentified.[7]

Subgroup Effects

The impacts of racial and ethnic groups were studied in the 1980s by, among others, Borjas (1986a, 1986b, 1987a), Stewart and Hyclack (1986), King et al. (1986), and DeFreitas (1988). The conclusions of those who have developed more or less direct evidence regarding the aggregate effects of immigration on native workers (as a whole) refute the segmentation hypothesis in its extreme form. Immigration appears to cause a decrease in employment of low-skilled, native-born persons, but only a small decrease. The wages of such workers probably fall also, but again only slightly. Subdividing of the domestic labor market and further refinements in classifying immigrant groups have led to similar conclusions of negligible or, at most, very small immigration impacts. Interestingly, these impacts are sometimes positive. DeFreitas' (1988) view of immigration, as a sequential process in which some newcomers integrate into ethnic job clusters and, over time, disperse from these enclaves to exert competitive pressures on low-skilled native workers, seems to be a plausible explanation for some of the observed coexistence of complementary and substitution relationships. However, it should be noted that analyses based on 1990 data are still rare. The large influx of the 1980s and its focus on California could have changed the various relationships.

Others have studied the effects of immigrants on young workers. Matta and Popp (1988) as well as Kimenyi (1989) argued that recent immigrants are substitutes for low-skilled native-born workers. Wingarden and Khor (1991) found only small effects of illegal aliens on teenagers' unemployment, but Borjas, Freeman, and Katz (1992) found a significant impact of trade and immigration on the most disadvantaged U.S. workers.

Industry-Specific Effects

Although the aggregate supply of unskilled labor may be quite inelastic and the aggregate demand for such labor is elastic, conditions may be considerably different in specific industries or occupations. Consequently, while the effects of immigrants on the total employment of unskilled persons and on their national average wage may be small, the effects on workers at a subnational level could be considerable, yet obscured in the aggregate.

Differences in age and educational composition, combined with less-than-perfect transferability of skills to the U.S. labor market, contribute to an occupational distribution of recent immigrants that is somewhat more oriented toward less-skilled occupations. The U.S. workforce as a whole is considerably more concentrated in the managerial and professional and in the technical, sales, and administrative support occupations than is the new immigrant population; immigrants are more concentrated in service and in operator, fabricator, and laborer occupations. Immigrants who have been in the United States for a longer period have an occupational distribution that is similar to that for all U.S. workers, which suggests either that the older immigrants had a different initial bundle of skills or that over time they were assimilated into the U.S. economy.

Industry-specific studies have been conducted for agriculture (Duffield 1990; Mines and Martin 1984); manufacturing (DeFreitas and Marshall 1984; Waldinger 1985; Maram and King 1983); and the service sector (Maram and King 1983). The many industry case studies are largely descriptive (as opposed to analytical) contributions, but taken as a whole, two conclusions emerge. First, in certain industries located in specific regions, such as Los Angeles and New York, employment displacement effects of immigrant workers are clearly evident.[8] These negative effects are frequently felt by earlier cohorts of immigrants, but native-born workers also suffer job displacement. Second, employers find immigrant hiring networks to be advantageous. No study has specifically analyzed why these networks are advantageous, but we can infer that relatively substantial cost savings must be realized through the use of network hiring.

Region-Specific Effects

The concentration of the foreign-born population of the United States differs considerably by census division and state. Whereas earlier immigrants of European origin tended to locate in eastern cities and then spread out from there, contemporary immigrants from Asia and the Americas tend to locate in western and southern areas. For example, in 1980, 40.9 percent of Miami's employees and 23.9 percent of Los Angeles's employees were foreign-born, but only 6.0 percent of Detroit's and 4.7 percent of Denver's. Such differential concentrations of the foreign-born suggest that the economic impacts of immigrants may differ in various regions of the United States, even though labor and capital flows along with interregional trade presumably spread and smooth the effects somewhat nationally. Studies of regional effects have included those of Smith and Newman (1977), Davila and Mattila (1985), Muller and Espenshade (1985), McCarthy and Valdez (1986), Card (1990), and LaLonde and Topel (1991a, 1991b).

In general, the empirical evidence appears to indicate that in areas where immigrant concentrations are particularly high (such as the southwestern border and Los Angeles), some wage-depressing effects are evident.[9] Moreover, some job displacement also seems to exist. These effects are most concentrated among the less-skilled and lower-income native residents of these regions.

More research is clearly required to identify the markets in which the immigrants compete, as well as to measure the relevant demand and domestic labor supply elasticities in these markets. One observation seems clear, however. The more narrowly defined the industrial sector and/or the region in question, the more likely are investigators to find negative consequences of immigration to native workers and earlier immigrant groups.

STUDIES BEYOND PRODUCTION THEORY

One of the major problems with most existing studies is that they focus on a single channel of immigrant influence, the production-theory channel; that is, they are concerned with whether immigrants and natives are substitutes or complements in production. However, immigrants may also influence native workers through a number of other channels, and these additional influences may offset or reinforce those exerted through the production-theory channel (Greenwood 1994; Greenwood and Hunt 1995). Another problem in many studies is that labor and capital mobility are not incorporated explicitly.

The production-theory effect can lead to either a decrease or an increase in aggregate labor income depending on whether immigrants and natives are complements or substitutes and the size of the relevant elasticities. Consequently, this effect can lead to higher or lower levels of local demand in an area. Moreover, the greater the wealth of the immigrants, the larger their sources of nonlabor income, and therefore the greater will be the stimulation of local final demand in an area due to immigrant settlement there.

Agglomeration effects—economies that accrue to an entire area due to increased population and scale—are rarely considered in the context of immigration, and the internal migrations caused by immigrants' effects on local wages are also seldom focused on. These channels of influence (and others) could be integrated into a single model, and two recent studies introduce channels of immigrant influence beyond the production-theory channel. The first of these is by Altonji and Card (1991), who developed a structural model that in addition to production theory includes output demand and exports from the metropolitan region. Their local demand effect occurs through increased population. Four skill categories of native labor are considered, and each is low-skilled. Altonji and Card did not econometrically estimate many of their model's parameters, did not explicitly include capital as an input, and did not explicitly incorporate labor mobility. They estimated parts of their model with 1970 and 1980 census data for 120 SMSAs. Although their econometric results are somewhat sensitive to the specification and estimation procedure used, their preferred results suggest that "a 1 percentage point increase in the fraction of immigrants in an SMSA reduced less-skilled native wages by roughly 1.2 percent" (p. 226).

The second recent study that introduces several channels of immigrant influence is by Greenwood and Hunt (1995). The main distinguishing features of this study are that it includes capital, explicitly models area supply-and-demand relationships in a structural manner, and incorporates several channels through which immigrants may affect natives, including production theory, local demand (including immigrant demand separately), net export demand, labor force participation, and migration. Both capital and labor are mobile.

Greenwood and Hunt used the recently available Gross State Product Accounts, which represent a more comprehensive database than that available to previous researchers, to estimate capital and output. Simulation results indicate that although immigrants and natives are substitutes in production, when other channels of influence are taken into account, the negative effects stemming from substitutability in production are substantially mitigated. Moreover, under certain assumptions the effects on native wages and employment are positive, which in turn leads to a positive correlation between native migration and immigration (similar to the observation made by Butcher and Card [1991] with respect to the 1980s).[10] However, increased immigration causes somewhat lower wages among the foreign-born, which is consistent with previous studies using alternative models.

IMMIGRANT COMPOSITION AND ITS IMPORTANCE

Immigrant composition is important, because who is permitted to enter may differentially affect the U.S. economy, native-born workers, and prior immigrants. The economic consequences of immigration to the United States are far-reaching, and they depend upon the characteristics of the immigrants. Given the fact that legal immigration is currently at or near historical highs, the compositional aspects of the immigrant population assume commensurate importance.

Gender is one of these important compositional aspects. Although little research has ever been conducted on the economic effects of immigrant females versus immigrant males, these effects are likely to be considerably different. First, females are less likely than males to be "economic migrants," or migrants motivated by economic advantages and costs. Female immigrants tend to have lower labor force participation rates and lower earnings than their male counterparts. Female immigrants therefore contribute less to taxes (such as income and Social Security taxes) than male immigrants. They tend to have a higher probability of part-time employment, and they sometimes compete in labor markets that are not common for males (e.g., day care, in-home cleaning services). Moreover, females have longer life expectancy than males, so those female immigrants who qualify for social services and generally for social benefits (such as Social Security and Medicare, as well as Supplemental Security Income) will, on average, demand them for a longer period of time. Finally, the child-bearing capacity of female immigrants increases the growth potential of the second-generation immigrant population and the U.S. population as a whole.

The age composition of immigration also is important. For instance, the age at which immigrants enter the United States is a determinant of the benefits that will be derived from their presence in the country. Other things being equal, immigrants who migrate at younger ages assimilate more rapidly into the U.S. labor force and therefore, since younger immigrants also have more years over which they contribute to the U.S. economy, they provide greater benefits to the United States. Furthermore, younger immigrants tend to be more proficient in English-language skills during their subsequent post-entry years than immigrants who enter at older ages. Greater proficiency in English-language skills further augments the immigrants' labor force productivity and also facilitates their more general social and cultural assimilation. In addition, the age composition of immigrants may influence the magnitude of the costs that immigrant families impose on the U.S. economy, since age composition importantly determines the dependency ratio within newly entering immigrant families. Immigrant families that arrive in the United States with young children may impose costs on social service providers (such as the public school system), but the returns to these investments (such as to education) may not accrue until many years in the future.

On the other end of the age spectrum, individuals who migrate at older ages may constitute a net burden on the U.S. economy, since they enter at ages at which their reliance on certain social services (e.g., health care) may be particularly high. Yet, age and human capital accumulation (in the form of formal education and job experience) go hand-in hand. Thus, in addition to implications for entrepreneurship and technical change, the immigration of older persons typically implies a potential direct impact on older native workers. They also have more nonlabor income, which more positively affects local labor demand, and their greater assets allow older immigrants to actively participate in housing and other (e.g., stock) markets. For these and other reasons, the age of immigrants is an important determinant of their economic impacts, but this aspect of immigration has not been extensively studied.

Finally, the skill composition of immigrants has many potential effects on the U.S. economy. The supply of highly skilled immigrant workers is often stressed as a matter of critical importance to the maintenance of a vibrant and competitive U.S. workforce in an economy that is increasingly becoming more globalized. Moreover, in an era of rapid technological change, highly skilled workers are necessary to keep productivity at the frontiers of technological developments. Yet, many of the studies that conclude that less-skilled immigrants have small but non-negligible impacts on the least-skilled domestic workers use data from 1970 and refer to immigration that occurred during the 1960s. Not only was immigration somewhat greater during the 1970s and 1980s than during the 1960s, but it also appears to have shifted toward less-skilled migrants. Several other studies have concluded that more highly skilled native workers are positively affected or perhaps are unaffected by immigration, again at least in the short run. In general, however, the literature is lacking in studies that identify precisely why the more highly skilled workers enjoy short-run benefits. Such benefits could result from factor complementarity, from the demand effects of the immigrants, from capital accumulation directly related to immigration, and/or from other causes.

In addition, migrant skill levels may be linked to many of the influences discussed earlier in the context of the age composition of migrants. Highly skilled workers are more economically productive than less skilled workers. Therefore, highly skilled workers add more to overall U.S. productivity, and their higher incomes contribute more to the private sector in the form of consumption expenditures and to the public sector in the form of tax payments. In addition to their higher incomes, highly skilled workers generally have higher levels of education. By virtue of their education and innate abilities, such workers are likely to be more proficient in English when they enter the United States, and if they are not, to learn English-language skills more quickly, and therefore they are able to assimilate more rapidly in the

U.S. economy. Given the linkage between skill level and income/education levels, the skill composition of immigrants also may influence the dependency ratio within immigrant families, as well as affect the overall U.S. fertility rate in subsequent years. Crime rates too are related to income and education levels. Therefore, the skill level of migrants should affect the extent to which immigrants impose a net cost on U.S. society.

OVERVIEW OF THIS STUDY

The research that is described here is based on a "human capital" approach to immigration. Although we attempt to account for factors such as political conditions and religion in source countries, much of our focus is on the benefits and costs of migrating legally to the United States. Such a focus entails explanatory variables such as relative per capita gross domestic product (GDP) and distance to the United States from source countries of immigrants. Because all sorts of institutional impediments inhibit free international movement, the force of economic incentives is blunted. Consequently, the models developed below attempt to control for institutional restrictions in two ways. First, we distinguish those immigrants who are numerically restricted under U.S. law from those who are exempt. Second, we introduce a number of "policy controls" as independent variables in our various models. These controls reflect such factors as naturalization to U.S. citizenship of persons born in different countries, as well as various programs (e.g., lotteries) that may have caused deviations from otherwise "normal" admission procedures.

Perhaps the most unique type of variable included in the study is a vector or set of source-country social program indicators. Four types of social programs are examined: 1) old-age pension systems, 2) sickness and maternity programs, 3) unemployment insurance programs, and 4) family allowances. We anticipate that because such programs involve transfers or redistributions between various groups in source countries, they influence the differential economic advantages of residing in various countries relative to residing in the United States. Thus, such programs will play a role in influencing not only the rate of legal migration to the United States, but also the gender, age, and skill composition of the migrants.

As an illustration of our thinking regarding the importance of social programs in source countries, consider unemployment insurance programs, which involve transfers from older workers with lower unemployment rates to younger workers with higher unemployment rates. In a typical country, the unemployment rate of persons in their twenties may be three times higher than that of persons in their forties. The younger workers also have migration propensities that are often three or four times higher than those of workers 20 years older. Thus, the benefits of unemployment insurance programs accrue differentially to an age class that otherwise has a high propensity to migrate. Consequently, such programs should discourage migration, and especially the migration of younger persons, while twisting the age composition of U.S. immigration toward older persons. Similar modes of thinking underlie many other social programs examined in this study.

The study is organized as follows. Chapter 2 sketches the history of U.S. immigration policy, and Chapter 3 provides a brief history of U.S. immigration. Chapter 4 provides details on the data that underlie the models that are estimated in Chapters 5 through 8. Chapter 5 discusses a model of the determinants of overall U.S. immigration. Chapters 6, 7, and 8 develop models of the gender, age, and occupational composition of U.S. immigration, respectively; the models also distinguish immigrants who are numerically exempt under U.S. law from those who are numerically restricted. Chapter 9 provides a summary and conclusions.

Notes

1. Also see Gordon (1975).
2. A CES production function requires that each elasticity of substitution between input pairs be equal, which in turn implies that no differential pattern of factor complementary exists.
3. Grossman's analysis is based on the assumption that characteristics of immigrants are similar to those of U.S. legal, employed residents in 1969. Since these characteristics may have changed over time, the conclusions may also have to be modified somewhat.

4. Greenwood, Hunt, and Kohli (1996) point out that her estimated production function is not well behaved and that it fails to satisfy the required concavity conditions.

5. Greenwood, Hunt, and Kohli suggest that the result appears to be consistent with findings regarding immigrant assimilation that indicate age-earnings profiles of immigrants that are initially lower than those of otherwise comparable native counterparts, but after a period of years catch up with and later surpass those of the natives. They are also consistent with declining immigrant quality over time.

6. Simon, Moore, and Sullivan (1993) report evidence of little or no observed increase in aggregate native unemployment, even in the relatively short run during which adjustment costs should be most severe.

7. Questions may also be raised concerning the relevance of the conclusions to the assessment of the impact of undocumented aliens on domestic workers. For evidence related to impacts of undocumented workers, see Bean, Lowell, and Taylor (1988), DeFreitas (1988), the companion U.S. General Accounting Office reports (1986, 1988), and Grossman (1984).

8. The fact that case studies reveal the most negative impacts on native and legal workers is not particularly surprising. Research employing the case-study methodology focuses on situations where researchers expect to find negative impacts. Regions and industries where negative impacts are likely to be found are generally known. For researchers knowledgeable about immigration in specific regions, occupations and even firms where negative effects might be found are also well known. Obviously, such knowledge frequently directs the researchers to cases that show adverse consequences for native and legal workers.

9. Topel (1994) concludes that, in the West, immigration of less-skilled Hispanics and Asian workers has adversely affected the wages of natives, especially less-skilled natives, thus contributing to the wage inequality observed in the West. This inference is indirect, however, since the Current Population Survey data that are used did not allow nativity status to be identified. Moreover, concerning the possible sources of the increase in the wage gap between highly educated and less educated individuals during the 1980s, Borjas and Ramey (1994) are unable to reject noncointegration between the college-to-high-school dropout wage series and the percentages of immigrants.

10. Filer (1992) describes a different pattern for the 1970s in which the location of immigrants in various places encourages out-migration of natives.

2 United States Immigration Policy

Immigration policy not only helps to determine how many persons may enter the United States during any given year; it also helps to influence the characteristics of U.S. immigrants: who they are, where they were born, when they may come, and with whom they may come. U.S. immigration policy has been characterized by three lengthy periods during which different emphases were placed on admission criteria: 1) the laissez-faire period that ended in 1921; 2) the national origin quota period from 1921 to June 30, 1968 (fiscal year 1967); and 3) the family reunification period beginning in 1968.

During the laissez-faire period, essentially no quantitative restrictions existed on immigration. Almost all persons were welcome to enter the United States with the exception of the Chinese (after 1882) and individuals such as criminals and prostitutes. Immigrants met at least two critical and related economic needs during the nineteenth and early twentieth centuries. First, they allowed the frontier to be developed without major labor shortages in eastern industrial centers, which could have been one cost of developing the frontier in the absence of immigration. Second, they satisfied the rapidly growing demand for unskilled and semiskilled labor in the nation's cities.

Between 1820 (when immigration statistics were first compiled) and 1921, 34.5 million persons were welcomed to the United States, an annual average of 337,843 immigrants.[1] The vast majority of these immigrants came from Europe, where famine, religious intolerance, political institutions, lagging employment opportunities, and relatively low wage rates in one way or another encouraged their flight. Moreover, many European nations were experiencing demographic transitions;[2] rural areas were especially overpopulated. Vialet (1980, p. 7) succinctly characterized the period: "The mass migration of the 19th century was the result of a near perfect match between the needs of a new country and overcrowded Europe."

During the second period of U.S. immigration policy, from 1922 through fiscal year 1967, 9.5 million immigrants entered the United

States, an average of 206,875 per year, or about 61.2 percent of the annual average during the laissez-faire period. This second period was characterized by the national origin quota system, which allocated visas in proportion to the national origins of the U.S. population, as defined from various censuses.

Vialet (1980) attributed the adoption of the first comprehensive quantitative restrictions on immigration (in the Quota Law of 1921) to a variety of immediate causes, including the fear of a flood of refugees from Europe following World War I, and the growing nationalism and isolationism that followed the war. The report of the Dillingham Commission (Joint Commission on Immigration), which painted a fairly negative picture of immigrants, undoubtedly also contributed to the Quota Law. Moreover, the adoption of restrictions was reinforced by what were at the time popular biological theories alleging the superiority of certain races (Congressional Research Service 1979, p. 8). Although the national origin quota system was reaffirmed in 1952, its philosophical basis was probably not one of racial superiority, but rather of contemporary sociological theories relating to cultural assimilation. The 1952 act introduced a preference system that recognized both needed skills and family reunification. In this way it was an antecedent of the Immigration Act Amendments of 1965 that were fully implemented in 1968.

The Immigration Act Amendments of 1965 ushered in a new era both for U.S. immigration policy and for U.S. immigration in general. The national origin quota system was abandoned at a time when national awareness of limitations on civil rights and civil liberties was acute. The new system, which is described in detail later in this chapter, was characterized by heavy emphasis on family ties as the main path to entry, although persons with needed skills and refugees also were provided opportunities to enter the United States. Between 1968 and 1995, 18.2 million persons were admitted to the United States as legal resident aliens, an annual average of 651,716. This average is 193 percent of that for the 1820–1921 period and 315 percent of that for the 1922–1967 period.

A BRIEF HISTORY OF U.S. IMMIGRATION POLICY

The Aliens Act of 1798 was the first federal law related to immigration, yet it was not until 1864 that Congress attempted to centralize control of immigration. This goal was achieved through the appointment by the President of a Commissioner of Immigration who served under the Secretary of State.

In 1875, Congress began for the first time to develop a policy of direct federal regulation of immigration in earnest. Direct regulation was accomplished by prohibiting the entry of undesirable persons (criminals and prostitutes).[3] Moreover, Congress prohibited bringing Oriental persons into the country without their free and voluntary consent and made contracting to supply coolie labor a felony. The Chinese Exclusion Act of 1882 suspended the immigration of Chinese laborers for 10 years, provided for the deportation of Chinese who were illegally in the United States, and barred Chinese from naturalization, among other provisions.[4] This act was later extended, and in 1904 it was reaffirmed and made permanent, with clarification of the territories from which Chinese were to be excluded.

The Immigration Act of 1907, among other things, established a Joint Commission on Immigration (the Dillingham Commission) that was charged with examining the U.S. immigration system. The Commission studied the effect of immigrants on the employment, wages, and working conditions of U.S. workers. In large part, the Commission's findings were responsible for the Immigration Act of 1917, which was a precursor of substantially more restrictive legislation enacted during the early 1920s.

The first quantitative restrictions on U.S. immigration were provided in the Quota Law of 1921,[5] which limited the number of immigrant aliens of any nationality to 3 percent of the foreign-born persons of that nationality who were living in the United States in 1910 (based on the decennial census of that year). The 1921 law had a clear effect on immigration, especially that from southern and eastern Europe. Table 2.1 shows the quotas that were in force for fiscal year 1921–22, as well as actual admittances during this year. The quotas were restrictive for virtually every country in southern and eastern Europe. For example, Italy had a quota of 42,057 and admittances from Italy were

Table 2.1 U.S. Immigration under the Quota Law of 1921 and Quotas under the Immigration Act of 1924 for Selected Countries

Country or place of birth	1921–1922			1924	
	Quota	Total admitted	Percentage of quota admitted	Quota	Percentage of 1921 quota
Austria	7,451	4,797	64.4	785	10.5
Belgium	1,563	1,581	101.2	512	32.8
Czechoslovakia	14,282	14,248	99.8	3,073	21.5
Denmark	5,694	3,284	57.7	2,789	49.0
Finland	3,921	3,038	77.5	471	12.0
France	5,729	4,343	75.8	3,954	69.0
Germany	68,059	19,053	28.0	51,227	75.3
Greece	3,294	3,447	104.6	100	3.0
Hungary	5,638	6,035	107.0	473	8.4
Italy	42,057	42,149	100.2	3,845	9.1
Netherlands	3,607	2,408	66.8	1,648	45.7
Norway	12,202	5,941	48.7	6,453	52.9
Poland	25,827	26,129	101.2	5,982	23.2
Romania	7,419	7,429	100.1	603	8.1
Russia	34,284	28,908	84.3	2,248	6.6
Sweden	20,042	8,766	43.7	9,561	47.7
Switzerland	3,752	3,723	99.2	2,081	55.5
United Kingdom	77,342	42,670	55.2	34,007	44.0
Yugoslavia	6,426	6,644	103.4	671	10.4
Irish Free State	–	–	–	28,567	–
Other	8,406	9,360	111.3	5,617	66.8
Total	356,995	243,953	68.3	164,667	46.1

SOURCE: Congressional Research Service (1980), Tables 7 and 15.

100.2 percent of this number; for Hungary, 5,638 and 107.0 percent. On the other hand, the old source countries of the "first wave" of immigrants in western and northern Europe had relatively high quotas, and their admittances during 1921–22 were relatively few: Germany, 68,059 (28.0 percent); and Sweden, 20,042 (43.7 percent). In total, only 68.3 percent of the overall quota of 356,995 was filled in fiscal year 1921–22, the first year in U.S. history that general quotas were in force. In 1922, the Quota Law of 1921 was extended for two years.

The Immigration Act of 1924

The Immigration Act of 1924 is one of the most important pieces of immigration legislation in U.S. history. It made permanent the national origin quota system and, in combination with the Immigration Act of 1917, it governed U.S. immigration policy until 1952. The 1924 law provided that until June 30, 1927, the annual quota of any quota nationality be set at 2 percent of the number of foreign-born persons of such nationality resident in the continental United States in 1890. The total annual quota was 164,667. From July 1, 1927, (but later postponed to July 1, 1929) until December 31, 1952, it set the annual quota for any country or nationality; the quota number had the same relation to 150,000 as the number of inhabitants in the continental United States in 1920 having that national origin did to the total population of the continental United States in 1920.

The 1924 act was far more restrictive than that of 1921, especially for countries of southern and eastern Europe. While the overall 1924 quota was 46.1 percent of that for 1921 (Table 2.1), the percentage for countries of southern and eastern Europe was much smaller: Hungary, 8.4 percent, and Italy, 9.1 percent. For first-wave countries, the percentages were much higher: Germany, 75.3 percent, and Sweden, 47.7 percent.

The change from a 1910 basis in the Quota Law of 1921 to an 1890 basis for defining country quotas in the 1924 law reflected nationality and ethnic tensions in the country during the 1920s. The major wave of immigration from southern and eastern Europe occurred after 1890. By establishing a basis date from a census before this wave, Congress effectively reduced the quotas of the new origin countries while maintaining relatively high quotas for the old source countries. In this way,

Congress hoped to preserve what it perceived as the nationality and ethnic balance of the United States as it existed prior to the second wave of immigration. It was precisely this type of discriminatory treatment that later laws would attempt to correct.

The 1930s and the 1940s were not particularly eventful in terms of immigration legislation. During the Depression of the 1930s, immigration was at a low ebb.[6] During the first half of the 1940s, immigration remained low because of World War II. In 1943, Congress repealed the Chinese Exclusion laws that began in 1882. After the war, immigration began to climb again, reaching 249,187 in 1950.

In 1952, Congress passed the Immigration and Nationality Act (McCarran-Walter Act) over a presidential veto. In many respects this 1952 act was a continuation of the laws of 1917 and 1924. It maintained the national origin quota system (though in a modified form); it kept in place the Asia-Pacific-triangle restrictions; and it contained no provisions to restrict Western Hemisphere immigration. However, the McCarran-Walter Act lifted various racial bars to naturalization, which removed race as a bar to immigration, and eliminated sex discrimination in immigrant admittances. Moreover, the act established a system of selective immigration that granted quota preference to skilled persons whose labor services met an urgent need in the United States. The 1952 act also maintained the policy established in the 1920s of exempting natives of Western Hemisphere countries from numerical restrictions.

Immigration and Nationality Act Amendments of 1965

The national origin system had been designed to preserve the ethnic balance of the U.S. population, but by the 1960s Congress began to recognize that the system was failing in this respect. First, those countries with the highest quotas were demanding only a fraction of their quota numbers. Second, between 1953 and 1964, approximately one-half million immigrants (of about 3.2 million total) were admitted under various special programs as exceptions to the national origin formula, which in the eyes of some members of Congress essentially resulted in the abandonment of the national origin system (Congressional Research Service 1979, p. 52). Between 1960 and 1965, of 1.7 million immigrants admitted to the United States, only 34.6 percent entered under a quota (Congressional Research Service 1980, p. 64). Finally, public perceptions regarding race and national origin were changed relative to what they were during the cold-war climate under which the McCarran-Walter Act was passed in 1952.

The Immigration and Nationality Act Amendments of 1965 were passed in October, and most provisions of the new law took effect on December 1, 1965. However, until June 30, 1968, certain vestiges of the national origin formula remained operational, and during this transition period, the unused quota numbers of undersubscribed countries could be absorbed by oversubscribed countries.

Because immigrants who legally entered the United States between 1972 and 1991 entered under the terms and conditions of the Immigration and Nationality Act Amendments of 1965 (with certain revisions enacted after 1965), the 1965 law is especially important in the context of the present study. This law had five major provisions.

1. It abolished the national origin quota system that had been established in 1924 and reaffirmed in 1952, thus eliminating national origin, race, or ancestry as a basis for exclusion.

2. It established a seven-category preference system for numerically restricted immigrants. These preferences (Table 2.2) provided for the reunification of families—the first, second, fourth, and fifth preferences, called the relative preferences—and for entry of persons with special occupational talents—the third and sixth preferences, which have come to be called the occupational preferences. (The seventh preference [not shown in Table 2.2], which related to refugees, was eliminated by the Refugee Act of 1980 after it became clear that this preference could not accommodate the flow of refugees who were being admitted under special legislation.) Visas not used in higher preference categories could be used under preferences two, four, and five. Nonpreference immigrants were to receive any remaining visas, but after a short time nonpreference visas were unavailable because preference visas accounted for the total allotment of restricted numbers. Numerically restricted immigrant visas were allocated on a first-come, first-served basis, but Western Hemisphere countries were not subjected to the preference categories.

Table 2.2 Immigrant Visa Allocation System (1968–1991)[a]

Preference/provision		Limit
Numerically limited immigrants: 270,000[b]		
1st:	Unmarried sons and daughters of U.S. citizens and their children	20% or 54,000
2nd:	Spouses and unmarried sons and daughters of permanent resident aliens	26% or 70,200[c]
3rd:	Members of the professions of exceptional ability and their spouses and children	10% or 27,000
4th:	Married sons and daughters of U.S. citizens, their spouses and children	10% or 27,000[c]
5th:	Brothers and sisters of U.S. citizens (at least 21 years of age) and their spouses and children	24% or 64,800[c]
6th:	Workers in skilled or unskilled occupations in which laborers are in short supply in the United States, their spouses and children	10% or 27,000
Nonpref.:	Other qualified applicants	Any numbers not used above[c]
Numerically exempt immigrants		
Immediate relatives of U.S. citizens		
	Spouses, children, parents of U.S. citizens at least 21 years of age	
Special immigrants		
	Certain ministers of religion	
	Certain former employees of the U.S. government abroad	
	Certain persons who lost U.S. citizenship	
	Certain foreign medical graduates	
Adjustments for refugees and those seeking asylum		

[a] As presented, this table refers to the law in 1991.
[b] Except for immediate relatives of adult U.S. citizens, an annual limit of 20,000 is imposed on each independent country.
[c] Numbers not used in higher preference may be used in these categories.

3. It established a group of immigrants exempt from quota limitations: a) immediate relatives of U.S. citizens, i.e., the spouses, children, and parents of U.S. citizens 21 years of age and older, and b) special immigrants, including ministers of religion and others.

4. It established an annual Eastern Hemisphere quota of 170,000 and a Western Hemisphere quota of 120,000. This was the first time that the Western Hemisphere was placed under a quota. However, the Eastern Hemisphere also was placed under a 20,000 per country limit on numerically restricted quota numbers, but this country limit was not applicable to the Western Hemisphere.[7]

5. Finally, it required that the Secretary of Labor certify that an alien attempting to enter as a worker would not replace a worker in the United States or adversely influence either the wages or working conditions of individuals similarly employed in the United States. This condition introduced a process known as labor certification that was applied to the third and sixth preference categories.

The single most important aspect of the 1965 amendments was the elimination of the national origin quota system, which had been in place for over 40 years. The second most important aspect was to bring the Western Hemisphere under a quota. The provision of a group of immigrants exempt from numerical restrictions was not new, but the three-tier system of numerically restricted immigration provided additional structure; the three tiers are hemisphere quotas (later, world quotas), country quotas, and preference-category quotas.

The Immigration Act of 1990

With legal immigration rising during the 1960s and 1970s, and with illegal migration thought to be high and perhaps also rising, the federal government began to study and discuss various immigration issues during the late 1970s. The result, in 1979, was a Select Commission on Immigration and Refugee Policy that proposed sweeping changes in the nation's immigration laws. During 1984, both the Senate and House passed the Immigration Reform and Control Act (Simpson-Mazzoli Bill), but this bill died in the conference committee established to reconcile differences between the two versions. The Simpson-Mazzoli Bill had three major provisions: 1) control of illegal migration, 2) legalization of alien status, and 3) reform of legal immigration. When it became clear in the next (99th) Congress that the entire package was not ready to be acted upon, the various provisions were unbundled. The result was the Immigration Reform and Control Act of 1986, which treated illegal migration, and the Immigration Act of 1990, which treated legal immigration.

The 1990 act bears a strong resemblance to the 1965 law it replaced.[8] Consequently, immigration under the previous law should provide a reasonable blueprint for likely U.S. immigration under the new law. Moreover, in a number of ways, the gender, age, and skill composition of immigrants under the new law should resemble that of their counterparts under the old law. For our purposes, the most important provisions of the Immigration Act of 1990 are the following.

1. The worldwide immigration ceiling was raised to 700,000 for fiscal years 1992, 1993, and 1994, falling to 675,000 for 1995 and later years. The ceiling is, however, flexible in the sense that while immediate relatives of U.S. citizens are included under the worldwide quota "cap," their number is unlimited.

2. Family-based immigration is guaranteed at least 226,000 visas. These are allocated per year to four preference categories (Table 2.3).

3. Employment-based preferences are allotted 140,000 visas annually and are grouped into five preference classes (Table 2.3).

4. The family-sponsored and employment-based preference visas made available to citizens of a single independent foreign state may not exceed 7 percent of the total number of visas for that state. Since family preferences are set at a minimum of 226,000 and the employment-based limit is set at a minimum of 140,000, the per-country ceiling for independent countries is raised to 25,620. Moreover, at least 77 percent of the visa allotment involving spouses, minor children, and unmarried sons and daughters of lawful permanent residents is designated for spouses and minor children, and three-quarters of these are not subject to per-country limits. Prior to the 1990 act, the per-country quota was set at 20,000.

5. So-called "diversity immigrants" were allocated 40,000 visas each in 1992, 1993, and 1994, with 1993 and 1994 gaining the unused numbers from the prior year. The diversity quota rose to 55,000 per year beginning in 1995. Diversity immigrants are those aliens born in countries adversely affected by the 1965 law and their spouses and children. The 55,000 visas are to be allocated to natives of countries that have sent fewer than 50,000 legal immigrants to the United States over the previous five years. No single country can receive more than 7 percent (3,850) of the number available worldwide. To be eligible for a diversity visa, a prospective immigrant must have at least a high school education or its equivalent and at least two years of work experience in an occupation that requires at least two years of training and experience (and this experience must be during the five years immediately preceding the date of application). Thus, diversity immigrants are a kind of occupational immigrant, but without specificity regarding the occupation. Clearly, diversity visas have considerable potential to affect the source-country composition of U.S. immigration.

Recent U.S. Policy

Until very recently, Congress has dealt with immigration through specifically designed laws. However, during 1996, Congress wrote provisions regarding immigrants into legislation that, at least on the surface, had little or nothing to do with immigration. The best example is the Personal Responsibility and Work Opportunity Reconciliation Act of 1996, which placed certain restrictions on the eligibility of legal aliens for federal public benefits (although certain of these restrictions were relaxed by Congress in 1997). Another example is the Anti-Terrorism Act, which provides for summary dismissal under certain circumstances.

Ten years after the passage of the Immigration Reform and Control Act of 1986, Congress enacted the Illegal Immigration Reform and Immigrant Responsibility Act of 1996 (IIRIRA) in an effort to control illegal migration, which was the primary goal of IRCA. The provisions of IIRIRA went into effect on April 1, 1997, but many of these

Table 2.3 Categories of Immigrants Subject to the Numerical Cap: Unadjusted and Fiscal Year 1996 Limits

Preference/provision	Unadjusted limit[a]		FY1996
Family-sponsored immigrants	**480,000**[b]		**565,819**[b]
Family-sponsored preferences	226,000		311,819
1st: Unmarried sons and daughters of U.S. citizens	23,400[c]		23,400[c]
2nd: Spouses, children, and unmarried sons and daughters of permanent resident aliens	114,200[d]		200,019[d]
3rd: Married sons and daughters of U.S. citizens	23,400[d]		23,400[d]
4th: Brothers and sisters of U.S. citizens (at least 21 years of age)	65,000[d]		65,000[d]
Immediate relatives of adult U.S. citizens (spouses, children, and parents) and children born abroad to alien residents	Not limited, but assumed to be 254,000		Not limited, but assumed to be 254,000
Employment-based preference	**140,000**[e]		**140,000**[e]
1st: Priority workers	40,040[e]		40,040[e]
2nd: Professionals with advanced degrees or aliens of exceptional ability	40,040[d]		40,040[d]
3rd: Skilled workers, professionals, needed unskilled workers and Chinese Student Protection Act	40,040[d]		40,040[d]
4th: Special immigrants	9,940		9,940
5th: Employment creation ("investors")	9,940		9,940

Preference/provision	Unadjusted limit[a]	FY1996
Diversity	**55,000**	**55,000**
Total	675,000[b]	760,819[b]

[a] The annual limit is adjusted based on visa usage in the previous year.
[b] The number of immediate relatives of U.S. citizens included in these figures is assumed to be 254,000. Immediate relatives may enter without any limitation; however, the limit for family-sponsored preference visa immigrants in a fiscal year is equal to 480,000 minus the number of immediate relatives admitted in the preceding year. The limit of family-sponsored preference visas cannot go below a minimum of 226,000 (the worldwide limit of 480,000 minus 254,000).
[c] Plus unused family fourth preference visas.
[d] Visas not used in higher preferences may be used in these categories.
[e] Plus unused employment fourth and fifth preference visas.

provisions are being challenged in courts of law. The IIRIRA legislation is regarded as a companion to the 1996 welfare reform legislation.[9]

IMMIGRATION POLICY AND THE COMPOSITION OF IMMIGRATION

U.S. immigration law has profoundly influenced the composition of U.S. immigration in numerous ways. The direct effects are written into the law, which historically has made special provisions for skilled persons and for certain males, for example. The indirect effects result from provisions of the law that affect from where immigrants may come or with whom they may come. Other aspects of U.S. law and U.S. policy that have nothing directly to do with immigration may also influence both the source countries of immigrants and the composition of various flows, especially gender and age composition.

One example of a direct influence is the emphasis that immigration law places on occupational skills relative to family reunification. The Immigration and Nationality Act Amendments of 1965 established two occupational preferences that in 1991 potentially accounted for 54,000 visas. In 1991, only 23,591 persons qualified for an occupational preference as "principals," as distinct from beneficiaries, who qualify as spouses and children of principals (31,358 in 1991). On the other hand, the Immigration Act of 1990, which took effect in November 1991, provides for 140,000 employment-based immigrants (and their spouses and children). In fiscal year 1992, 51,787 employment-based principals were admitted; in fiscal year 1996, 51,079. Thus, the new law shifted considerably more emphasis to occupational skills.

A second example—one that potentially could have influenced gender composition—is found in the Immigration Act of 1924. In this act, Congress made clear its desire for families not to be separated and for reunification of those families that were separated. Wives and unmarried children under 18 of U.S. citizens were granted nonquota status. Moreover, preference quota status was granted to the spouses and unmarried children under 21 of U.S. citizens aged 21 and over, as well as to the wives and dependent children under age 16 of permanent resident aliens. Harper and Chase (1975, p. 13) argue that in its original form this law discriminated against women, because "an alien wife preceding her husband could not confer preference quota status on him, and an American citizen wife . . . could only confer preference quota status on her alien husband." Although amendments were made at later dates to lessen the impacts of these conditions, some degree of discrimination remained until the enactment of the Immigration and Nationality Act of 1952. Moreover, by granting "preference quota status" to wives of quota immigrants aged 21 and over who were skilled in agriculture, the 1924 law made a further distinction based on gender. The Immigration and Nationality Act of 1952 (the McCarran-Walter Act), among other things, eliminated discrimination between the sexes as a basis for exclusion.

The indirect influences of the law on immigrant composition are more subtle than those exerted directly, but they are no less important. For example, historically the occupational preferences have strongly favored the admittance of males, especially as principals. Such gender tilting is due in part to males in source countries having a higher probability of being "economic migrants" (persons who respond to economic incentives) because of their higher labor force participation rates. The gender tilting is also due to the higher probability that males in most source countries will have more education than females, as well as claim to more personal resources to finance an international move.

Another important indirect effect of immigration law is on the source-country composition of immigrants. Because different countries will provide immigrants who have, on average, different personal or family characteristics (such as years of schooling, occupational experience, and number of dependents), legal preferences or barriers to immigration from various parts of the world have almost certainly tilted immigrant composition in one way or another.

U.S. immigration policy in combination with foreign policy can also indirectly affect both the gender and age composition of immigration. For example, for many years, the United States has had a significant military presence in certain foreign countries such as Germany, Korea, and the Philippines. Because historically the military has been predominately male, foreign-born spouses of military personnel have been primarily female. Consequently, countries with a significant U.S. military presence have relatively many young women qualify for permanent resident alien status as the wives of U.S. citizens. Moreover, after residing continuously in the United States for at least five years, a permanent resident alien can qualify for naturalization. Upon obtaining citizenship, any naturalized citizen who is at least 21 years of age is eligible to reunite with her (or his) parents, who are exempt from numerical restrictions. Thus, from the same countries that are sources of relatively many young female immigrants come relatively many older immigrants. In the modeling effort described below, we attempt to account for such countries.

Notes

1. These figures relate to gross immigration, not net immigration. Especially during the late nineteenth and early twentieth centuries, return migration was considerable, amounting to perhaps 33 percent of gross immigration (Warren and Kraly 1985).
2. The "demographic transition" refers to a society's passage from traditional to modern economic and social conditions. During this passage, both birth and death rates, which are initially quite high, fall. However, in many (but not all) cases during the transitional phase, death rates fall first and, because birth rates remain high for a time, population grows rapidly. Many possible reactions to the high rate of population growth are possible, including internal migration from rural to urban areas and emigration. See McNamara (1982).
3. In 1882, those persons deemed likely to become a public charge were added to the list of excluded persons, and in 1891, persons suffering from certain contagious

diseases were placed on the list, along with polygamists and aliens assisted by others through the payment of passage. Anarchists, or persons who believe in, or advocate, the overthrow by force or violence of the government of the United States, or of all government, or of all forms of law, or the assassination of public officials were barred in 1903. Knowledge of English was made a requirement of naturalization in 1906. In 1907, imbeciles, feeble-minded persons, and persons with physical or mental defects that could affect their ability to earn a living were barred from entry. In 1917, illiterate aliens were excluded from admission.

In 1940, past as well as present membership in proscribed organizations became grounds for barring entry. In 1950, present or past membership in the Communist party was added to the list. The exclusion or expulsion of aliens who persecuted others on the basis of race, religion, national origin, or political opinion under the direction of the Nazi government of Germany or its allies was authorized in 1978. Certain grounds for exclusion, especially based on health considerations, were repealed in 1990.

4. Higman (1984) discussed the circumstances that led to the banning of Chinese. Among the factors that he noted are the completion of the Union Pacific Railroad in 1869 that resulted in what he calls "a large floating labor supply" (p. 34), a serious recession in the mid 1870s, cultural differences with persons of European ancestry, and the fact that the Chinese did not migrate freely but rather were controlled by Chinese societies, which appeared to be a new kind of slavery.

5. Goldin (1994) discussed the reasons why restrictive legislation was not adopted much earlier in the 1890s. She concluded (p. 255) that "shifting political interest, generally favorable economic times, and a lot of good luck" (for those who came between 1890 and 1921) were the main reasons.

6. Of the 528,431 persons accepted as legal resident aliens during the 1930s, 250,000 are estimated to have been refugees from Nazi persecution (Vialet 1980).

7. The Immigration and Nationality Act Amendments of 1976 placed the Western Hemisphere under the annual 20,000 per country ceiling as well as under the preference categories. A later amendment in 1978 combined the separate Eastern and Western Hemisphere ceilings into a single worldwide ceiling of 290,000, which in 1980 was reduced to 270,000 in connection with the Refugee Act of 1980.

8. The new law, like the old, provides for the unrestricted immigration of certain immediate relatives of U.S. citizens. The new law places more emphasis on employment considerations, but the old occupational preferences (3rd and 6th) emphasized many of the same types of considerations. Legal resident aliens are still able to reunite with immediate relatives under a preference (though with an expanded number of available visas).

9. The 1996 welfare reform bill defines a new eligibility category for legal aliens, called qualified aliens, which includes lawful permanent residents, refugees, and those granted asylum, as well as certain others. Most qualified aliens were barred initially from food stamps and supplemental security income (SSI), which is a federal cash assistance program (supplemented in certain states) for the elderly, blind, and disabled. Moreover, the welfare reform law initially barred qualified

aliens admitted to the United States before the law's enactment on August 22, 1996, from all means-tested federal programs for their first five years in the United States. However, in 1997, Congress changed its position and approved the continuation of SSI and Medicaid for those legal immigrants who were in the United States on August 22, 1996. It also approved such benefits for those legal immigrants who were in the United States on this date but were not receiving these benefits, if they subsequently become poor or disabled. States also are permitted to deny qualified aliens Temporary Assistance to Needy Families (TANF), which replaced Aid to Families with Dependent Children (AFDC), Medicaid, and various federally funded state programs such as child care and services for the elderly. Certain exceptions are made, including refugees and those granted asylum during their first five years in the United States (extended to seven years in 1997). Naturalized citizens are eligible for the benefits available to native-born citizens, but naturalization typically requires five years as a permanent resident alien.

Most federal public benefit programs have not been available to illegal migrants, but the law was silent on such eligibility for certain (minor) programs. The 1996 law defines "not qualified aliens" to include illegal migrants and bars their use of federal public benefit programs, as well as state and local programs. If states wish to make benefits available to nonqualified aliens, they must pass a law that allows them to do so. The Congressional Budget Office estimates that 0.5 million aliens who presently receive SSI benefits could lose their eligibility, along with 1.0 million aliens currently using food stamps.

3 A Brief History of U.S. Immigration

Table 3.1 provides a decade-by-decade breakdown of U.S. immigration from the 1820s to the 1990s.[1] Historically, the years of heaviest immigration were early in this century, when the annual gross flow exceeded one million during six different years with a peak at 1.3 million in 1907. Between 1901 and 1910, 8.8 million immigrants were admitted to the United States, a figure unrivaled by any other decade in the nation's history. However, during the 1980s, 7.3 million persons entered. The recent surge of immigration has continued during the 1990s; in 1991 alone over 1.8 million persons were admitted as legal permanent residents, and between 1991 and 1996, 6.1 million persons were admitted.[2]

WAVES OF IMMIGRATION

The First Wave

During U.S. history, the source-country composition of immigration has changed considerably. Muller and Espenshade (1985), following others, characterized this changing composition as consisting of four overlapping waves (though the third of these four refers to internal migration and not directly to immigration). The first major wave began in earnest during the 1830s, when the number of arrivals jumped to 599,125 from 143,439 during the 1820s. During the 1840s, arrivals totaled over 1.7 million, and this wave peaked during the 1880s.

Although immigration during the mid to late nineteenth century was certainly due to some combination of economic and social conditions in Europe and the promise of a better life in America, technological improvements in transporting people by sea, which allowed large numbers of persons to move relatively quickly, safely, and cheaply, were also important. Thomas (1973, p. 36) indicated that the first Cunard steamships were placed in service during 1840, revolutionizing ocean

**Table 3.1 Immigration to the
United States, by Decade,
1821–1996**

Period	Number
1821–1830	143,439
1831–1840	599,125
1841–1850	1,713,251
1851–1860	2,598,214
1861–1870	2,314,824
1871–1880	2,812,191
1881–1890	5,246,613
1891–1900	3,687,564
1901–1910	8,795,386
1911–1920	5,735,811
1921–1930	4,107,209
1931–1940	538,431
1941–1950	1,035,039
1951–1960	2,515,479
1961–1970	3,321,677
1971–1980	4,493,314
1981–1990	7,338,062
1991–1996	6,146,213

SOURCE: U.S. Immigration and Naturalization Service (1997), Table 1.

transport, although Scott (1972, p. 36) reported that in 1856, about 95 percent of the immigrants who arrived in New York still came by sail. By 1873, however, the majority came by steam.[3] Gould (1979) noted three important consequences of the substantial reduction in the duration of the crossing. First, the opportunity cost of not working while on board the ship was greatly reduced. Second, the physical hardships of lengthy voyages, including hunger, thirst, sickness, and death, were eased by the faster crossing. Third, knowledge about opportunities in

America, transmitted through private correspondence and through advertising by steamship lines, spread more rapidly.

The first wave originated in Europe, specifically in western and northern Europe. The Potato Famine (which struck continental Europe as well as Ireland), social and economic problems, demographic transitions, and religious intolerence were common motivating factors for this wave of immigrants. Ireland was a major source country. Between 1815 and 1845, an estimated 850,000 Irish crossed the Atlantic (Taylor 1971).[4] During the 1850s, 2.6 million immigrants arrived in the United States, 35 percent from Ireland. The 1850 U.S. Census reported 962,000 persons born in Ireland; the 1890 Census, 1.9 million persons.

Immigration from Germany, which had begun during the 1830s and had continued to build during the 1840s, outstripped that from Ireland during the 1850s, when Germany supplied 37 percent of U.S. immigrants. As the nineteenth century wore on, Germany far exceeded Ireland as a source of U.S. immigrants, and the United Kingdom also became an important source. During the 1860s, the United States had over 2.3 million arrivals, with Germany accounting for 34 percent, the United Kingdom for 26 percent, and Ireland for 19 percent. These three countries of western Europe accounted for almost 80 percent of immigrant arrivals during the 1860s, but during this decade, immigration from Norway and Sweden also began to grow significantly.

The source-country pattern of U.S. immigration began to change during the 1870s. While the three traditional source countries remained important (accounting for about 61 percent of the arrivals), eastern and southern Europe for the first time began to supply significant numbers, and immigration from northern Europe continued to grow. For example, Austria-Hungary, Italy, and the Soviet Union accounted for about 168,000 immigrants during the 1870s, and Norway-Sweden accounted for another 211,000.[5] Both numbers were to grow markedly during the following four decades.

During the 1880s immigration increased sharply—5.2 million arrivals compared with 2.8 million during the 1870s—with rising numbers of immigrants from virtually every European country except France and Spain. For example, movement from Germany more than doubled, from about 0.7 million during the 1870s to 1.5 million during the 1880s. Major increases also occurred from Austria-Hungary, the Soviet Union, Italy, the United Kingdom, Ireland, and Belgium. Arrivals from Norway, Sweden, and Denmark increased from 243,016 during the 1870s to 656,494 during the 1880s. Immigration from the Americas was also of some significance; movement from Canada and Newfoundland amounted to 776,944 during the 1870s and 1880s.[6] (Land arrivals from Mexico were not completely enumerated until 1908, and between 1886 and 1893 no data whatsoever are available for Mexico, so the number of immigrants from Mexico is largely unknown for the nineteenth century.)

The Second Wave

The second wave of immigration noted by Muller and Espenshade was from southern and eastern Europe. This wave began seriously during the 1870s and 1880s, but it was overshadowed by movement from western and northern Europe. During the 1890s, total arrivals fell to 3.7 million; yet during this decade, movement from the Soviet Union and Italy more than doubled, with 0.5 million arrivals for the former and almost 0.7 million for the latter. Austria-Hungary sent another 0.6 million. Together, these source countries accounted for 47.5 percent of U.S. immigration during the 1890s. On the other hand, migration from Germany declined by almost 1.0 million persons, that from the United Kingdom by well over 0.5 million, and that from Ireland by almost 0.3 million.

The reasons for emigration from southern and eastern Europe were many. Just as the steamship was a permissive factor in the earlier emigration from western European countries that had easy access to the Atlantic, the railroad was a permissive factor in later emigration from southern and eastern Europe because it provided relatively cheap, safe, and fast transport to Atlantic ports (Taylor 1971). Moreover, these countries were experiencing rapidly changing technology (and thus economic change), institutions, and ideas. Gould (1979, p. 617) noted that the "eastward march of personal freedom was obviously an important part of the explanation of the corresponding geographical shift of the sources of European emigration as the nineteenth century ran its course."[7] Demographic transitions occurring in these countries also encouraged immigration to the United States.

The first decade of the twentieth century stands out as the decade with the most immigrant arrivals in U.S. history: between 1901 and

1910, 8.8 million persons entered the country. During this decade, Austria-Hungary supplied the United States with 2.1 million immigrants, the Soviet Union with 1.6 million, and Italy with 2.0 million, these three accounting for two-thirds of all arrivals.

With continued heavy movement from eastern and southern Europe, the 1911–1920 period promised to be another decade of mass immigration. Over 4.1 million persons arrived in the four years from 1911 to 1914, but with the beginning of World War I, immigration was sharply curtailed. Only 1.6 million persons arrived between 1915 and 1920. With the imposition of the first binding entry quotas during the early 1920s (the Chinese exclusion laws excepted), immigration declined to 4.1 million during the 1920s, 2.3 million (or 56 percent) of which came during the first four years of the decade. The temporary quota restrictions of 1921 and 1922, followed by the first permanent restrictions embodied in the Immigration Act of 1924, spelled the effective end to the "second wave" of U.S. immigration. However, the quota restrictions imposed during the 1920s did not apply to Western Hemisphere countries, and partially as a consequence, Canada and Newfoundland (924,515) and Mexico (459,287) ranked first and second among source countries of U.S. immigration during the 1920s.[8]

The Third Wave

Picking up on an earlier theme of B. Thomas (1973), Muller and Espenshade argued that black migration from the rural South to northern cities began to grow significantly when immigration, which had been primarily directed to northern U.S. cities, declined. This northward internal migration, which is the third wave, in fact was general and not restricted to blacks. It also coincided with significant movement from farms and into urban areas and was motivated by growing job opportunities. In earlier years, these opportunities had been taken by low-skilled immigrant laborers, who were presumably good labor-market substitutes for less skilled blacks and whites from the South.

With the worldwide depression of the 1930s, immigration fell sharply: only 538,431 persons entered the United States during the decade, and net emigration probably occurred (Gemery 1994). Because of World War II, only 170,952 immigrants arrived during the first half of the 1940s. However, with the end of the war, immigration again began to build.

The Fourth Wave

The fourth wave of migration consists primarily of Hispanics and Asians. Immigration from Mexico and the Caribbean began to grow significantly during the 1940s and 1950s. In 1943, Congress provided for the importation of temporary agricultural laborers from North, South, and Central America. This law formed the legal basis for the "Bracero" program, which involved the importation of agricultural workers from Mexico. Between 1942 and 1964, 4,646,399 contracts were written for Mexicans to work temporarily in U.S. agriculture (Congressional Research Service 1980, Table 30). A continuing flow of migrants (legal and illegal) since 1964 makes Mexico today the single most important source of U.S. immigrants.

After restrictions on immigration from Asia were phased out beginning in 1965, movement from this part of the world to the United States increased dramatically; clearly, the earlier entry restrictions had produced a pent-up demand. Thus, the sources of U.S. immigration shifted strongly away from Europe and strongly toward Asia and the Americas.

During the 1970s, as the numerically restricted component of U.S. immigration grew at high annual rates due to the family reunification provisions of the law, illegal migration (especially from Mexico but from elsewhere as well) was gathering momentum. Furthermore, refugee admittances, particularly from Southeast Asia, were sufficiently important that in 1980 specific legislation was passed to deal with them (Refugee Act of 1980). During the 1981–1990 period, the United States admitted 7.3 million persons as permanent resident aliens. In only one other decade (1901–1910) has the nation admitted more immigrants (8.8 million), and this decade is often characterized as one of "mass" migration.

During the 1970s and 1980s, U.S. birth rates were low. Consequently, changes in the foreign-born population contributed importantly to overall U.S. population growth. Increases in the foreign-born population between 1980 and 1990 and between 1970 and 1980 of 5.7 and 4.5 million, respectively, were the two largest decadal increases in the nation's history (Table 3.2). During the 1980s, the foreign-born population contributed 25.7 percent of the increment in U.S. popula-

Table 3.2 Foreign-Born and Native Components of Population Change by Decade, 1870–1990

Years	Change in total population	Change in foreign-born	Change in native	Contribution of foreign-born to total change (%)	Contribution of native to total change (%)
1870–1880	11,597,412	1,112,714	10,484,698	9.59	90.41
1880–1890	12,791,931	2,569,634	10,222,297	20.09	79.91
1890–1900	13,046,861	1,091,699	11,955,162	8.37	91.63
1900–1910	15,977,691	3,174,610	12,803,081	19.87	80.13
1910–1920	13,738,354	404,806	13,333,548	2.95	97.05
1920–1930	17,064,426	283,457	16,780,969	1.66	98.34
1930–1940	8,894,229	-2,609,253	11,503,482	-29.34	129.34
1940–1950	19,028,086	-1,250,531	20,278,617	-6.57	106.57
1950–1960	27,766,872	-683,398	28,450,270	-2.46	102.46
1960–1970	24,747,690	-41,665	24,789,355	-0.17	100.17
1970–1980	23,333,879	4,460,604	18,873,275	19.12	80.88
1980–1990	22,164,068	5,687,410	16,476,658	25.66	74.34

SOURCE: U.S. Bureau of the Census (1975); also 1980 and 1990 censuses.

tion, a considerable contrast to the 1930–1970 period, when the foreign-born population declined absolutely.

The 1990s started with the admission of 1.8 million legal immigrants in 1991, 1.1 million of whom had been illegal aliens who were given legal status under terms of the Immigration Reform and Control Act of 1986. Moreover, in 1990 Congress passed the Immigration Act of that year, which became effective in October of 1991 (fiscal 1992) and greatly increased the immigration quota ceilings. Thus, immigration promises to remain significant through and beyond the 1990s, and the composition of immigrant flows will surely have a role in the national debate on immigration.

SOURCE REGIONS OF IMMIGRANTS

Table 3.3 clearly shows the changing geographic sources of U.S. immigrants. During the 1850s, 94.4 percent of U.S. immigration was from Europe, and only 4.5 percent was from Asia and the Western Hemisphere. During the first decade of the twentieth century, Europe still contributed 91.6 percent of the immigrants, but by the 1950s, the European share had fallen to just over half. By the 1980s, not only had the volume of immigration increased appreciably, but the source-country composition of immigration also had changed dramatically. As a different view of this change, of the 45.2 million immigrants admitted to the United States as of 1970, 78.7 percent had a country of last residence in Europe; of the 17.1 million admitted between 1971 and 1995, 13.6 percent came from Europe, 48.7 percent came from the Americas, and 34.6 percent came from Asia.

Layard et al. (1992) discussed how the changing political and economic situation in Europe may ignite a major East-West migration, with some of the migrants seeking entry into the United States. Indeed, migration from Europe to the United States appears to be building once again. Immigration from Europe grew each year from 1987 (61,174) through 1994 (160,916). Between 1991 and 1994 alone, 222,585 persons were admitted from the Soviet Union (based on place of birth), and 100,597 from Poland. However, admittances from Europe declined to 128,185 in 1995.

Table 3.3 Source Regions of U.S. Immigration for Selected Decades[a]

Region	1851–1860	1901–1910	1951–1960	1981–1990
Europe	2,452,577 (94.4%)	8,056,040 (91.6%)	1,325,727 (52.7%)	761,550 (10.4%)
Asia	41,538 (1.6%)	323,543 (3.7%)	153,249 (6.1%)	2,738,157 (37.3%)
Americas	74,720 (2.9%)	361,888 (4.1%)	996,944 (39.6%)	3,615,225 (49.3%)
Africa	210 (0%)	7,368 (0.1%)	14,092 (0.6%)	176,893 (2.4%)
Oceania	158 (0%)	13,024 (0.1%)	12,976 (0.5%)	45,205 (0.6%)
Not specified	29,011 (1.1%)	33,523 (0.4%)	12,491 (0.5%)	1,032 (0%)
Total	2,598,214	8,795,386	2,515,479	7,338,062

SOURCE: U.S. Immigration and Naturalization Service, *1990 Statistical Yearbook of the Immigration and Naturalization Service*, U.S. Government Printing Office: Washington D.C., 1991, Table 2.
[a] These data reflect country of last residence.

HISTORICAL U.S. IMMIGRATION: GENDER, AGE, AND SKILL

Many aspects of immigrant composition are important in terms of the demographic structure of the United States and the effects of immigration on the U.S. economy. This study focuses specifically on gender, age, and skill composition, each of which has been important in shaping the historical consequences of immigration in the United States. In this section, we briefly discuss the historical context of the contemporary compositional measures that we analyze later.

Gender Composition

In the first detailed analysis of migration using census data, Ravenstein asserted that "woman is a greater migrant than man" (1885,

p. 196).   His seventh law of migration is that females are more migratory than males (p. 199).   Ravenstein's analysis concerned lifetime migration in the United Kingdom and used 1871 and, especially, 1881 census data.[9]

In most major international migration flows of the nineteenth and twentieth centures, males commonly have made up more than half of the immigrants and frequently have accounted for far more than half. This gender composition characterized U.S. immigration through the entire nineteenth century and through the first 30 years of the twentieth (Table 3.4).   From a high of 230.2 during the 1901 to 1910 period, this ratio fell steadily to 67.7 (the decadal low) during the 1941 to 1950 period and remains below 100 in the 1990s.

The crossover from male-dominated to female-dominated immigration occurred in 1930 and appears, at least in part, to have been due to the imposition of binding immigration quotas by the United States during the 1920s (though the ratio had been falling steadily for some years).   The immigration quotas of the 1920s were particularly restrictive for immigrants from southern and eastern Europe, and flows from these countries were extreme in their orientation toward males.   During the 1901 to 1910 period, the sex ratio for immigration from Greece was 1703.2; comparable ratios for Italy, Austria-Hungary, and the Russian Empire were 372.6, 238.5, and 185.6, respectively.   On the other hand, the Irish ratio was 90.1.[10]   By curtailing flows from countries with traditionally high sex ratios, the immigration laws of the 1920s had an important effect on the immigration sex ratio that continues today.

Another factor that contributed to high sex ratios around the turn of the century was that many male migrants apparently entered the United States with the intention of residing here only temporarily and later returning home; this was particularly true of migrants from Italy.   The data suggest that migrants from Greece and other countries of southern and eastern Europe also may have intended their stays to be temporary. Indeed, a large fraction of those from such countries did return home, but those males who stayed later reunited with their wives and families, which caused a subsequent reduction of sex ratios, especially after binding quotas were enacted.   The tendency for early flows from a given source to be predominantly male and for later flows to be characterized by family reunification and falling sex ratios is common today.

Table 3.4 Gender of U.S. Immigrants, 1821–1994

Period	Males	Females	Sex ratio
1821–1830[a]	78,196	35,173	222.3
1831–1840[a]	378,725	210,628	179.8
1841–1850[a]	1,014,196	693,189	146.3
1851–1860[a]	1,500,132	1,094,439	137.1
1861–1870[a]	1,480,646	965,982	153.3
1871–1880[a]	1,808,228	1,136,482	159.1
1881–1890[a]	3,169,839	2,024,300	156.6
1891–1900[a]	2,361,836	1,442,383	163.7
1901–1910[a]	6,309,062	2,741,181	230.2
1911–1920[a]	3,612,772	2,111,186	171.1
1921–1930[b]	2,282,988	1,824,221	125.1
1931–1940[b]	229,150	299,281	76.6
1941–1950[b]	417,987	617,052	67.7
1951–1960[b]	1,155,421	1,360,058	85.0
1961–1970[b]	1,487,611	1,834,066	81.1
1971–1980[b,c]	1,859,302	2,103,373	88.4
1981–1990[d,e,f]	2,659,019	2,678,507	99.3
	[3,415,032]	[3,281,564]	[104.1]
1991–1994[f,g]	1,486,857	1,705,775	87.2
	[2,507,657]	[2,001,683]	[125.3]

[a] From Ferenczi and Willcox (1929), Table VII.
[b] From Houstoun, Kramer, and Barrett (1984), Table A–1.
[c] Excludes 1980.
[d] From U.S. Immigration and Naturalization Service (1991), Table 11.
[e] Excludes 1981.
[f] Excludes persons legalized under the provisions of the Immigration Reform and Control Act of 1986. Numbers in brackets include IRCA legalizations.
[g] From U.S. Immigration and Naturalization Service (1996), Table 12.

Age Composition

Immigrant age composition is more difficult to track over long periods of history than is gender composition because of changed age groupings in reported data. Table 3.5 shows the young adult age class as 15–40, 14–44, 16–44, and 15–44 for different periods. Nevertheless, certain generalizations can be made about the age composition of historical immigration to the United States.

Between the 1830s and the 1880s little change occurred in the aggregate age composition of U.S. immigrants; for example, the percentage in the 15–40 age class ranged between 66.3 and 68.4 (Table 3.5), which is a very narrow band for a five-decade period. However, during the 1890s, as immigration from southern and eastern Europe surged, those who were 15 to 40 increased to 77.6 percent (1891–98). After the 1920s, the percentage in the 16–44 class fell, while the percentage of persons over 44 increased dramatically from 9.2 percent (1921–30) to 18.4 percent (1941–50). After a decline in the 1950s, the percentage of immigrants who are older has continued to rise: in 1995, 19.4 percent of U.S. immigrants were over 44 years of age.

Skill Composition

In a number of papers, Borjas has argued that the skills or human capital embodied in successive immigrant cohorts declined during the post-World War II period.[11] Regarding immigration toward the end of the nineteenth century, Spengler (1956, p. 281) made the same claim:

> The southward and the eastward shifts of the sources of immigration were accompanied by changes in the composition of the immigrant stream and in the nature of its impact on the American economy. An increasingly large proportion of the immigrants came from relatively underdeveloped agricultural countries, with the result that the occupational composition of the immigrants came to be increasingly inferior to that of an American population.

Available data regarding skill composition are not clean-cut. Occupational classifications have changed over time. Moreover, occupations were for the most part self-reported, and different occupations could carry different connotations for people from different parts of the world. Perhaps most importantly, however, over time different percentages of immigrants actually reported an occupation. For example,

Table 3.5 Age Composition of U.S. Immigration, 1921–1994 (%)

Period	Age 15–40	14–44	16–44	15–44	Over 40	Over 44
1821–1830	71.3				11.3	
1831–1840	66.3				9.8	
1841–1850	66.8				9.9	
1851–1860	68.4				10.5	
1861–1870	68.2				11.8	
1871–1880	67.0				12.6	
1881–1890	68.1				10.5	
1891–1898	77.6				7.9	
1899–1900		81.4				5.7
1901–1910		83.0				5.0
1911–1917		80.0				6.5
1918–1920			70.6			10.4
1921–1930			73.3			9.2
1931–1940			66.3			17.1
1941–1950			60.0			18.4
1951–1960			63.5			13.6
1961–1970			60.8			13.8
1971–1980			59.4			14.8
1981–1990				66.3		15.8
1991–1994				68.8		16.4

SOURCE: For 1820–1957, U.S. Bureau of the Census (1975), Series C133-138, p. 62; for later years, various annual reports and statistical yearbooks of the Immigration and Naturalization Service.

during the 1901–10 period, 74.3 percent of the immigrants reported an occupation, whereas during the 1861–70 period, only 38.8 percent reported one.

Table 3.6 reports two measures of skill composition and lists them in two ways. First, it identifies immigrants classified as professional, commercial, or skilled and refers to this group as "skilled." Second, it breaks out the first two classes, professional and commercial, into a group called "highly skilled." For each group, percentages are reported relative to all immigrants and also to only those who reported an occupation. These occupational classifications are used by decade, beginning with 1821–30, but this classification scheme ends with 1898 data. After 1898, the occupational groupings are professional, technical, and kindred workers; managers, officials, and proprietors, except farm; and craftsmen, foremen, operatives, and kindred workers. These three groups at least roughly match those for the 1821–98 period, which can be observed by noting how similar the figures for 1899–1900 are compared to the corresponding figures for 1891–98.

From each measure of skill reported in Table 3.6, basically the same conclusions may be drawn. First, as immigration from Ireland began to surge during the 1840s, skill composition declined sharply in terms of the percentages of immigrants classified as skilled and as highly skilled. Second, when immigration from Germany began to build during the 1850s and 1860s, the skill composition rebounded. Third, the data affirm Spengler's assertion that when immigrant origins shifted toward southern and eastern Europe, the skill composition of the flows was low: the lowest percentages reported in Table 3.6 are for the period from 1881 to 1910. However, the downward shift appears to have occurred earlier, during the 1861–70 and 1871–80 periods, before movement from southern and eastern Europe became maximal. Fourth, after the imposition of entry quotas and during the period when immigration was at a low level for other reasons, the skill composition increased once again during the 1930s and 1940s.

The gender, age, and skill composition of historical U.S. immigration have been described in some detail (Ferenczi and Willcox 1929), but virtually no effort has been made to formally model these compositional aspects. This observation parallels our earlier observation that compositional models of migration are rare even in the contemporary context.

Table 3.6 Skill Composition of U.S. Immigration, 1821–1990 (%)

Period	Skilled[a]	All immigrants Highly skilled[b]	Percentage declaring an occupation	Those declaring an occupation Skilled	Highly skilled
1821–1830	28.5	14.1	30.2	94.1	47.5
1831–1840	21.5	7.7	38.7	55.6	20.0
1841–1850	13.2	3.0	45.3	29.0	6.6
1851–1860	14.6	5.1	39.0	37.4	13.2
1861–1870	17.8	5.0	38.8	45.9	12.8
1871–1880	14.7	2.8	50.8	28.9	5.6
1881–1890	12.3	2.0	50.4	24.4	4.0
1891–1898	15.0	2.2	58.2	25.8	3.7
1899–1900	14.7	2.4	67.9	21.7	3.6
1901–1910	16.2	3.0	74.3	21.9	4.0
1911–1920	16.6	3.7	70.4	23.6	5.3
1921–1930	19.2	4.8	60.8	31.7	8.0
1931–1940	21.8	13.7	41.9	51.9	32.6
1941–1950	25.0	11.7	45.3	55.2	25.9
1951–1960	23.9	9.4	47.2	50.6	20.0
1961–1970	23.3	12.2	44.1	52.8	27.6
1971–1979	22.7	12.6	41.6	54.6	30.2
1982–1988[c]	–	9.3	34.0	–	27.3
1989–1990[d]	–	7.8	55.8	–	14.0

[a] For the 1821–1898 period, *skilled* refers to "professional," "commercial," and "skilled," whereas for the period beginning 1899, *skilled* refers to "professional, technical, and kindred workers," "managers, officials, and proprietors, except farm," and "craftsmen, foremen, operatives, and kindred workers."

[b] *Highly skilled* refers to the first two categories listed in note "a" for the respective periods.

[c] Occupational information is unavailable for 1980 and 1981 in published INS reports. For 1982–85, what had previously been called "professional, technical, and kindred" was called "professional specialty" and for 1986–90, "professional specialty and technical." The *skilled* group is not comparable for the period after 1982 due to changes in published occupational classifications.

[d] Due to the inclusion of persons legalized under the Immigration Reform and Control Act of 1986 in the 1989 and 1990 figures, these years are not comparable to earlier years. Thus, they are reported separately.

Notes

1. Although "official" data such as those presented in this chapter frequently are used with no misgivings regarding their quality, the numbers are far from flawless. Immigrant records were not maintained consistently. For example, the definition of an "immigrant" changed several times during the nineteenth and early twentieth centuries, which is at least in part responsible for U.S. immigration figures that do not coincide with (U.S.-bound) emigration figures provided by source countries. Moreover, immigrants arriving by sea were not always counted accurately, and migration over U.S. land borders often went unreported. See Gould (1979) for a discussion of certain shortcomings of historical U.S. immigration data.

2. Of the 1.8 million figure for 1991, over 1.1 million were legalized under the terms and conditions of the Immigration Reform and Control Act of 1986. During 1992, 1993, and 1994, a total of 193,642 were so legalized. The legalized individuals were not new entrants to the United States but rather had entered the country legally and overstayed or had entered without documents. During 1992–1994, 141,690 additional persons entered as "legalization dependents."

3. During the 1820s, an average voyage from Liverpool to New York by sailing ship required 40 days, but because of weather conditions, many voyages took much longer, even more than twice as long (Gould 1979, p. 613). In 1867, the average crossing for a sailing ship was 44 days, whereas that for a steamship was 14 days. During the 1870s and 1880s, the average crossing by steamship had fallen to 7–10 days. The shorter time in passage greatly reduced sickness and the loss of life. Scott (1972, p. 29) reported death rates for arriving vessels of almost 25 percent during the late 1840s and illness rates of over 30 percent. However, these figures appear to be high, perhaps focusing on what Mokyr referred to as "coffin ships," on which between 30 and 45 percent of the passengers died at sea; many more died soon after arrival. During 1847, on-board mortality was quite high, but during 1848 such mortality probably did not exceed 2 percent (Mokyr 1983, pp. 267–268).

4. According to Mokyr (1983, p. 230), until the early 1830s about two-thirds of the Irish emigrants preferred Canada as a destination, but after 1835 about three-fifths preferred the United States.

5. Of course, the Soviet Union did not exist as such during the 1870s, but the U.S. Immigration and Naturalization Service reports historical data in this way.

6. Although some fraction of this number no doubt originated in Canada and Newfoundland, many ships bearing immigrants destined to the United States arrived in Quebec. Ships carrying raw materials from Canada to Europe found a profitable backhaul in migrant traffic (Gould 1979). Thus, data reporting country of last residence could distort figures for country of birth.

7. Gould (1979, p. 616) noted that British restrictions on the emigration of skilled labor were lifted in 1825. Legal impediments to emigration were severe in eastern and central Europe until much later in the nineteenth century.

8. Migration between Mexico and the United States has occurred during four major periods, the first of which coincided with the second wave of European migration to the United States (Weintraub et al. 1998). The Mexico-born population of the United States increased from approximately 100,000 in 1900 to about 1.0 million in 1930, due primarily to the northward movement of seasonal agricultural laborers (along with refugees from the Mexican Revolution and some others).

    During the 1930s, approximately 600,000 Mexico-born persons moved from the United States back to Mexico, with the consequence that the Mexico-born population of the United States declined to about 400,000 in 1940. This reverse flow makes up the second major period of migration between Mexico and the United States.

    Weintraub et al. characterized the organized bilateral recruitment of Mexicans to work in U.S. agriculture (1942–1964) as the third major period of migration between Mexico and the United States. Even after the discontinuation of the Bracero program in 1964, flows of legal immigrants and illegal migrants from Mexico continued and grew as ties with family and friends in the United States expanded (Massey et al. 1987), thus constituting the fourth major period of Mexico-United States migration.

9. "Lifetime migration" refers to persons who were residing in area j at time t and were born in some other area.

10. Data used to calculate the 1901–1910 sex ratios have been drawn from Reports of the Immigration Commission (1911, pp. 41–44). Some confusion appears to exist concerning the volume number of the report cited here. The Immigration Commission published 42 volumes. The volume referenced above is listed in the publication itself as "Vol. 20" and carries the title *Statistical Review of Immigration 1820–1910—Distribution of Immigrants 1850–1900*. But in the "list of reports of the Immigration Commission" this title is shown as volume 3; volume 20 is shown as *Immigrants in Industries: Pt. 23, Summary Report on Immigrants in Manufacturing and Mining*.

11. Much of this research is summarized in Borjas (1990).

4 The Immigration Data

The immigration patterns described in Chapter 3 are based primarily on census data. Although census data, particularly the Public Use Microdata Samples (PUMS), provide much detail on the foreign-born population of the United States, for the purposes of this study they have at least three serious shortcomings with respect to tracking immigrant composition. First, census data relate to the foreign-born population as enumerated every 10 years. The foreign-born population consists of immigrants (legal resident aliens), nonimmigrants (such as visitors for pleasure and students), and illegal resident aliens. The present study focuses on legal immigrants only and thus requires an alternative data set.

Second, census data reflect only the "residual" foreign-born population. A large fraction of those immigrants who legally enter the United States are thought to subsequently depart. Warren and Kraly (1985) argued that of the 30 million legal immigrants admitted to the United States between 1900 and 1980, about 10 million subsequently emigrated from the United States. Studying the 1971 U.S. immigrant cohort, Jasso and Rosenzweig (1982) showed that the fraction of immigrants that subsequently departs is a function of the country of birth, meaning that the residual foreign-born population enumerated in the census is self-selected because of the selective emigration of prior immigrants.

Third, the census involves a count only every 10 years. Consequently, with the possible exception of examining specific entry cohorts of the foreign-born, changes over time in the various compositional patterns of migration cannot be traced in any detail.

Due to these factors and others involving econometric procedures, we have chosen to use the U.S. Immigration and Naturalization Service (INS) data in this study. Because these data are annual and include a record for every legal resident alien granted entry into the United States, the analyst is able to study annual swings in compositional patterns that may be due to economic, social, and political conditions in source countries and to economic conditions in the United States.

For many years the INS has published annual data on persons admitted to the United States as legal resident aliens.[1] These publications also include information on persons naturalized and on those admitted as nonimmigrants. The published data have been widely used for descriptive purposes, but less commonly for analytical purposes. More recently, the INS has begun to make microdata available. The INS Public Use Tapes contain considerable detail on each person admitted as a legal resident alien. In spite of the fact that the microdata tapes include much valuable information, they have not been widely used for at least two reasons. First, and probably most importantly, the data for certain years are flawed, which has the potential to seriously interrupt any time series created from the tapes. Second, for the years included in the data, the number of microdata files is enormous because the United States admits immigrants in very large numbers. Partially as a consequence of these numbers and partially for other reasons, the INS Public Use Tapes are extremely cumbersome to use.

This chapter, which draws heavily from Greenwood, McDowell, and Trabka (1991), describes the INS Public Use Tapes (referred to also as "INS data") and their strengths and weaknesses. One of the major strengths of the data is the possibility of developing an annual time series on many variables relating to U.S. immigration. We document the frequency and severity of certain flaws in the data, which are clearly a major source of weakness, including the years and the number of records for which the data are flawed. We also discuss methods of "correcting" the problems inherent in the data, so as to allow the use of a continuous time series in the panel-data models estimated below. Finally, we discuss changes over time in the gender, age, and skill composition of U.S. immigration, based on the INS data.

NUMBER OF RECORDS AND TYPES OF INFORMATION

The United States is the world's major country of immigration. Between 1991 and 1995, over 5.2 million persons were accepted as legal resident aliens. Consequently, the number of records in the INS data is enormous, even for a single year. Table 4.1 reports the annual number of U.S. immigrants beginning in 1972, which is the earliest year for which the Public Use microdata are available.[2] This table also subdivides the numbers for the two broad immigrant classes defined under U.S. law, namely, numerically restricted and numerically exempt. It further splits the exempt group into its two major components, which are refugees and immediate relatives of U.S. citizens. Not only are the numbers large even for the year with the smallest number of admittances (1972, 384,685); the numbers are also growing. The number of legal immigrants admitted in 1991 (1,827,167) was the highest annual total in U.S. history.[3]

The INS data contain a record on each alien legally admitted to the United States for permanent residence. For individuals who are classified as "new entrants," the data are drawn from the U.S. Department of State form VISA OF-155 (Immigration Visa and Alien Registration), which is filled out at the time the individual is processed for admittance. For those who were already in the United States in a temporary status but who were adjusted to legal permanent resident after petitioning the INS, INS Form I181 is used.

The INS Public Use Tapes contain the following information on each alien who became a legal permanent resident of the United States between 1972 and 1991: port of entry, month of admission, year of admission, class of admission, country of chargeability, country of birth, country of last permanent residence, nationality, sex, age, marital status, occupation, state and area of intended residence, most recent nonimmigrant class of entry, most recent nonimmigrant year of entry, and labor certification. Almost 300 ports of arrival are listed in the data, as are the locations of INS District offices in the United States and in U.S. territories (such as Agana, Guam, and San Juan, Puerto Rico).

Immigrant class of admission refers to the specific condition that entitles the person to become a permanent resident of the United States. Information on class of admission contains considerable detail, such as preference category and/or precise type of family relationship under which admittance was gained, new arrival versus adjustment of status, the refugee act under which admittance was gained, and type of special immigrant. For particular categories of immigrants, both the person qualifying for admission and his or her dependents are counted against the category; consequently, principals are distinguished from beneficiaries.

58

Table 4.1 Immigrants by Type of Admission, 1972–1991

Fiscal year	Total	Subject to numerical limitations	Exempt from numerical limitations		
			Total[a]	Immediate relative of U.S. citizens	Refugee and asylum adjustments[b]
1972	384,685	283,666	101,019	86,332	–
1973	400,063	282,911	117,152	100,953	–
1974	394,861	274,131	120,730	104,344	–
1975	386,194	281,561	104,633	91,504	–
1976	398,613	284,773	113,840	102,019	–
1976TQ[c]	103,676	72,511	31,165	27,895	–
1977	462,315	276,500	185,815	105,957	–
1978	601,442	341,104	260,338	125,819	122,472
1979	460,348	279,478	180,870	138,178	32,049[d]
1980	530,639	289,479	241,160	151,131	75,835
1981	596,600	330,409	266,191	147,148	107,244
1982	594,131	259,749	334,382	162,968	156,601
1983	559,763	269,213	290,550	172,006	102,685
1984	543,903	262,016	281,887	177,783	92,127
1985	570,009	264,208	305,801	204,368	95,040
1986	601,708	266,968	334,740	223,468	104,383
1987	601,516	271,135	330,381	218,575	96,474
1988	643,025	264,148	378,877	219,340	110,721

1989	1,090,924	280,275	810,649[e]	217,514	84,288
1990	1,536,483	298,306	1,238,177[e]	231,680	97,364
1991	1,827,167	293,846	1,533,321[e]	237,103	139,079

SOURCE: United States Immigration and Naturalization Service, *Annual Report* (1966–1977) and *Statistical Yearbook of the Immigration and Naturalization Service* (1978–1991).

[a] This column includes immediate relatives of U.S. citizens, refugee and asylum adjustments, and special immigrants. The last of these is given by the difference between the "total" column and the sum of the two columns to its right.

[b] Data prior to 1978 are not comparable because most refugees entered as numerically restricted. During 1978, 1979, and 1980, refugees also entered as restricted, but their numbers were dwarfed by those who entered as numerically exempt under special legislation.

[c] TQ = transitional quarter.

[d] Includes only Cuban refugees, Indochinese refugees, and other.

[e] The 1989 figure was inflated by the legalization of almost 478,814 resident aliens under the provisions of the Immigration Reform and Control Act of 1986. During 1990, 880,372 persons were legalized, and during 1991, 1,123,162 persons were legalized. These individuals are not included on the INS Public Use Tapes.

For those who adjust their status, the INS data report the most recent nonimmigrant class of entry, of which 35 separate designations are included; among these designations are temporary visitor for pleasure, temporary visitor for business, temporary worker, exchange visitor, student, and many more. The most recent year of nonimmigrant entry also is given.

Country of chargeability is the independent country to which the immigrant is credited; country of chargeability is almost always country of birth. Each independent country was limited to 20,000 numerically restricted immigrants per year under the immigration law that is studied here (the Immigration and Nationality Act Amendments of 1965), whereas in 1991 dependencies of independent countries were limited to 5,000 per year of the 20,000 limit. Over 230 separate codes are included for various countries of birth. Country of citizenship is reported under nationality.

PRACTICAL PROBLEMS

The Volume of the Data

The first problem encountered in working with the INS data involves sheer volume. In addition to dealing with a very large number of observations (totaling well over 10 million for the period 1972–1991), users of the data are confronted with a mind-boggling array of variables that must somehow be organized. The possible combinations of characteristics that might be used as variables for purposes of analysis are far in excess of one billion.

We were guided in our choice of information by two thoughts, namely, the goals of the study and the theoretical model or models that yielded hypotheses to be tested. The objective of our study is to analyze the gender, age, and skill composition of legal U.S. immigrants. To meet this goal, we specified models that required information on country of birth, year of admission, class of admission (numerically restricted or numerically exempt), gender, age (three groups), and occupation (three groups). Our models also require that this information be cross-tabulated. For example, we not only needed to retain the number of male immigrants, but also the number of these males who were numerically restricted, aged 20-34, and professional and technical workers. The lack of the necessary data on the independent variables of the model limited us to a maximum of 60 countries. In order to produce an annual time series for each of the 60 countries of birth for 20 years (1972–1991), we aggregated individuals from each country into 36 cells (two classes of admission times two gender distinctions times three age groups times three occupational groups), which is a manageable number of variables.

Immigrant Source Countries

For every immigrant, the INS Public Use Tapes contain three types of information on source country or countries: country of birth, country of last permanent residence, and country of nationality. Because the objective of our research is to explain various compositional aspects of U.S. immigration, some countries had to be eliminated because information on the explanatory variables of our models simply is not available. We exhaustively sought data for as many countries as possible. We finally had to settle on 60 source countries for which we had information on all the necessary variables (Table 4.2). The various continents and regions of the world are reasonably well represented among the set of 60 countries.

Periodicity of the Data

The INS data are available on a fiscal-year, rather than a calendar-year, basis. This means that for the years 1972–1976, the data refer to immigrants who entered the United States from July through June of the following year (e.g., 1972 data are for July 1971 through June 1972). The year 1976 included a transitional quarter (July, August, September), which is specifically identified as a separate period.[4] After this, the data refer to October of the previous year through September of the fiscal year in question.

Refugees

From an analytical perspective, the presence of refugees in the data file has the potential to cause serious problems. As shown in Table 4.1,

Table 4.2 The 60 Source Countries Used in This Study[a]

Region/Country	Region/Country
Africa	Europe (continued)
Botswana	Ireland
Burundi	Italy
Egypt	Netherlands
Kenya	Norway
Liberia	Spain
Malawi	Sweden
Mauritius	Switzerland
Swaziland	United Kingdom
Tanzania	Yugoslavia
Tunisia	North and Central America
Zimbabwe	Barbados
Asia	Canada
India	El Salvador
Indonesia	Haiti
Israel	Honduras
Japan	Jamaica
Korea	Mexico
Malaysia	Nicaragua
Pakistan	Panama
Philippines	Trinidad & Tobago
Singapore	Oceania
Sri Lanka	Australia
Thailand	Fiji
Europe	New Zealand
Austria	South America
Belgium	Argentina
Denmark	Brazil
Finland	Chile
France	Ecuador
Germany	Paraguay
Greece	Uruguay
Hungary	Venezuela
Iceland	

[a] In the analytical work that follows, Israel is not included in "Asia," but rather is grouped with "Europe"; also, "Western Hemisphere" refers to the groups of "North and Central America" and "South America" in this table.

aggregate refugee admittances have been quite irregular; for example, 122,472 were admitted or adjusted in 1978, 32,049 in 1979, and 156,601 in 1982. This irregularity is compounded because during certain years, refugees tend to have been admitted or adjusted in large blocks from specific source countries (e.g., 67,985 from Cuba in 1977, but 3,885 in 1982; 86,777 from Vietnam in 1978, but 1,435 in 1977; 25,476 from Haiti in 1988, but only 5 in 1985). The arrival of refugees in the United States is not actually listed in the INS data; the refugees appear only when they adjust their status to permanent resident (and some refugees may never adjust their status). Thus, refugees have some potential to overwhelm the normal immigration numbers for certain countries, causing tremendous spikes in the annual series.

The movement of refugees to the United States is probably motivated by reasons different than those of other migrants, although they also presumably seek better employment opportunities and higher wages. To a larger extent than with other immigrants, however, refugee admittances are discretionary on the part of U.S. authorities, who must decide which potential immigrants qualify as refugees, how many to accept in any given year, and from where to accept them. It is precisely this discretion and the resulting irregular admittances of refugees from different countries that has the potential to overwhelm any effort to empirically estimate a model using the INS data.

The problem of refugees can be eliminated in either of two ways. First, the major source countries of the refugees can be eliminated from the database, because country of birth is one of the variables in the INS data. In our research, we took this approach not so much because of refugees themselves, but because of the unavailability of other information on those countries, such as gross domestic product per capita, measures of educational attainment, etc. Second, because refugees can be specifically identified according to their entry class, they can be selectively eliminated from the data for any country of birth included in the researcher's working data set.[5] We also used this approach, even though for most of our 60 countries very few refugees remained in our data set because their major countries of origin had been eliminated.

As shown in Table 4.3, when refugees and IRCA legalizations are removed from the data, the 60 countries in our sample accounted for between 58.2 and 73.6 percent of all nonrefugee immigrants 20 years of age and older. A definite downward trend exists in this percentage,

64

Table 4.3 Annual, Adjusted Annual, and 60-Country Annual Immigration, 1972–1991

Year	Immigrant total	Excluding refugee/legalized		60-county set	
		All	Aged 20 and over	Aged 20 and over	As % of "excluding refugee/legalized aged 20 and over"
1972	384,685	355,886	229,902	169,203	73.6
1973	400,063	369,155	233,675	168,982	72.3
1974	394,861	369,211	230,794	166,770	72.3
1975	386,194	351,529	222,834	160,976	72.2
1976	398,613	358,627	235,152	170,188	72.4
1977	462,315	383,830	259,853	179,499	69.1
1978	601,442	468,661	318,127	223,293	70.2
1979	460,348[b]	364,465	242,551	163,562	67.4
1980	530,639	442,582	307,904	205,124	66.6
1981	596,600	489,025	334,395	232,300	69.5
1982	594,131	486,201	335,138	201,178	60.0
1983	559,763	456,895	322,202	206,826	64.2
1984	543,903	451,759	317,948	206,967	65.1
1985	570,009	474,969	340,790	222,476	65.3
1986	601,708	497,325	356,383	234,837	65.9
1987	601,516	509,608	367,631	242,545	66.0
1988	643,025	561,293	419,005	290,687	69.4

1989	1,090,924	527,340	377,839	242,747	64.2
1990	1,536,483	558,737	395,474	241,406	61.0
1991	1,827,167	564,921	398,665	231,977	58.2

SOURCE: U.S. Immigration and Naturalization Service, *1994 Statistical Yearbook of the Immigration and Naturalization Service*, Table 1; INS Public Use Tapes, 1972–1991.

[a] Excludes refugees and legalizations under the Immigration Reform and Control Act of 1986. Detail in the INS *Statistical Yearbooks* may not match the totals shown here because some classes of refugees are not labeled specifically in the *Yearbook*, but they can be found in the Public Use Tapes by the Act under which they were admitted.

[b] The total number of immigrants shown here differs from that reported in the INS *Statistical Yearbook* due to a problem with the data for 1979. Neither measure is accurate; the total in the *Yearbook* contains duplicate records, and the total shown here represents approximately 85 percent of total immigration in 1979 because the duplicate records have been eliminated.

presumably because the source countries became more diversified over the 20-year period. These 60 countries account for a sufficiently high fraction of all immigrants that considerable confidence can be placed in any empirical results obtained by using them. Countries excluded from the list that have been the source of important nonrefugee movements in recent years include the Dominican Republic, China, and Iran.

Age Detail

In the INS data, a single age is reported for each immigrant. Although some immigrants may not know their exact age (a problem that is not uncommon around the world), we have no reason to believe that this is a serious problem in the INS data.

The models developed below emphasize individual decision making, assuming rational agents who seek to maximize their utility. Because children typically do not make their own decisions about whether or not to migrate to the United States, we have eliminated children from the immigration data that we analyze: specifically, all persons in the INS files who were under 20 years of age at the time of entry have been removed from the data. Within the group 20 and over, we identify three age classes: 20–34, 35–54, and 55 and over. Our empirical work especially focuses on the groups of age 20–34 and 55 and over.

Occupational Information

The occupational information in the INS data has some potential problems.[6] First, the occupation listed by the immigrant is self-reported. Some experts argue that different occupational titles may mean different things in different countries, thus perhaps making a given occupational title noncomparable across source countries. Second, a large fraction of the immigrants either had no occupation or chose to report none, perhaps because they were not entering under an occupational preference and were therefore not required to give one. Moreover, for those immigrants who enter as principals under the third and sixth (occupational) preference categories, reported occupation refers to the job they were to be taking in the United States and not their last job.[7] For everyone else, the occupation refers to the last job held in the country of last permanent residence. For those who adjust their status, this last job could be in the United States.[8]

The first problem (if indeed it is a problem) can be addressed by grouping occupations into broad categories. Thus, only intentional misreporting that would significantly misrepresent a person's occupation would present a problem, and misreporting does not appear to be a concern. Perhaps a second reason for using broadly defined occupations is that the number of cross-classifications of the data is held to manageable proportions. This is especially true when the data are split into two genders, three age groups, and two classes of immigrants (i.e., numerically restricted and numerically exempt). Thus, two broad occupations are defined in our work: 1) professional, technical, and kindred workers plus managers, officials, and proprietors (not including farm proprietors); and 2) craftspersons and laborers. The second group includes everyone who declared an occupation and is not included in the first group. A third category includes occupation not reported, homemakers, the unemployed or retired, and students (not including those under 20, who were eliminated from our data set).

The second problem, of not reporting an occupation, is potentially more serious. For each of 60 source countries, Table 4.4 reports the average percentage of persons 20 years of age and older who reported an occupation over the period 1972–1991. These percentages vary widely. The problem for analytical purposes is one analogous to selectivity and results in measurement error. Moreover, these percentages may differ because labor force participation rates differ across countries, or because different proportions of men and women are included in the flows (the latter being related to labor force participation). In the empirical work on skill composition that is reported in Chapter 8, we include in each regression a variable for the percentage of the immigrants from country i in year t who fail to report an occupation. This variable is treated as endogenous (that is, assumed to be correlated with unobserved country-specific effects) and thus provides a control for the percentage who do not report an occupation.

Table 4.4 Persons 20 Years Old and Over Who Reported an Occupation: 1972–1991 Country Means (%)

Region/Country	Mean	Region/Country	Mean
Africa		Europe (continued)	
Botswana	57.1	Ireland	67.4
Burundi	56.3	Italy	53.6
Egypt	59.5	Netherlands	59.5
Kenya	62.4	Norway	58.9
Liberia	62.0	Spain	51.1
Malawi	58.4	Sweden	59.9
Mauritius	63.3	Switzerland	63.7
Swaziland	70.1	United Kingdom	59.6
Tanzania	63.1	Yugoslavia	55.6
Tunisia	60.5		
Zimbabwe	64.4	North and Central America	
		Barbados	80.6
Asia		Canada	59.7
India	51.8	El Salvador	69.0
Indonesia	51.1	Haiti	70.1
Israel	60.4	Honduras	61.8
Japan	41.0	Jamaica	78.7
Korea	39.4	Mexico	62.6
Malaysia	60.8	Nicaragua	54.7
Pakistan	55.1	Panama	51.5
Philippines	56.0	Trinidad & Tobago	69.1
Singapore	56.3		
Sri Lanka	62.9	Oceania	
Thailand	49.4	Australia	65.2
		Fiji	74.7
Europe		New Zealand	65.9
Austria	60.1		
Belgium	53.2	South America	
Denmark	60.1	Argentina	58.2
Finland	56.4	Brazil	52.9
France	58.2	Chile	58.0
Germany	47.4	Ecuador	65.5
Greece	56.8	Paraguay	57.6
Hungary	60.9	Uruguay	65.6
Iceland	49.1	Venezuela	45.5

FLAWS IN THE INS DATA

For certain years, two types of flaws are present in the INS Public Use Tapes, and because each could cause a discontinuity in the time series on immigrant admittances from various source countries, each must be addressed.

Missing Records for 1979

The data for 1979 are not complete: only about 85 percent of total admittances are included in the file. The INS discovered eight years later that a number of 1979 entries were exact duplicates (one immediately following the other with the same immigrant identification number) and concluded that these were due to a conscious human act. The INS then purged the file of all such duplicate observations. (The INS *1979 Statistical Yearbook* erroneously includes these duplicate entries.) The INS determined that the duplicate records were substituted for actual immigrants and based on preference-category expectations determined that about 15 percent of all 1979 immigrant records were lost.

Because there is no way of restoring the missing information, we felt it necessary to carefully examine the 1979 data to determine, to the best of our ability, whether any bias was introduced by what might have been the systematic exclusion of a certain group or groups. We studied aggregate time-series information on many variables, such as gender, age by gender (with 12 specific age classes identified), and occupation. We found no indication that 1979 data were unusual, in the sense that no break occurred in the temporal patterns of the fractions of all immigrants who were accounted for by our various groups.

Thus, we used the 1979 data as we received them. In our analytical model, we control for unobserved temporal effects that, among other things, could account for any anomaly for 1979. We feel that, for our purposes, the problem with the 1979 data is not a major obstacle.

Missing Information for Certain Years

The second flaw in the INS data is perhaps more serious, but unlike the 1979 problem, it is correctable. For the years 1980–1983, information on gender, occupation, country of last permanent residence, port of entry, marital status, nationality, state and area of intended residence, nonimmigrant class of entry, and nonimmigrant year of entry is missing from a number of records. Experts at INS, who were not working for the agency when the problem occurred, have no idea what caused the information to be lost.[9] Elimination of refugees from the sample removes many of the incomplete records, but for the 60 countries used in our study, a large number of observations (Table 4.5) remain with no information on gender and occupation, which are critical variables for our study.[10]

For the records with missing information, gender was imputed in the following way. First, for the observations with no missing data, gender was transformed into a dummy variable (1 = female; 0 = male) and was regressed on other immigrant characteristics for which information was complete. The independent variables in this regression were preference category (six dummies, one for each of the six preference categories), age, principal immigrant versus beneficiary (dummy), new arrival versus adjustment of status (dummy), and labor certification or not (dummy). For certain years, two different labor certification variables were used. These regressions were estimated separately for each of the 60 countries and for each year (for a total of 240 regressions; for exceptions, see Appendix A, Table A1). The R^2 values for each country and each year for which data were imputed are reasonably high, with almost all in excess of 0.40 and most at or above 0.50 (Table A1). These regressions were then used to predict gender for the observations for which this information was missing. For predicted values of 0.5 and higher, 1.0 was assigned to the observation (female); for those with a predicted value of less than 0.5, zero was assigned (male).

The same procedure also was followed in an attempt to impute the missing values for occupation. However, this effort was unsuccessful. For every source country, the percentage of total immigration accounted for by those who reported no occupation far exceeds the percentage who reported one of the two broad occupational groupings with which we worked. Consequently, based on predicted values, the regression assigned the category with the highest probability, which was almost always "no occupation reported."

As an alternative, we compared the observations with missing data to those with complete data for the entire sample and several of the

Table 4.5 Detail on Incomplete INS Records for 1980–1983

Year	Total immigrants	Total records with missing data	Share of total (%)	60-country sample	Records in sample with missing data	Share of sample (%)
1980	530,639	132,541	25.0	300,006	52,541	17.5
1981	596,600	130,351	21.8	348,170	40,674	11.7
1982	594,131	21,512	3.6	287,495	13,680	4.8
1983	559,763	22,680	4.1	289,249	13,921	4.8

largest source countries. For the most part, the percentage of immigrants in each classification was found to be very similar. For example, in the complete group, 1.4 percent are first-preference immigrants, 41.0 percent are numerically exempt, and 24.5 percent are adjustments of status; the respective percentages for the missing group are 1.4, 41.4, and 24.2.[11] We thus assumed that the occupational distribution also was comparable between the two groups, and we allocated the same percentage of the incomplete observations to each of the three occupational groups as that group represents of the complete observations.

This procedure was followed separately for each country and for each year. This approach obviously has the shortcoming of not assigning occupations to the micro observations, as we did with gender, which prevents occupations from directly being cross-tabulated with other variables. When we needed to cross-tabulate information (for 240 cells), the same procedure was followed, with the missing observations assigned to the 240 cells in the same proportion that those cells represented in the complete sample. This procedure, however, overwrites the individual gender estimates by assigning all attributes (numerically restricted/exempt, gender, age, and occupation) of the cell.

As shown in Table 4.6, for 1981 the observations for which information is missing are strongly biased toward adjustments of status. The same is also true for 1982 and 1983, although the bias is not quite as strong. For 1980, new arrivals and adjustments have virtually the same distribution. For 1981, 1982, and 1983, the observations with partial information lean toward the numerically exempt category relative to

Table 4.6 Comparison of Missing and Complete Records for the 60-Country Sample, 1980–1983 (%)

	1980		1981		1982		1983	
	Missing	Complete	Missing	Complete	Missing	Complete	Missing	Complete
New arrivals	75.8	75.5	28.4	86.3	48.8	75.7	38.9	77.6
Adjustment of status	24.2	24.5	71.6	13.7	51.2	24.3	61.1	22.4
Preference category								
Numerically restricted	58.6	59.0	52.5	67.4	47.1	55.2	47.9	54.9
First preference	1.4	1.4	1.1	1.3	1.5	1.9	1.6	2.0
Second preference	23.6	23.9	15.6	20.3	16.9	23.6	15.8	23.0
Third preference	5.3	4.4	9.5	3.3	10.0	6.1	11.7	6.1
Fourth preference	1.6	1.8	2.1	3.1	3.7	3.9	3.0	3.7
Fifth preference	18.2	18.4	7.7	17.9	8.5	13.6	8.5	13.9
Sixth preference	5.4	5.4	7.2	4.8	5.3	5.5	7.0	6.2
Other	3.1	3.8	9.3	16.7	1.3	0.8	0.4	0.1
Numerically exempt	41.4	41.0	47.5	32.6	52.9	44.8	52.1	45.1

the numerically restricted category, although the bias is not as strong as for new entrants/adjustments. Table 4.6 also reports differences within preference categories.

The INS is certain that the missing information relates to specific months during which individuals gained legal resident alien status. This type of omission is not as serious as one related to other variables, such as port of entry, because here the omissions would have been systematically biased toward specific source countries.

GENERAL ASSESSMENT OF THE INS DATA

Compared to cross-sectional data, time-series data on migration are quite rare. However, even when time series data are available, they rarely provide detailed migrant characteristics (e.g., gender, age, marital status, education, employment status, and earnings). For example, for the United States, the major time-series data set relating to internal migration is the Internal Revenue Service file. These data provide considerable spatial detail (states and counties), and income class, but contain no information on gender, age, or any other demographic measure of interest.

A major advantage of the INS data is that they have both a temporal (year) and a cross-sectional (source-country) dimension. Moreover, they provide considerable demographic detail. Economic information on the immigrants is largely lacking, which is a serious drawback to economists, but the INS Public Use Tapes are the best available data source for the study of U.S. immigration by immigrant class. Although the INS Public Use Tapes have shortcomings, these data also present a great research opportunity.

COMPOSITION OF U.S. IMMIGRATION, 1972–1991

In Chapter 3, we considered historical trends beginning in 1821 in gender, age, and skill composition. Here we focus on the 1972–1991 period and (for the most part) on the 60 countries that make up our sample. During this 20-year period, noteworthy aggregate changes occurred in each measure of composition that we study. For specific countries, the changes were often quite pronounced.

Immigrant Gender

Although many believe that immigration is dominated by young males, and although this belief is accurate for international migration in parts of the world, it is not true for legal immigration to the United States, at least with respect to legal immigration over the last 25 years (Table 4.7).[12] Through the 1970s, the gender composition favored females by between 7.2 percentage points (1976) and 4.4 percentage points (1979). However, during the 1980s, the flows began moving toward equality and during most years slightly favored males. This change was due in part to the increased admittance of refugees, which tend to be strongly oriented toward males. For example, in 1984, 56.6 percent of 92,127 refugees were males; corresponding figures for 1986 and 1988, respectively, are 56.0 percent of 104,383 and 55.2 percent of 81,719.[13]

During the early 1990s, the gender composition shifted strongly toward males. In 1990, the differential favored males by 6.6 percentage points; in 1991, almost two-thirds of the legally admitted immigrants were male. However, this shift was transitory and was associated with the legalization of previously illegal migrants under IRCA. Persons of Mexican birth were the primary beneficiaries of legalization (in 1991, 79.0 percent of 946,167 persons born in Mexico who received legal status were male).[14]

An important aspect of gender composition is immigrant class of entry. Table 4.8 reports, by gender, immigrants who entered as numerically restricted and numerically exempt from our 60-nation set. These data exclude both refugees and persons legalized under IRCA. Several points are noteworthy. First, the 60-country sample favors females more than does overall immigration. The percentage of females in the sample never falls below 50.3 percent for any year. Second, the pattern seen earlier, in which the female share falls toward 50 percent and then begins to rise again, is more characteristic of numerically exempt immigrants than numerically restricted immigrants. In many years, the

Table 4.7 Gender of U.S. Immigrants, 1970–1996 (%)

Year	Male	Female
1970	47.4	52.6
1971	46.6	53.4
1972	46.7	53.3
1973	46.6	53.4
1974	46.7	53.3
1975	46.8	53.2
1976	46.4	53.6
1977	46.9	53.1
1978	47.6	52.4
1979	47.8	52.2
1980	47.9[a]	52.1[a]
1981	47.6[a]	52.4[a]
1982	50.3	49.7
1983	50.7	49.3
1984	50.5	49.5
1985	50.2	49.8
1986	50.0	50.0
1987	49.9	50.1
1988	50.5	49.5
1989	50.4	49.6
1990	53.3	46.7
1991	66.4	33.6
1992	51.0	49.0
1993	46.9	53.1
1994	46.3	53.7
1995	46.3	53.7
1996	46.2	53.8

SOURCE: U.S. Immigration and Naturalization Service, *Statistical Yearbook of the Immigration and Naturalization Service*, various years.

[a] Number is taken from INS Public Use Tapes and does not include refugees.

Table 4.8 Gender of Numerically Restricted and Numerically Exempt U.S. Immigrants Aged 20 and Over for 60 Countries, 1972–1991 (%)

Year	All		Restricted		Exempt	
	Male	Female	Male	Female	Male	Female
1972	44.8	55.2	48.2	51.8	36.8	63.2
1973	44.4	55.6	47.1	52.9	38.7	61.3
1974	44.2	55.8	47.3	52.7	38.3	61.7
1975	44.5	55.5	47.6	52.4	38.1	61.9
1976	43.7	56.3	48.2	51.8	35.5	64.5
1977	44.6	55.4	48.3	51.7	38.8	61.2
1978	44.1	55.9	48.6	51.4	36.0	64.0
1979	44.4	55.6	49.4	50.6	38.2	61.8
1980	45.5	54.5	49.1	50.9	41.4	58.6
1981	45.3	54.7	47.8	52.2	41.4	58.6
1982	46.7	53.3	49.6	50.4	44.1	55.9
1983	47.9	52.1	50.5	49.5	45.7	54.3
1984	48.2	51.8	50.0	50.0	46.9	53.1
1985	47.9	52.1	50.1	49.9	46.2	53.8
1986	47.6	52.4	50.0	50.0	46.0	54.0
1987	47.9	52.1	49.9	50.1	46.3	53.7
1988	49.7	50.3	50.4	49.6	49.4	50.6
1989	46.6	53.4	50.1	49.9	43.9	56.1
1990	44.4	55.6	50.1	49.9	40.1	59.9
1991	43.5	56.5	49.6	50.4	39.0	61.0

differential favors exempt females by over 10 percentage points and in some cases by over 20.

Immigrant Age

The age composition of U.S. immigration also has changed over time (Table 4.9). The percentage of male immigrants accounted for by the youngest age class (under 10 years old) has fallen regularly since 1970 (in 1970, 19.0 percent, but in 1992, only 9.8 percent). The percentage of male immigrants of age 50 and over has risen regularly, from 7.9 percent in 1970 to 11.3 percent in 1992. The percentage aged 20–29 first increased (from 24.5 percent in 1970 to 30.0 percent in 1982) and then declined (to 26.9 percent in 1988).

As is the case for males, the percentage of females under 10 years old has fallen steadily, from 16.7 percent in 1970 to 9.9 percent in 1992 (Table 4.9).[15] The percentage of females aged 50 and over increased from 9.2 percent in 1970 to 14.4 percent in 1992. The percentage of women in this age class consistently has been greater than the percentage of men. The longer life expectancy of females is one explanation for their relatively heavier representation in the older age classes. Notable is the decline in the percentage of female immigrants aged 20–29, who accounted for 31.3 percent of female immigrants in 1976 but 26.6 percent in 1992. This decrease, as well as decreases for each younger age class, was offset by increases for each of the older age groups, not just for the group 50 and over.

As with gender composition, age composition is highly sensitive to whether the immigrants are numerically restricted or numerically exempt (Tables 4.10 and 4.11). For the 60-country sample, the age composition of males and females within each class of entry is quite similar. However, for each year, the exempt group has far larger shares of persons in the 55–64 age class than the restricted group, which is due to the family reunification provisions of U.S. law. Moreover, among exempt immigrants, the age group 55–64 has grown quite dramatically, to more than 20 percent of each gender in 1991. This growth has been mainly at the expense of the youngest age group reported (20–34), because the 35–54 age class also has increased over time. Differences in age composition between numerically restricted and

Table 4.9 Age of Male and Female U.S. Immigrants (%)

Age (years)	Males					Females				
	1970	1976	1982	1988	1992	1970	1976	1982	1988	1992
Under 10	19.0	16.5	14.3	10.7	9.8	16.7	14.4	13.8	10.8	9.9
10 – 19	18.5	19.1	20.2	16.3	17.5	18.2	17.3	18.6	15.6	17.0
20 – 29	24.5	28.2	30.0	26.9	28.3	30.4	31.3	29.0	27.3	26.6
30 – 39	20.1	17.8	18.2	22.5	22.5	16.7	15.5	17.2	20.4	21.2
40 – 49	9.9	8.2	8.0	11.5	10.7	8.8	8.0	8.2	10.7	10.8
50 – 59	4.6	5.0	4.6	6.3	5.8	4.9	6.4	6.3	7.6	7.1
60 – 69	2.4	3.6	3.2	4.1	3.8	3.1	4.8	4.6	5.3	5.1
70 – 79	0.7	1.4	1.3	1.4	1.4	1.0	1.9	1.9	1.9	1.8
80 and over	0.2	0.3	0.3	0.3	0.3	0.2	0.4	0.4	0.5	0.4

Table 4.10 Age of Numerically Restricted Male and Female Immigrants Aged 20 and Over for 60 Countries, 1972–1991 (%)

Year	Males 20–34	Males 35–54	Males 55–64	Females 20–34	Females 35–54	Females 55–64
1972	65.1	29.8	5.1	64.5	28.9	6.6
1973	63.4	31.0	5.6	63.7	29.0	7.4
1974	64.7	30.4	4.9	65.5	27.9	6.6
1975	65.1	29.9	5.0	64.8	28.4	6.8
1976	66.2	28.5	5.3	65.0	27.2	7.8
1977	65.1	29.1	5.8	63.9	28.0	8.1
1978	61.9	32.3	5.9	64.0	29.5	6.6
1979	62.0	33.2	4.8	63.6	32.1	4.3
1980	65.2	30.6	4.2	64.6	30.8	4.6
1981	59.0	35.5	5.5	63.6	31.3	5.1
1982	64.2	32.4	3.4	64.9	31.6	3.5
1983	63.0	33.0	3.9	64.3	32.5	3.2
1984	61.3	34.4	4.3	63.3	33.3	3.5
1985	62.8	33.3	3.9	64.6	32.3	3.1
1986	60.3	35.6	4.1	63.8	33.0	3.2
1987	60.8	35.0	4.2	64.1	32.8	3.1
1988	58.0	37.4	4.7	62.5	34.3	3.3
1989	60.0	35.6	4.4	63.0	33.8	3.2
1990	57.6	37.3	5.1	61.4	35.0	3.6
1991	58.0	36.8	5.2	61.7	34.6	3.7

**Table 4.11 Age of Numerically Exempt Male and Female Immigrants for
60 Countries, 1972–1991 (%)**

	Males			Females		
Year	20–34	35–54	55–64	20–34	35–54	55–64
1972	70.9	15.7	13.5	70.7	16.6	12.7
1973	73.5	15.3	11.2	70.7	17.3	12.1
1974	72.0	16.0	12.0	68.4	18.0	13.6
1975	69.2	16.2	14.7	65.4	18.2	16.4
1976	66.4	14.8	18.8	64.8	16.5	18.7
1977	64.2	15.7	20.1	60.7	17.3	22.1
1978	65.0	16.4	18.7	61.3	18.7	20.0
1979	60.2	16.3	23.5	56.7	18.9	24.5
1980	63.8	17.2	19.0	57.4	18.6	24.0
1981	61.3	16.7	22.0	55.1	18.8	26.1
1982	63.5	18.5	18.0	55.9	20.2	23.9
1983	66.4	17.7	15.9	57.3	20.2	22.5
1984	68.1	17.1	14.8	58.6	19.9	21.6
1985	67.0	18.0	15.0	58.4	20.1	21.5
1986	65.9	18.4	15.7	57.5	20.1	22.5
1987	64.5	20.0	15.5	57.1	20.6	22.3
1988	52.3	33.5	14.3	51.1	29.1	19.9
1989	58.7	23.2	18.1	56.1	22.1	21.9
1990	56.8	22.4	20.8	57.0	20.9	22.1
1991	55.5	22.3	22.2	56.1	21.4	22.5

numerically exempt immigrants again serve to emphasize the importance of disaggregating along these lines.

When we move beyond these aggregate figures to study the gender
and age composition of immigration from specific countries, we
uncover considerable variability. Table 4.12 reports gender and age
composition in broad terms for 1972 and 1988 for selected countries.
(We report 1988 data because they include no legalizations, in contrast
to 1989–1991 [see Table 4.1]). Four observations are noteworthy.
First, wide variations in gender composition exist across countries for a
given year. For example, in 1972, 70.8 percent of immigrants from
Germany were female, versus 45.4 percent from India; in 1988, 72.1
percent from Germany and 41.1 percent from Haiti were female. Second, for any given country of birth, considerable changes have occurred
over time in gender composition. In 1972, 54.3 percent of immigrants
from Haiti were female, but in 1988, only 41.1 percent; from the U.K.,
58.9 percent were female in 1972, and 49.6 percent in 1988.

Third, for any given year, gender-specific age composition also varies widely among countries. For example, in 1988, 3.6 percent of the
female immigrants from Germany were 50 years of age or older, versus
23.8 percent from India. For the same year, only 11.0 percent of the
male immigrants from Haiti were less than 20 years of age, versus 42.9
percent from Korea. Fourth, for any given country of birth, considerable changes have occurred in gender-specific age composition over
time. India and the Philippines provide strong support for this observation. In 1972, 1.5 percent of the male immigrants and 1.5 percent of
the female immigrants from India were 50 and over; by 1988, the comparable figures were 20.3 percent and 23.8 percent. For the same
years, the percentage of male immigrants 50 and over from the Philippines grew from 6.1 percent to 20.4 percent, and the percentage of
females from 7.1 percent to 21.9 percent. The countries reported in
Table 4.12 were chosen because they are or have been particularly
important sources of U.S. immigrants; other countries may have even
greater ranges.

Skill Composition

For numerically restricted immigrants 20 years of age and over in
our 60-country sample, Table 4.13 reports annual data for our three

82

Table 4.12 Gender and Age of U.S. Immigrants from Selected Countries, 1972 and 1988

Country	Total immigration		Female (%)		Aged 50 and over (%)				Aged less than 20 (%)			
					Male		Female		Male		Female	
	1972	1988	1972	1988	1972	1988	1972	1988	1972	1988	1972	1988
Germany	6,848	6,645	70.8	72.1	6.1	6.4	6.8	3.6	45.8	31.5	27.4	18.6
Haiti	5,809	34,806	54.3	41.1	7.5	9.4	12.1	9.7	57.3	11.0	50.9	16.3
India	16,926	26,268	45.4	49.4	1.5	20.3	1.5	23.8	18.5	22.6	23.5	24.0
Korea	18,876	34,703	61.8	56.9	3.8	13.4	3.9	16.6	37.4	42.9	32.5	34.3
Mexico	64,040	95,039	49.3	43.9	5.4	10.3	7.2	13.8	49.9	17.6	48.2	20.9
Philippines	29,376	50,697	60.1	58.4	6.1	20.4	7.1	21.9	40.3	35.0	26.2	24.2
U.K.	10,078	13,228	58.9	49.6	10.2	8.0	11.2	8.2	37.7	24.4	28.1	24.5

SOURCE: U.S. Immigration and Naturalization Service, *1972 Annual Report of the Immigration and Naturalization Service*, Table 9; *Statistical Yearbook of the Immigration and Naturalization Service, 1988*, Table 12.

Table 4.13 Numerically Restricted U.S. Immigrants Aged 20 and Over, by Gender and Occupation for the 60-Country Sample, 1972–1991 (%)

Year	Males PTK[a]	Males Other	Males No occupation	Females PTK[a]	Females Other	Females No occupation
1972	40.6	51.6	7.8	21.2	22.1	56.8
1973	34.9	55.6	9.5	19.9	19.5	60.6
1974	31.1	58.0	10.9	17.7	21.3	61.0
1975	33.2	57.1	9.7	19.3	21.4	59.3
1976	34.3	53.9	11.8	19.7	21.6	58.7
1977	37.0	48.9	14.2	18.3	26.4	55.3
1978	29.9	56.7	13.4	12.9	30.1	57.0
1979	33.7	51.2	15.2	15.4	30.0	54.6
1980	35.7	47.5	16.8	13.0	32.7	54.3
1981	27.4	58.6	14.0	14.0	32.5	53.5
1982	35.6	45.1	19.3	14.8	31.6	53.6
1983	32.4	48.3	19.3	15.9	30.9	53.3
1984	31.6	45.7	22.8	15.7	30.7	53.6
1985	31.4	44.4	24.2	14.3	30.1	55.6
1986	30.8	44.4	24.9	14.6	29.8	55.6
1987	31.3	44.7	24.0	15.4	30.6	54.0
1988	29.3	50.4	20.3	15.6	32.0	52.4
1989	29.6	48.8	21.6	16.1	31.1	52.8
1990	31.0	46.7	22.3	17.3	30.0	52.7
1991	30.6	46.4	23.0	16.5	29.7	53.8

[a] PTK = professional, technical, and kindred plus managers, officials, and proprietors.

occupational groups (i.e., professional, technical, and kindred workers, as well as managers, officials, and proprietors; all others who report an occupation; and no occupation reported, homemakers, unemployed and retired persons, and students). Table 4.14 shows the same data for numerically exempt immigrants. To ascertain the significance of any trend in the data reported in Tables 4.13 and 4.14, we estimated the following simple regression for each share:

Eq. 4.1 $PCT_i = \alpha_i + \beta_i T + e_i,$

where PCT_i is the percentage point share for each group identified in the two tables and T is a simple linear time trend (i.e., $T = 1, 2, \ldots, 20$). The regression results are reported in Table 4.15; all estimated constant terms and coefficients are highly significant.

Among numerically restricted males, the share of the highest skill class fell significantly, but so did the share of immigrants with less skills (Table 4.15). The percentage reporting no occupation increased. Among numerically restricted females, the share of the group with the highest skills also declined significantly, but the share in the lower skill class increased significantly and the share reporting no occupation declined (Table 4.15).

The highest-skilled numerically exempt males behaved much like numerically restricted males in that their share also declined, but it fell much more rapidly between 1977 and 1988. The share of less-skilled immigrants also declined and those who reported no occupation increased (Table 4.15). The pattern for numerically exempt females in the highest skill class increased significantly over the 1972–1991 period, but the overall share for this group is not large, as indicated by the relatively low constant term (α_i) reported in Table 4.15. As with numerically restricted females, the share of numerically exempt females with less skills increased, and the share reporting no occupation declined.

As suggested by Borjas (e.g., 1990) in connection with census data, the fraction of males with the highest skills declined significantly over the 1972–1991 period. However, the fraction with lower skills also declined. One explanation that Borjas offers for declining skill composition is that immigrants have increasingly originated in countries with

Table 4.14 Numerically Exempt U.S. Immigrants Aged 20 and Over, by Gender and Occupation for the 60-Country Sample, 1972–1991 (%)

Year	Males PTK[a]	Males Other	Males No occupation	Females PTK[a]	Females Other	Females No occupation
1972	21.1	64.7	14.2	6.7	13.2	80.0
1973	20.9	66.0	13.1	6.9	14.6	78.4
1974	19.8	66.5	13.7	6.6	16.4	77.0
1975	22.3	62.3	15.4	7.8	15.9	76.4
1976	23.2	58.5	18.4	7.2	15.9	76.9
1977	23.9	58.0	18.0	8.8	18.4	72.9
1978	23.1	59.1	17.8	10.5	22.6	66.9
1979	21.5	59.7	18.8	9.1	21.4	69.3
1980	21.1	56.2	22.7	9.0	19.8	71.2
1981	21.3	57.4	21.4	9.4	20.8	69.8
1982	21.7	55.9	22.4	10.1	20.4	69.6
1983	17.6	61.3	21.2	9.5	22.2	68.3
1984	16.4	59.9	23.7	8.9	22.1	69.0
1985	16.4	56.9	26.8	9.3	22.4	68.3
1986	15.8	55.9	28.3	9.1	22.5	68.4
1987	14.8	56.6	28.6	8.7	22.0	69.3
1988	15.3	54.5	30.2	7.6	33.3	59.0
1989	15.8	53.9	30.4	8.7	20.7	70.6
1990	18.7	45.1	36.2	11.4	17.9	70.7
1991	19.5	42.7	37.8	11.1	17.0	71.9

[a] PTK = professional, technical, and kindred plus managers, officials, and proprietors.

Table 4.15 Simple Linear Regressions for Trends in Immigrant Skill Shares, 1972–1991[a]

Immigration class	α_i	β_i	Adjusted R^2
Numerically restricted			
Males			
PTK[b]	34.65***	–0.23***	0.21
Other	57.01***	–0.63***	0.47
No occupation	8.36***	0.85***	0.82
Females			
PTK[a]	18.48***	–0.20***	0.21
Other	22.41***	0.55***	0.53
No occupation	59.14***	–0.36***	0.61
Numerically exempt			
Males			
PTK[a]	23.19***	–0.35***	0.47
Other	66.27***	–0.83***	0.68
No occupation	10.54***	1.18***	0.94
Females			
PTK[a]	7.40***	0.14***	0.32
Other	16.37***	0.36***	0.19
No occupation	76.11***	–0.49***	0.35

[a] *** Indicates absolute $t \geq 1.96$.

[b] PTK = professional, technical, and kindred plus managers, officials, and proprietors.

less-skilled occupational structures. Since our sample of countries is large, this is also a possible explanation for our observation.

The overall percentage of females in the highest skill class fell, but that for the relatively small group of numerically exempt females increased (Table 4.15). Although the number of females in the highest skill class remained relatively low, it increased by a factor of almost 4 between 1972 and 1991. The percentage of females who reported no occupation decreased, but the corresponding percentage of males increased fairly substantially (Table 4.15). We do not know exactly why this latter increase occurred. It probably was in part the result of the increased fraction of older males who entered the United States, but other factors were undoubtedly also operating.

Notes

1. See U.S. Immigration and Naturalization Service, *Statistical Yearbook of the Immigration and Naturalization Service*, for data from 1978 to the present. For earlier years, a limited number of variables is available in various INS annual reports.
2. Although 1971 data are not available on the INS Public Use Tapes, they have been used to conduct quite innovative research. See Jasso and Rosenzweig (1982).
3. The figure for 1991 includes 1,123,162 immigrants who were legalized under the terms of IRCA. Such legalized immigrants are not represented in the data used in this study; we analyze "normal" immigration.
4. In our analytical work, this quarter is not included in any way.
5. Using refugee designations in the microdata files, we were able to exclude certain individuals who are not discernible in the published INS data.
6. For 1972 and 1973, immigrant occupations correspond to the occupations reported in the 1960 census. For 1974–1982, immigrant occupations correspond to those used in the 1970 census. For 1983–1991, the categories correspond to those given in the 1980 census, which relative to the previous censuses used far-more-aggregated categories.
7. For these individuals, the prospective U.S. employer actually reports a job title in the labor certification process, and this title yields occupation.
8. Regarding occupation coding, Michael D. Hoefer of the Demographic Statistics Branch of INS writes that "since new arrivals are coded at a central location . . . their quality is better than for adjustments. I have reason to believe that this is true based on comparing the occupational distributions by visa type. The percentage of unknown occupations is lower for new arrivals than adjustments; and this holds even for labor qualifying immigrants, who have the same source document for both adjustments and new arrivals" (private correspondence to M.G.).

9. Partial information regarding the lost files was created by INS through the use of separate records. However, the information on these records was not as extensive as that on the lost files.

10. For example, for 1980, of 132,541 records with missing data, 55,500 are for refugees.

11. A particularly large discrepancy does occur in 1981, with 71.6 percent of the missing observations being adjustments of status compared with only 13.7 percent in the complete group. However, even for 1981 the approach used here could not have been badly misleading. The vast majority of observations with missing information are from countries that supplied the United States with relatively many immigrants, and for these countries the observations with missing information were only a small fraction of the total. Thus, the distributions were based on relatively large fractions of the total, not on relatively small fractions.

12. A widely distributed U.N. document concerned with international migration asserts that "generally, migrants have included a larger number of males than females and have been over-represented in the working age and under-represented in the ages of childhood and old age, compared to the total population" (United Nations 1979, p. 54).

13. More recently, however, the gender composition of refugees has become more equal. In 1993, 51.0 percent of 127,343 refugees were male; in 1994, 50.9 percent of 121,434 refugees were male; and in 1995, 51.5 percent of 114,664 were male (U.S. Immigration and Naturalization Service 1997, p. 92).

14. U.S. Immigration and Naturalization Service 1992, p. 52.

15. Although in more recent years the male and female shares of children in the U.S. immigration flow have converged, in general the male share under 10 years old is greater than the female share in this age class. Many explanations are possible for this phenomenon, ranging from more purely demographic to more purely economic. For example, due to gender-selective abortions and infanticide, many countries around the world are known to have female population deficits. The same forces that favor such behavior could also cause female children to be left behind when part of a family migrates. Preferences for male adoptees in the United States could have the same result. Finally, such a phenomenon could be part of family long-term investment strategies that favor sending male children to the United States.

5 Modeling Flows of U.S. Immigration

"Determinants" of migration is a term used to broadly describe the factors that influence decisions to migrate. An empirical model of the determinants of U.S. immigration assesses which factors are statistically significant and which are not in shaping migration flows to the United States.

The importance of two types of characteristics may be assessed. First, personal characteristics (such as age, gender, schooling, marital status, English language ability, and many more) are of interest, but the data set that we use contains a limited number of personal characteristics. Second, place characteristics are potentially important. Because we know the country of birth of each legal resident alien allowed to enter the United States, we are able to develop a fairly rich set of information concerning where the migrants came from.

The models developed in this study are based on the immigrant's country of birth for two main reasons: 1) under U.S. immigration law, country of birth is a primary consideration for admission as a (numerically limited) legal resident alien; and 2) most legal immigrants have a country of last permanent residence that is the same as their country of birth.[1]

PRIOR MODELS

Much of the research on the determinants of U.S.-bound migration has focused on the nation's laissez-faire period, when institutional impediments to immigration were either nonexistent or few and when restrictions on emigration from source countries were low. This focus is perhaps chosen because binding immigration constraints (such as were put in place during the early 1920s) blunt the economic forces underlying migration.

From an economist's perspective, differential economic opportunity plays a key role in explaining international migration in general and

U.S. immigration in particular. The usual starting point for most economic analyses of the determinants of international migration is the expected utility model, in which an individual economic agent (i.e., a potential migrant in a particular source country) is assumed to maximize a utility function subject to a budget constraint. Money or real wage (or income) differentials are presumed to reflect opportunities for utility gains. Correspondingly, various measures of job opportunities are presumed to reflect the probability of employment. The potential immigrant is then assumed to select from among alternative destination countries the one that maximizes expected utility net of the costs of moving.[2] Of course, most potential migrants stay where they are either because the benefits of moving to another country are sufficiently low or because the costs are sufficiently high.

In the context of nineteenth and early twentieth century migration from Europe to the United States, two related questions have been at the center of the debate regarding the determinants of the movements: 1) Were migration flows from Europe to America caused by economic conditions in Europe (the push of low wages and lagging employment opportunities) or by economic conditions in America (the pull of relatively high wages and attractive employment opportunities)? 2) Were differential job opportunities more or less important than differential wages in determining the volume of transatlantic migration?

Economic historians, demographers, and others have long debated these questions.[3] The debate has typically concerned transatlantic migration until the early 1920s, when entry barriers in North America appear to have significantly curbed the flows.[4] Jerome (1926) was one of the first to study this issue. He examined immigration from Europe over a 100-year period up to the imposition of U.S. immigration quotas in the 1920s. He concluded that economic conditions in the United States were primarily responsible for short-cycle movements in European emigration to the United States. Kuznets and Rubins (1954) agreed with Jerome's findings.

Long cycles in transatlantic migration also have been studied.[5] Thomas's (1973) basic theme was that the interaction between the United Kingdom and the United States played a crucial role in these cycles. Thomas viewed the Atlantic economy of the period as consisting of Great Britain and a periphery of developing countries, including the United States, Canada, Argentina, and Australia. Thomas did not downplay the role of the United States in determining transatlantic migration, but rather placed Great Britain on a more equal footing. He felt that before 1870, conditions in Europe were probably more important than those in the United States, but after 1870 these positions were probably reversed.

Because long swings in European migration to the United States seem to have coincided for most source countries, Kuznets (1958) leaned strongly toward the importance of economic forces in the United States: "Since it is highly unlikely that the timing of either birth cycles or 'push' elements was the same in so many different parts of the world, the similarity must be ascribed to some 'pull' factors" (p. 31). Easterlin (1961) also argued for the dominance of conditions in the United States.

Swedish migration to the United States during the late nineteenth and early twentieth centuries has been studied intensely, starting with D.S. Thomas (1941). Contrary to the generalizations of Kuznets and others, she concluded that economic conditions in Sweden were relatively more important than those in the United States. Wilkinson (1967), in his analysis of long swings in Swedish emigration to the United States, found that changes in U.S. labor demand were more important than those in Sweden. On the other hand, Quigley (1972), studying migration from the agricultural and nonagricultural sectors of Sweden to the United States between 1867 and 1908, came down squarely on the side of Thomas. His regression analysis shows that "the influence of both Swedish agricultural and industrial conditions was as important as corresponding conditions on the United States" (p. 121). Quigley's findings suggest that emigration from the agricultural sector was at least as sensitive to Swedish agricultural wages as to those in the United States. Industrial wages in the United States provided a strong attraction, but emigration from the Swedish industrial sector was very sensitive to Swedish industrial wages. U.S. agricultural and industrial wages are significant in Quigley's regression, but the coefficients are not nearly as high as that for Swedish industrial wages.

Wilkinson (1970) developed annual time series data (1870–1913) on immigration from Denmark, Germany, United Kingdom, Sweden, Italy, Russia, and France, as well as data relating to output and income in the various countries. In his regression analysis, he also used a measure of migrant stock (the number of persons born in country i and living in the United States at time t) as an explanatory variable. An important distinguishing feature of Wilkinson's study is that he specifically tests for the relative importance of income and job opportunities, where the latter variable is proxied by output. Wilkinson concluded that "European migration to the United States prior to World War I was significantly influenced by both employment opportunities in the particular European country . . . and the gain in real income to be achieved by migration to the United States" (p. 277). He found that employment opportunities in the United States were much less important than real wages. Moreover, the stock of past migrants proves to be critical for each country he studied except Russia. In addition, Wilkinson concluded that output expansion in the United States had no influence on migration from either the United Kingdom or Germany to the United States. Because the United Kingdom and Germany were major sources of U.S. immigrants during the nineteenth century, these findings appear to be in sharp contrast to those of Kuznets and others, and they have not gone unchallenged.

Gallaway and Vedder (1971), using British data that report annual migration flows (1860–1913) from the United Kingdom to the United States, as well as to Australia, Canada, and South Africa, developed regression results somewhat different than those of Wilkinson. They found that higher unemployment rates in the United Kingdom were marginally significant in explaining migration to the United States, but unemployment rates and changes in wage levels in the United States were not significant. However, four of five dummy variables that depict various "panics" in the United States are negative and highly significant, suggesting that business conditions in the United States were indeed important. Gallaway and Vedder attribute the differences between their findings and Wilkinson's to what they judge to be an inappropriate use of lagged variables by Wilkinson. On balance, Gallaway and Vedder concluded that both push and pull forces were operating to drive transatlantic migration, but the pull forces were dominant.

Hatton and Williamson (1994) argue that no consensus exists on the push versus pull issue, in part because the issue is a "false one." Potential migrants almost certainly base their decisions on a comparison of alternatives (including the present location), but ad hoc models combined with shaky data have yielded conflicting conclusions.

In general, historical studies of migration from Europe to the United States and Canada suggest that economic conditions in the destination countries, especially high wage rates and employment opportunities, were attractive. Economic conditions in Europe also were of some important in explaining the flows, and demographic conditions in source countries almost certainly played a role. The costs of migrating were important as well. In this respect, past settlement was a key determinant of migration flows, because family and friends who previously migrated provided not only information about America, but also cultural, linguistic, and religious ties to the former place of residence.

MODELING THE DETERMINANTS OF MIGRATION TO THE UNITED STATES

Numerous motives obviously underlie the decisions about whether and when to move to the United States. The model developed here emphasizes the importance of both differential economic advantage between various source countries and the United States, as well as the ease with which a prospective migrant can transfer accumulated occupational skills to the U.S. labor market (Greenwood and McDowell 1991). Moreover, we presume that, *ceteris paribus*, the presence or absence of different types of social programs in source countries will influence differential economic advantage, because these programs entail income transfers between various groups in those countries.

Potential migrants are assumed to be optimizers who choose their utility-maximizing location subject to their budget constraint. The potential migrant's utility in the home country is a function of income and the relative "attractiveness" of the home country. The individual decides to move to the United States when expected maximum utility, which is a function of expected market earnings, income transfers, and amenities, exceeds anticipated utility in the home country by an amount greater than the costs associated with migration.

The ease or difficulty of migrating to the United States is influenced importantly by U.S. immigration policy. U.S. entry requirements may alter the force of economic and other types of influences in numerous ways. For example, a large and growing group of immigrants has been exempt from the quota limitations of U.S. law, and they incur lower costs of moving to the United States both because they need not wait for a preference visa and because of their family ties. Another group has already entered the United States as nonimmigrants and has already borne many of the costs associated with migration; certain members of this group are able to "adjust" their status to legal resident alien (i.e., immigrant).

An important aspect of this chapter is to estimate the magnitudes of the influence of various determinants of U.S. immigration. In the model that follows, immigrants who are numerically restricted are distinguished from those who are numerically exempt. The models estimated in this study contain several vectors of variables, including differential economic opportunity, the cost of migration, the political attractiveness and religion of potential source countries, U.S. immigration policy, and social programs in origin countries, as well as certain features of these programs. (See Appendix B for definitions of the variables.) The models are of the following general form:

Eq. 5.1 $\qquad m_{it} = \beta_j \, v_{ijt} + e_{it}$

where

$\quad m_{it}$ = the rate of U.S. immigration from country i during year t, and the rate is defined relative to the population of i during t;

$\quad \beta_j$ = j vectors of estimated coefficients;

$\quad v_{ijt}$ = j vectors of explanatory variables relating to country i during year t; and

$\quad e_{it}$ = error terms.

Differential Economic Opportunities

The differential economic opportunity vector contains five elements: per capita gross domestic product (GDP) of country i relative to that of the United States, measured in U.S. dollars; the rate of growth of real GDP in country i averaged over the three previous years relative to a comparable rate for the United States; country i's central government revenues, expressed as a percentage of i's GDP; the percentage of i's population residing in urban areas; and the percentage of country i's labor force that is female.

Countries with a relatively high per capita GDP have smaller earnings differentials relative to the United States, which should reduce emigration. In countries with relatively rapid growth of real GDP, job prospects in the country ought to be more attractive, again reducing emigration. Central government revenue as a percentage of GDP measures the extent of government taxes (and perhaps of government transfer activity) within a country. The burdens of taxes fall most heavily on workers, who tend to be those individuals in the age groups with the highest propensities to migrate. Given that we directly control for numerous types of transfers (which are discussed in detail below), we expect higher levels of government revenues to encourage migration.

The percentage of the source-country's population that is urban provides a measure of economic development; *ceteris paribus*, the rate of migration to the United States ought to be lower from more highly urbanized and developed countries. Female participation in formal labor markets is proxied by the percentage of country i's labor force that is female. Where jobs in formal labor markets are relatively more available to women, their employment prospects at home should be better, with the consequence that their emigration should be discouraged. However, higher female labor force participation should also reflect a larger pool of potential economic migrants from country i to the United States, thus clouding the expected direction of its influence. Therefore, we do not specify *a priori* a sign on female labor force in the immigration-rate regressions.

Migration Costs

The vector for the costs of migration to the United States contains six variables, three associated with direct entry costs and three associated with the costs of transferring skills. Direct entry cost variables include distance (the estimated airline mileage between the principal city of country i and the nearest major U.S. city); country i's crude birth rate; and a measure of the number of U.S. armed forces personnel (as well as U.S. citizen employees of the military) who were stationed in country i during year t, relative to the population of i during year t.

Distance serves as a proxy for the money costs (as well as the non-money costs) of moving farther away from relatives and friends. High birth rates are likely to be associated with larger family size, and the larger the family, the higher the migration costs. Finally, spouses of U.S. military personnel enter the United States as numerically exempt from immigration quotas, and, after a five-year wait and meeting other requirements, they may qualify for U.S. citizenship. As U.S. citizens 21 years of age and older, they may reunite with their parents, who are also exempt from quota restrictions. Therefore, potential immigrants from source countries with higher direct costs (e.g., more distant, higher birth rate, few U.S. military persons) should, on average, have lower propensities to migrate to the United States.

Migration costs are also incurred because some portion of an immigrant's accumulated human capital (knowledge and skills) may not be perfectly transferable internationally. Three variables are included to capture these losses: a dummy variable that equals 1 if country i's official U.N. language is English; a measure of country i's education level, which is proxied by the number of students at the third level (i.e., universities and other institutions of higher education) expressed as a fraction of total population (and then multiplied by 100); and the number of natives of country i who attended a U.S. university during t, as a proportion of the country's population aged 20 to 24.

Expected skill losses should be lower for potential migrants from English-speaking countries. Better educated individuals generally have higher propensities to migrate, and they also should be better able to adapt to the requirements of a new occupational environment; a higher general level of education also may reflect an occupational mix that is more like that of the United States. Finally, receiving an education at a U.S. university should enhance the ease with which an individual can transfer job skills to the United States. Because lower skill losses should encourage migration, immigration to the United States ought to be greater from English-speaking countries, from countries with a relatively high level of education, and from countries that send relatively many students to the U.S. schools.

Political Attractiveness and Religion

The political attractiveness of a country is presumed to be reflected by its political competitiveness, which is measured by an index of political rights ranging from 1.0 for countries with a fully competitive electoral process to 7.0, indicating least free (Gastil 1987). Countries with politically competitive systems are considered to be relatively attractive. Political repression should be a push factor for emigration, but, if domestic political repression is associated with emigration restrictions, emigration will be reduced.

The measures of religion used here distinguish countries that are primarily Catholic or Muslim, where a country is designated as Catholic (Muslim) if the country's population is made up of at least 50 percent Catholics (Muslims). Since Catholicism is the single largest religious denomination in the United States, we expect immigrants from countries designated as Catholic to find social assimilation easier, which should encourage their migration. We do not specify a sign for the influence of being from a Muslim nation.[6]

U.S. Immigration Policy

U.S. immigration policy clearly can influence the rate of migration to the United States. We believe that because of policy impacts on both the cross sections (i.e., source countries) and time series (i.e., years), controls must be introduced for U.S. immigration policy (Greenwood and McDowell 1991).[7]

To account for policy differences and changes in the law, our model includes variables that reflect the spatial and temporal aspects of U.S. policy. We distinguish three regions of the world: Asia (not including Israel), the Western Hemisphere (1972–1976), and all other countries. The last group is the benchmark, and immigration from the Western Hemisphere (1972–1976) and from Asia is examined by the use of two regional dummies. One dummy variable equals 1 for Western Hemisphere countries for the years 1972 through 1976, and the other equals 1 if country i is in Asia. These dummies are included to account for differential treatment, possible non-policy-related discrimination, divergence between policy guidelines and implementation, and the importance of intervening alternative destinations for potential migrants to the United States.

Other aspects of U.S. immigration law affect the costs of entry into the United States. For instance, the law facilitates the entry of foreign-born relatives of U.S. citizens and legal resident aliens. Migration costs are thus lower for persons who have citizen relatives in the United States, as proxied by the number of recent naturalizations of persons born in country i. The number of U.S. naturalizations of persons born in country i are summed over year t and the prior four years and are expressed relative to the population of i during t.

During the period 1977–1982, 147,538 preference numbers were issued under the Silva program, which was instituted under court order to provide replacement visas for numbers originally used for Cuban refugee adjustments. Visas available under the Silva program went to independent Western Hemisphere countries and were assigned in addition to the annual worldwide ceiling. As a practical matter, Mexico was allocated the majority of Silva visas, receiving 117,045 (79 percent). The numbers of such visas received by Mexico in the years 1977–1982 were 3,629, 49,481, 6,333, 4,242, 53,168, and 192, respectively (U.S. Department of State 1987, Table VIII). To account for the Silva program, a dummy variable is included that indicates a large number of Silva admittances from country i during year t (equals 1 for Mexico in 1978 and 1981).

The Immigration Reform and Control Act (IRCA) of 1986 provided for 5,000 nonpreference visas in both 1987 and 1988. Nonpreference (lottery) visas had not been available for some years, but the IRCA legislation made them available over and above the normal allotment of numerically restricted visas for aliens born in countries from which immigration had been adversely affected by the 1965 Amendments to the Immigration and Nationality Act.[8] A dummy variable is used to control for the influence of these lottery issuances. This dummy variable equals 1 if the number of NP-5 and OP-1 lottery issuances charged to country i was greater than 5 percent of the number of numerically restricted immigrants for year t who were born in that country.

Social Programs in Source Countries

We are unaware of any previous attempt to introduce an extensive set of social program indicators for source countries into a model of U.S. immigration. Neither are we aware of any effort to include such variables in a model of migration to any other country, in spite of the fact that many countries, especially in Europe, have social program systems that are more extensive and more generous than that of the United States. To study the importance of such programs, we had to develop the data set ourselves, drawing the basic information from the

Social Security Administration's *Social Security Programs throughout the World*. In the various models that we estimate, the social program vector includes several variables relating to the population covered by the specific program (coverage) and, given coverage, includes other variables relating to various features of the programs (features).

The basic idea that underlies the inclusion of these social program variables in the model is that the presence or absence of different types of social programs will influence differential economic advantage, since the programs entail income transfers among groups in the source countries. The extent to which benefits are provided to various groups depends on the particular program, program coverage, and other specific program features.

Eleven variables are included in the vector of social programs in country *i*. The social programs considered include those providing old-age pensions, sickness-related benefits, unemployment benefits, and family allowance subsidies. Old-age pension programs ordinarily take the form of pensions payable for life (or at least a considerable number of years). Old-age pension programs may provide pensions that are universally available (to all residents or citizens) or that are employment-related (available only to wage earners and salaried employees). Universal and employment-related programs also generally differ in terms of financing: whereas universal pension programs are usually financed from general government revenues, employment-related systems generally are financed through some combination of employer and employee contributions.

To distinguish the characteristics of old-age pension programs, we include three variables: a dummy variable that equals 1 if a country has a program providing pensions that are universally available; a dummy variable that equals 1 if a country has an employment-related pension program that operates as a social insurance system; and a dummy variable that equals 1 if a country has an employment-related pension program that operates as a provident funds system.[9] We also include a control indicating if a country has an old-age pension program containing a stipulation that the pension is not payable abroad or is payable abroad only under "limited" conditions.

Sickness-related programs also can be either universal or employment-related. One variable is used to indicate whether coverage is universally available to all residents or citizens. Three additional variables are included to identify specific program features: 1) those for which cash sickness benefits are paid when short-term illnesses prevent the insured individual from going to work; 2) programs providing maternity benefits that are paid to working mothers during some designated period before and after the birth of a child; and 3) programs providing health-care benefits, which are usually provided in the form of medical, hospital, and pharmaceutical benefits.

The unemployment-benefits programs included are those that generally provide compulsory insurance of a fairly broad scope, covering the majority of employed persons, regardless of the type of industry, or at least covering those workers in industry and commerce. Family allowance programs provide regular cash payments to families with children. Such payments may be either universal (provided to all resident families with a specific number of children) or employment-related (provided only to the families of wage and salary workers). In certain countries these programs may also include school grants, birth grants, maternal and child-health services, and sometimes even allowances for adult dependents. Two variables are included to indicate whether either a universal or employment-related family allowance program is available in country i.

To determine the effect of the various social programs on the (normalized) volume of immigration from a source country, we must first determine the programs' net cost-benefit impacts on natives of the country, particularly those natives who are the most likely to migrate. Other things being equal, young workers are more likely to migrate than older individuals. While old-age pension programs may provide attractive benefits to all individuals who ultimately receive them, such benefits are generally available only after some lengthy period of employment or residence. Therefore, the tax and/or wage contribution burdens imposed on younger workers may actually induce a larger volume of migration. Such an impact may be particularly pronounced in situations where old-age pensions are universally available. In such cases, not only are their benefits delayed to some future period, but the younger workers (through either tax or wage effects) also bear a substantial current burden of paying for the benefits received by other individuals. Thus, we anticipate that the presence of a universal old-age pension program in country i will encourage a higher rate of emigration.

For employment-related pension programs, this expectation is less certain. For instance, to the extent that younger workers anticipate that the present values of their future old-age benefits outweigh the current costs being imposed on them, the presence of such programs will not increase their propensity to migrate. Indeed, compared with the alternative of no pension program, employment-related pensions may serve to reduce migration. Moreover, a provident funds system does not entail an obvious transfer from younger to older workers. Such programs may stimulate migration, in that they provide an opportunity to save resources necessary to cover the costs of relocation. However, for individuals who have a vested interest in an old-age pension program, constraints on the ability to internationally transfer the pensions should discourage migration.

Programs that provide maternity benefits, employment-related family allowances, and unemployment insurance are the most likely to provide net benefits to young workers and their families. Consequently, we expect the presence of these programs to reduce the rate of immigration to the United States. The same expectation also may be attached to universal family allowance programs, though it is less clear here given the nature of transfers in programs providing universal benefits.

The effects of programs relating to sickness are not clear. For instance, in countries in which cash benefits are paid to individuals with illnesses that prevent them from working, these benefits are generally available to all workers. While the potential for such illnesses may increase with age, we cannot determine the net costs and benefits to particular groups of workers because those costs and benefits are generally tied to earnings. Without a more detailed characterization of the benefits and financing of such programs, we are unable to anticipate their effect on the rate of migration. Health care in the form of medical, hospital, and pharmaceutical benefits most likely assists older individuals, because sicknesses that result in such medical expenses generally increase with age. On the other hand, those benefits are also of value to young families, especially those with children. However, if such benefits are universally provided, we expect the cost burden imposed on workers to induce a higher rate of migration.

EMPIRICAL FINDINGS

This model has been estimated by means of a number of econometric techniques that are appropriate for panel data, including random effects, one-way fixed-effects–time, one-way fixed-effects–countries, and the Hausman-Taylor instrumental variable technique. These techniques are described in Appendix C. Depending upon the specific technique used, the resulting estimates differ somewhat. In this and subsequent chapters, we focus on the Hausman-Taylor estimates. The Hausman-Taylor approach (Hausman and Taylor 1981) uses instrumental variables, accounts for both temporal and country-specific effects, and is particularly appropriate when temporally invariant variables (labeled z) are included in the model and when certain variables may be endogenous. Variables that vary both temporally and among countries are labeled x. A subscript 1 indicates an exogenous variable, and a subscript 2 indicates and endogenous variable. (For comparative purposes, Appendix C reports estimates using other econometric approaches.)

The Hausman-Taylor approach specifically accounts for variables that vary only cross-sectionally (i.e., across countries). Distance, English language, the control for Asian nations, and the religion controls are obvious candidates for this set of variables. Moreover, although the social program measures may vary through time for any given country, in practice they need not do so. Thus, each social program variable was checked for each country. In no instance did any social program variable fail to change in any country. Thus, each of these variables was treated as temporally varying.

The Hausman-Taylor approach also requires a distinction between variables that potentially may be correlated with unobservable country-specific effects (endogenous variables) and variables that are not so correlated (exogenous variables). Frequently, no theory underlies the partitioning of the endogenous and exogenous variables; however, we wished to develop an underlying rationale. Our key to making the partition was to ask which variables could reflect "choice" (and consequently a taste for the U.S. lifestyle) and which could relate to potential work ethic or desire for education. Any such variable could be correlated with the unobservables. For example, naturalizations could reflect a taste for the United States. English language could lead to better knowledge about the United States through education, movies, newspapers, and television, thus leading to a correlation with the country-specific effects. Similar arguments could be made with regard to the education level in the source country, as well as to the number of foreign students from country i and U.S. military personnel in country i. We interpret our notion of choice broadly to include social choice. As a consequence, government revenue, political competitiveness, birth rate, female labor force participation, and the various social program variables are treated as endogenous, or potentially correlated with country-specific effects. Thus, the vector (x_1) for time- and country-varying exogenous variables includes relative per capita income; relative growth of GDP; percentage of population in urban areas; the control for the differential treatment of the Western Hemisphere natives during the 1972–76 period; the lottery program visas; and the Silva program. For temporally invariant exogenous variables, the vector (z_1) includes distance; the control for Asian nations; and the two controls for the primary religion being either Catholic or Muslim. Our division of variables between exogenous and endogenous has the practical consequence of placing a heavy burden on the estimation technique.

Table 5.1 contains Hausman-Taylor estimates of the basic model of U.S. immigration (with no social program variables), as well as three models that include the vector of social program variables so that we can see how the inclusion of the social program variables contributes to explaining the determinants of U.S. immigration. (Appendix D, Table D1 contains means and standard deviations for all variables used in the study, and Table D.2 contains t-statistics corresponding to Table 5.1). The following discussion focuses only on the regressions that include the social program vectors (right-most three columns in Table 5.1), and all statements of effects should be read with the implicit qualification, *ceteris paribus*.

Wage or income differences between the United States and source countries have frequently proven to be significant determinants of U.S. immigration (Greenwood and McDowell 1991; Lucas 1976). Higher per capita income (or related measures) in source countries or smaller differences relative to the United States discourage migration to the United States. Whether with respect to historical or contemporary U.S. immigration, such measures have rarely failed to provide significant

Table 5.1 The Rate of Migration to the United States, 1972–1991: Hausman-Taylor Instrumental Variable Estimates[a,b]

Vector/variable	Basic model[c]	All immigrants[d]	Numerically restricted[d]	Numerically exempt[d]
Diff. Econ. Opportunity				
Relative per capita income (x_1)	-0.016	0.005	0.080	-0.068*
Relative growth of GDP (x_1)	0.603**	0.425*	0.379*	0.066
Government revenues (x_2)	0.288*	0.399***	0.348***	0.045
% Urban (x_1)	-1.707***	-2.003***	-1.321***	-0.460***
% Female in labor force (x_2)	-1.304**	0.835	0.929*	-0.168
Migration costs				
Distance from U.S.A. (z_1)	-0.324***	-0.300***	-0.209***	-0.092***
Birth rate (x_2)	-2.550***	-3.131***	-2.112***	-1.023***
U.S. military presence (x_2)	0.074***	0.037	0.036*	0.003
Education (x_2)	0.298	0.347*	0.425**	-0.041
English language (z_2)	2.100***	-0.025	0.167	0.115
U.S. college students from i (x_2)	-0.307***	-0.250***	-0.227***	-0.021
Polit. attract. and religion				
Political competitiveness (x_2)	0.034***	0.032***	0.022***	0.010***
Catholic (z_1)	0.274	-0.362	-0.260	0.042
Muslim (z_1)	0.282	0.023	0.097	0.069
U.S. immigration policy				
Per capita naturalizations (x_2)	0.056***	0.057***	0.030***	0.027***
Lottery visas (x_1)	0.073*	0.080**	0.096***	-0.013

Silva visas (x_1)	0.160	0.154	0.220	-0.065
Western Hemisphere 1972–76 (x_1)	-0.260***	-0.270***	-0.200***	0.068***
Asia (z_1)	0.637***	-0.117	-0.193	0.112
Social programs				
Universal old-age (x_2)	–	0.009	0.055	-0.017
Employment-related old-age (x_2)	–	-0.050	-0.047	-0.017
Provident fund old-age (x_2)	–	-0.049	-0.011	-0.049
Old-age pension not portable (x_2)	–	-0.089*	-0.051	-0.037*
Universal sickness (x_2)	–	-0.015	-0.058	0.046
Cash sickness benefits (x_2)	–	-0.560***	-0.276***	-0.269***
Maternity benefits (x_2)	–	0.174***	0.143***	0.032
Medical benefits (x_2)	–	-0.084*	0.036	-0.118***
Unemployment insurance (x_2)	–	-0.840***	-0.779***	-0.050
Universal family allowance (x_2)	–	-0.154	-0.151*	0.015
Employment family allowance (x_2)	–	-0.174*	-0.141*	-0.020
Control				
Population of i (x_1)	-0.152***	-0.058	-0.010	-0.038*

a *** Indicates $t \geq 1.96$; ** indicates $1.67 \leq t < 1.96$; * indicates $1.29 \leq t < 1.67$. Appendix Table D2 contains the actual t-statistics that correspond to this table.

b The interpretation of the coefficients reported in this table for the rate model are not directly comparable to those for the composition models reported in the following chapters.

c No social program variable.

d Includes social program variables.

explanations. Thus, our results, which show the coefficient on relative income to be statistically insignificant in the regression for all immigrants, are somewhat surprising. This finding appears to be due in part to our choice of an econometric estimator, because (as indicated in Appendix C, Table C1) the more common one-way fixed-effects–time estimate of relative income is negative and highly significant. We believe that we are appropriately picking up country-specific effects with the Hausman-Taylor estimator and thus better controlling for such effects. Nonetheless, the lack of significance of relative income is surprising.

However, for those who are numerically exempt, the coefficient on relative income is negative and marginally significant. Thus, those persons who are not subject to entry restrictions (and thus the most likely to reflect the force of economic incentives) have some tendency to come from countries with lower relative incomes.

The coefficients of relative economic growth are positive and reflect marginal significance (Table 5.1); we had anticipated a negative sign. One possible explanation for the positive sign is that economic growth provides assets that help potential migrants pay the costs of an international move, but this explanation is not entirely satisfactory. Thus, our two key measures of differential economic opportunity behave disappointingly. Government revenue has the expected sign and is highly significant for all immigrants and for numerically restricted immigrants, but not for those who are exempt. Thus, higher tax and transfer activity encourages the departure of young and highly mobile individuals. Percent urban has the expected negative sign and is highly significant in each regression (Table 5.1). Thus, U.S. immigrants have a strong tendency to originate in less-urbanized and presumably less-developed countries. Female labor force participation does not have a particularly strong influence on migration rate in any regression including social program variables (perhaps because the marriage-market scenario is gender-specific and our data, at this point, are not decomposed by gender).

The migration costs vector performs somewhat better than that for differential economic opportunity. Distance and the associated higher costs of moving significantly discourage migration to the United States. Higher birth rates in source countries also significantly discourage migration, presumably by raising the cost of family migration.

Countries having a significant U.S. military presence send more migrants to the United States, but the relationship is only significant (marginally) in the numerically restricted regression.

While the influence of education is positive in three regressions (Table 5.1), it is significant only for the numerically restricted immigrants. Although the influence of English language is positive and highly significant in the basic model, this variable is not statistically significant when social programs are introduced. Thus, although English language and level of education play some role in influencing immigration to the United States, they do not play a particularly prominent role. This finding has important policy implications, because it suggests that numerically exempt immigration is not from countries with relatively high levels of educational attainment. If the migrants from such countries reflect source-country characteristics, exempt immigration is not keeping pace with restricted immigration in terms of providing the United States with well-educated newcomers.

Finally, contrary to expectations, countries that send more students to the United States (as nonimmigrants) tend to have lower rates of restricted immigration. This finding is surprising, but it may reflect a strategy to circumvent U.S. immigration restrictions: for countries with long waits for legal resident alien status, moving as a student may provide an alternative means of entering the United States.

Researchers have long known that political conditions in potential source countries provide a major inducement for immigration to the United States. Clearly, refugees are one example, but refugees are not included in this study. The coefficient on political competitiveness is positive and highly significant, which suggests that even "normal" flows to the United States are driven to some extent by dissatisfaction with suppressive political regimes. On the other hand, religion does not appear to directly influence decisions to move to the United States.

Parents, spouses, and children of U.S. citizens 21 years of age and older are exempt from numerical restrictions on immigration; thus, persons who have become naturalized U.S. citizens greatly facilitate movement to the United States. The variable for per capita naturalizations is positive and highly significant, reflecting the importance of this legal avenue for U.S. entry. The lottery program of the late 1980s also boosted U.S. immigration, especially numerically restricted immigration. Because the lottery recipients entered as restricted and not as exempt, this finding makes sense. However, the Silva program does not appear to have influenced the immigration rate.

During the first five years studied, U.S. entry requirements for Western Hemisphere immigrants were not as stringent as they were for natives of Eastern Hemisphere countries. Thus, the coefficients indicating that this differential treatment is associated with fewer immigrants is somewhat surprising. However, when the demand for entry from Western Hemisphere countries was low, the political cost to the United States of sustaining a good neighbor policy was also low. As the demand for immigrant visas from these countries increased, the cost of maintaining such a policy rose. Consequently, Congress placed Western Hemisphere countries under essentially the same admission criteria as Eastern Hemisphere countries. This argument suggests that entry restrictions favoring natives of Western Hemisphere countries were themselves endogenous with the flows from these countries.

The unique variables in this study are those relating to social program availability in source countries. Among these variables, that for the availability of unemployment insurance programs particularly stands out: the coefficients on this variable in both the "all immigrants" and the "numerically restricted" regressions have the highest t-value of any variable in these Table 5.1 regressions (see Appendix D, Table D2). The presence of unemployment insurance significantly discourages migration to the United States, and because the incidence of unemployment is highest among those labor force members in their low to mid twenties, unemployment insurance discourages migration by the individuals who have the highest propensity to migrate.

Numerically exempt immigrants tend to be considerably older than restricted immigrants (because the exempt group contains parents of U.S. citizens), and perhaps as a consequence, unemployment programs are not significant in the regression for exempt immigrants.

Old-age pension programs have little influence on the rate of immigration; the only effect of such programs involves portability. For countries where pension programs are not portable, the rate of migration to the United States is lower, particularly for exempt immigrants, who are presumably older; i.e., U.S. citizens—probably naturalized citizens, because their parents had been living abroad—are more likely to bring their parents to the United States if the parents are not required to give up their pension benefits.

Sickness and maternity programs also play a role in shaping immigration to the United States. In the regression for all immigrants, a significantly lower rate of immigration is evident from countries providing cash sickness benefits, and a significantly higher rate from countries with maternity benefits. The influence of the availability of medical benefits is negative and marginally significant. The influence of cash sickness benefits is strongly negative for both restricted and exempt immigrants; maternity benefits stimulate only the flow of the restricted group, and medical benefits appear to only retard the flow for the exempt group. Thus, the availability of both cash sickness benefits and health-care benefits discourages movement to the United States. The fact that the influence of medical benefits is negative and significant only for exempt immigrants (primarily of spouses and parents of U.S. citizens and who are generally older) is noteworthy. Although we anticipated a negative sign on the variable for maternity benefits, for reasons that are not clear, maternity benefits provide a push, especially for the numerically restricted group.

The family allowance variables suggest a modest retarding effect on migration to the United States, especially for numerically restricted immigrants. Such programs provide benefits to families with relatively young children, where the parents are in those age classes with fairly high migration propensities. The younger numerically restricted group is deterred by such programs, whereas the older numerically exempt group is unaffected by them.

SUMMARY

In this chapter we have developed a model of the determinants of immigration that contains vectors of variables reflecting differential economic opportunity, migration costs, political conditions in source countries, U.S. immigration policy, and social programs in source countries. The last of these is unique. Using panel data for 60 countries of birth of U.S. immigrants and for 20 years (1972–1991), we obtained Hausman-Taylor instrumental variable estimates of the parameters of the model.

The model generally performs well. Other things being equal, U.S. numerically restricted immigrants tend to come from countries that are growing relatively fast and that have high government revenues as a percentage of GDP. More of all U.S. immigrants came from countries that have relatively suppressive political regimes and that have relatively many naturalized U.S. citizens from the country. Source-country factors discouraging migration include distance from the United States, a high birth rate, a sickness and medical benefits system, relatively many students from the country studying in the United States, and an unemployment insurance system. Family allowance systems tend to discourage numerically restricted migration to the United States, but the influence of such programs is not great.

When immigrants are distinguished as numerically restricted versus numerically exempt, differences in the empirical results are generally as anticipated. The group that is the least constrained in expressing its economic motivation is the exempt group, and this group has a tendency to originate in countries with lower incomes relative to the United States. Because the exempt group is made up primarily of spouses and parents of U.S. citizens, it tends to be somewhat older. Probably as a consequence, the exempt group is not significantly discouraged from migrating due to the presence of an unemployment insurance program, whereas the restricted group is strongly discouraged. Moreover, the availability of health-care benefits discourages the migration of the exempt group, as does the lack of portable pension benefits. Finally, whereas greater distance and the associated higher costs of migrating discourage each group from moving to the United States, the coefficient on the distance variable is over twice as high in absolute value for numerically restricted immigrants. Not only do older exempt immigrants have greater assets to cover the costs of moving over longer distances, but also their costs of moving are likely to be subsidized by U.S. citizen relatives living in the United States.

In subsequent chapters, we use essentially the same variables to develop models of the gender, age, and skill composition of U.S. immigration.

Notes

1. The movement from country A to B to C is sometimes called "geographically indirect" movement from A to C. The term "indirect immigration" has also frequently been used when an individual moves from country A to country B, but in country B gains nonimmigrant status. At a later date, the person may adjust his/her status to legal resident alien, in which case the immigrant is called "indirect." The "indirect" here obviously refers to legal status in the receiving country and not to the actual geographic path the individual took to get there.

   Greenwood and Trabka (1991) used the INS Public Use Tapes to show that between 1972 and 1987 the percentage of geographically indirect migration to the United States ranged from 7.2 percent (1981) to 14.8 percent (1984). The increased number of geographically indirect moves during the 1980s was clearly due to the increased number of refugees accepted by the United States (Greenwood and Trabka 1991). Refugees were even more responsible for the increase in legally indirect movement, which tripled in number and doubled in percentage between 1972 and 1987. As noted in Chapter 4, refugees have been removed from our data set. Their removal greatly reduces any problems stemming from differences between countries of birth and countries of last permanent residence. Thus, our choice of country of birth as the country of an immigrant's origin appears to be acceptable for most migratory moves to the United States that we study here.

2. Most migration models fail to incorporate information about alternative opportunities and focus solely on the chosen destination. This is particularly true of models of the determinants of international migration, in large part due to shortcomings of available data.

3. Gould (1979) provided a fairly comprehensive survey of the causes of European emigration, with special emphasis on efforts to empirically model the determinants of European intercontinental movements. Hatton and Williamson (1994) surveyed more recent studies of international migration that in many cases incorporate improved historical data.

4. We use the term "appear" because some scholars argue that the flows were already tapering off by the early 1920s and thus that immigration restrictions did not have the force they may have had in earlier years. However, if the effects of World War I are taken into account, the flows do not appear to have begun to fall. In 1921, before the temporary entry restrictions that were imposed in that year became effective, 805,228 persons entered the United States.

5. The term "Kuznets cycles" has also been used to denote long swings, which are thought to be 15 to 25 years in length.

6. Tyree and Donato (1985) argued that fewer females immigrate to the United States from Muslim countries. If their position is correct, we should be able to detect this influence in our gender models.

7. Policy controls that have only a temporal dimension are picked up by the equivalent of the temporal fixed effects that we employ in estimating the model and can-

not be introduced otherwise. However, certain temporal policy effects discussed below apply only to specific sets of countries, and thus dummy variables reflecting these policies may be included.

8. The NP-5 program created by IRCA allotted visas on a first-come, first-served basis. The OP-1 program was established by Section 3 of the Immigration Amendments of 1988, and visas allotted under it were based on a bona fide lottery. Each program involved nonpreference visa allocations.

9. Pension programs that operate as social insurance systems base eligibility for pensions on the length of employment, and the amount of individual pensions is usually related to the level of the worker's prior earnings. Such programs are financed largely from special contributions (e.g., a percentage of earnings) by workers and employers and in most instances are compulsory. On the other hand, provident funds systems are essentially compulsory savings programs in which regular contributions withheld from employees are matched by those of their employers. These contributions are set aside in a special fund and then later repaid to the worker, as a general rule, in a single lump sum.

6 The Gender Composition of U.S. Immigration

The gender composition of U.S. immigration is important for several reasons. First, females are less likely than males to be "economic migrants," migrants motivated by economic advantages and costs; females are more likely to be "tied movers" as defined by Mincer (1978). Partly as a consequence, female immigrants tend to have lower labor force participation rates and lower earnings than their male counterparts. Second, the child-bearing capacity of female immigrants increases the potential for growth of the second-generation immigrant population. Because neither the 1980 nor the 1990 census asked a question concerning the nativity of parents, we are not able to easily assess the number of persons who in 1990 had foreign-born mothers. Third, females have a longer life expectancy than males. Consequently, those female immigrants who qualify for social services and benefits (such as Social Security and Medicare) will, on average, demand them for a longer period of time.

In this chapter, we discuss factors that influence the gender composition of immigrant flows. Understanding the gender composition requires consideration of the incentives surrounding the various "modes" by which an immigrant may enter the United States. First, an immigrant can enter independently, presumably with economic incentives primarily in mind. While such economic migrants often are thought to be male, the gender composition of immigrant flows varies across source countries depending upon source-country characteristics (Donato 1992). Alternatively, immigrants may enter as either non-economic or tied migrants. Non-economic migrants move for the purpose of family reunification or to form a family, for instance, as the spouse of a U.S. citizen. Thus, consideration must be given to source-country characteristics that determine the gender composition of immigrants who marry U.S. citizens (Jasso and Rosenzweig 1990). Tied migrants enter the United States as part of an immigrant family unit. Given independent economic migrants as primarily male and tied migrants as primarily female, variations in the gender composition of immigration from various source countries will be a function of the relative incentives of family-unit migration (Borjas and Bronars 1991; Mincer 1978) versus single-unit independent migration.

THE GENDER COMPOSITION MODEL

The general form of the model is that of Eq. 5.1. In addition to the variables summarized in Chapter 5, the gender composition equation includes two variables expected to specifically reflect the propensity of females to migrate: the population sex ratio in country i (the ratio of males to females in the indigenous population); and the relative education of females as compared with males (the percentage of country i's female population that is at the third level relative to the percentage of country i's male population at that level). The sex ratio controls for the gender composition of source country i's indigenous population; the relative education of females is substituted for the general population's education level, which is used as the control for educational attainment in the rate regression.

Consider economic migrants. The propensity of females to migrate internationally is expected to be a function of their educational attainment and the degree to which they are economically active. Other things being equal, highly educated individuals have higher propensities to migrate, so as females attain higher levels of education relative to males, the female share of the migration flow should increase. If we view migration as another form of human capital development, economically active individuals are more likely to migrate than individuals who do not participate in the formal labor market. Therefore, as the extent of female labor force participation rises, the probability that they will become international migrants is enhanced.

Economic migrants should be particularly responsive to the factors that reflect differential economic advantage and relative migration costs. For economic migrants, whether male or female, lower costs and/or greater returns to migration should cause a larger flow. Ideally, within the set of potential economic migrants, to distinguish between the migration propensity of women versus men, we would want to know gender-specific differences in the costs and returns to migration.

For example, if the wage differential between the United States and the country i were greater for women than for men, a larger proportion of the flow should be women. Unfortunately, gender-specific data pertaining to source countries are generally unavailable.[1]

A distinction between female and male migration does exist, however: males are generally presumed to be economic migrants, but the same is not true of females. As noted by Tyree and Donato (1986, p. 40) "the majority of immigrant women do not move alone, but are married and move with their husbands." Whereas the extent of this characterization may have changed over time, and although it may be different for different source countries, females still are characterized frequently as either non-economic or tied migrants in international migration flows. Given this characterization of females, the proportion of total immigrants that is female should vary with the ratio of economic to non-economic/tied migrants: as the ratio falls, the proportion of total immigrants who are females should rise.

The factors included in the differential economic opportunities vector are expected to be of particular importance in influencing the ratio of economic to non-economic migrants. For example, a higher level of development should lower the propensity to migrate of economically active individuals (mostly male), and higher source-country income should increase the relative flow of non-economic migrants (mostly female) because higher income retards the flow of economic migrants. Thus, such factors should cause an increase in the proportion of migrants that is female.[2]

The effect of migration costs on the gender composition of migrants should vary. For instance, given that a high birth rate in country i is associated with larger family size, there will be higher migration costs for family-unit migration, which should cause fewer females to come from nations with high birth rates. Certain other migration costs (e.g., skill losses) will be relevant only for economic migrants. The higher the migration costs incurred by economic migrants (but not by non-economic migrants), the lower the ratio of economic to non-economic migrants. Thus, migration flows from source countries where skills are relatively less transferable to the United States should have a greater share of females. Moreover, certain evidence (e.g., Duleep and Sanders 1993; Long 1980) suggests that family investment strategies may be used to facilitate adjustments for expected skill losses—during the initial years in the United States, the husband invests in U.S.-specific skills, and the wife works to support these investments—thus relatively more family-unit migration (and consequently more tied female migrants) is induced under circumstances where skill losses are expected to be greatest.

English-speaking persons typically bear lower costs of adjusting to the U.S. labor market, and so English-speaking nations should have a greater share of males in their migrant flows. However, this expectation is somewhat ambiguous, since language familiarity facilitates social and cultural assimilation, which are also important to non-economic migrants. Receiving an education at a U.S. university should make it easier to transfer job skills to the United States. Hence, nations with relatively large numbers of students attending U.S. universities should have a greater share of males in their migrant flows. Jasso and Rosenzweig (1990) argue that the number of immigrant husbands of U.S. citizens would reflect the origin country's number of students in the United States, and that immigrant wives of U.S. citizens would be disproportionately drawn from countries that host U.S. military installations.

The expected relationship between the costs imposed on all migrants (e.g., political considerations, distance) and the gender composition of migration can be complicated by a number of factors. For example, countries with relatively unattractive political environments also may have restrictions, such as emigration barriers, that distort (in unknown ways) migration flows. A plausible argument exists for more immigrant wives than husbands coming from more distant nations (e.g., Jasso and Rosenzweig 1990), but other considerations also may be at work. If men are disproportionately represented in the pool of potential economic migrants, distance may actually discourage male migration, because distance (among other factors) proxies intervening opportunities and thus the opportunity costs of migrating to any given destination; that is, the greater the distance, the greater or better are likely to be the alternative opportunities within the given radius of a move.

The Roman Catholic Church has the largest membership of any single denomination in the United States and may be expected to play an important role in the social and cultural assimilation of immigrants, which would seem of particular relevance for non-economic migrants.

Moreover, in countries where Catholicism is the principal religion, the maintenance of family units may play a more prominent role in determining migration decisions. Thus, we expect more family-unit migration, and consequently relatively more females, from countries where Catholicism is the primary religion. On the other hand, in countries dominated by Muslim religious beliefs, females may feel inhibitions regarding emigration, especially emigration as single and unattached.[3]

Of the U.S. institutional considerations, the number of prior immigrants from country i who have become U.S. citizens should be of particular relevance in determining the gender composition of U.S. immigration. An increased number of prior immigrants from country i lowers the direct entry costs for potential migrants in i, which should be particularly relevant for non-economic migrants. Hence, the number of prior immigrants who become U.S. citizens should positively influence the proportion of females in the flow.

In terms of social program variables, consider first the coverage of the various programs. Programs that are universally available should provide benefits that are of particular importance to potential non-economic migrants. Moreover, since universal programs are generally financed from general government revenues and therefore supported by taxes, the economically active population will bear the burden of paying for the benefits. Therefore, universal social programs should stimulate the flow of economic migrants and reduce the number of female migrants, *ceteris paribus*. The effect of employment-related programs will vary. For instance, the presence of unemployment benefits should retard the flow of economic migrants and thus increase the proportion of female migrants. On the other hand, a family allowance program is likely to be of particular importance in family-unit migration decisions, and the female share of migration flows should be lower from countries where such programs are available.

There is less certainty about the effects of sickness programs. To the extent that these programs are employment-related and provide net positive benefits to their participants, sickness programs should reduce the flow of economic migrants and increase the proportion of females who migrate. On the other hand, the availability of maternity benefits in country i should retard the flow of female migrants.

Old-age programs are not typically gender-specific; however, they can influence the ratio of economic to non-economic migrants.

Because universally available old-age programs would be of particular importance to potential non-economic migrants, the share of female migrants from countries having such programs should be lower. Old-age programs related to employment (and thus primarily affecting economically active individuals) may retard migration, in the sense that these individuals anticipate future benefits. However, once received, such benefits may actually provide older individuals with the wealth necessary to cover the costs of relocation. Where these old-age benefits are not payable abroad, the flow of individuals who have been economically active should be reduced if the old-age program is employment-related.

ESTIMATION OF THE GENDER EQUATION

The methodology we used to examine immigrant composition has long been employed by economists to analyze systems of consumer demand/expenditure equations (e.g., Leser 1961; Pollak and Wales 1969; Parks 1969; and Barten 1977), as well as systems of cost-share equations (e.g., Berndt and Wood 1975). We are unaware of any previous attempt to use such an approach to study the composition of migration, except for Greenwood, McDowell, and Waldman (1996). In the context of immigration to the United States, the sum over various components gives total immigration during a given year (e.g., sum over g gender groups, n age groups, or m occupational classes). The approach also allows a natural transition to various subgroups. For example, the immigrant population may first be distinguished by gender, and then each gender group may be distinguished by age.

Let i represent source country, j represent the variable ($j = 1, \ldots, n$), t represent the year, and g represent the gender. The approach employs total immigration of a given type as the dependent variable and can be expressed in the following way, where IMM_{igt} represents total immigration from country i, of gender g, during year t:

Eq. 6.1 $\text{IMM}_{igt} = \beta_g \Sigma_{g=1}^{2} \text{IMM}_{igt} + \Sigma_{j=1}^{n} \beta_{gj} X_{igjt} + e_{igt},$

where

$$\Sigma^2_{g=1} \beta_g = 1 \text{, and}$$

$$\Sigma^2_{g=1} \beta_{gj} = 0, \forall \beta_j.$$

The conditions state that the coefficients on the control total (in this case, total immigration) must sum to 1.0 across the two gender equations. Moreover, the coefficients on each independent variable must sum to zero. Thus, if each independent variable were set at zero, the gender shares would sum to 1.0, as they logically must. Furthermore, any change in an independent variable that increases (decreases) one share (say, for males) must correspondingly decrease (increase) the other so that the shares continue to sum to 1.0. The coefficients on the various independent variables are interpreted as a change in the absolute number of immigrants of type g due to an incremental change in the independent variable. Note, however, that β_g provides an estimate of the share of total allocated to each gender. Each composition equation is estimated as a system of equations.[4]

Estimation of the gender composition model is accomplished by pooling time-series and cross-section data, and several econometric issues arise. These issues were discussed in Chapter 5 in reference to the estimation of the rate equation, and they remain equally relevant within the current context. We have tested for appropriateness of the random effects versus the within estimator. Since the null hypothesis (that the random effects and the right-hand-side variables are uncorrelated) is rejected, we employ the Hausman-Taylor estimator described in Appendix C.[5]

EMPIRICAL FINDINGS

Table 6.1 reports coefficients and significance levels for all male and female U.S. immigrants. Table 6.2 reports comparable findings for female numerically restricted and numerically exempt immigrants. Although the gender-specific regressions presented in Table 6.1 for all males and females are almost mirror images, we have reported both to clearly show the properties of the modeling approach described above.

Table 6.1 Gender Composition of Total U.S. Immigrants: Hausman-Taylor Instrumental Variable Estimate[a]

Variable	Male	Female
Diff. econ. opportunity		
Relative per capita income	142.90*	−142.90*
Relative growth of GDP	−222.03	222.03
Government revenues	0.12	−0.12
% Urban	−5.92*	5.92*
% Female in labor force	32.80***	−32.80***
Migration costs		
Distance to U.S.A.	105.38**	−105.38**
Birth rate	−11.94***	11.94***
U.S. military presence	−82.52***	82.52***
Relative female education[b]	−91.52*	91.52*
English language	−2195.82***	2195.82***
U.S. college students	51.94	−51.94
Polit. attract. and religion		
Political competitiveness	−1.33	1.33
Catholic	−780.93***	780.93***
Muslim	539.28	−539.28
U.S. immigration policy		
Per capita naturalizations	−8.18	8.18
Lottery visas	90.84**	−90.84**
Silva visas	−2717.11***	2717.11***
Western Hemisphere 1972–76	−50.44	50.44
Asia	−1805.99***	1805.99***
Social programs		
Universal old-age	−139.94	139.94
Employment-related old-age	66.49	−66.49
Provident fund old-age	−3.86	3.86
Old-age pension not portable	38.10	−38.10
Universal sickness	9.94	−9.94
Cash sickness benefits	−186.96**	186.96**

Variable	Male	Female
Maternity benefits	−96.63*	96.63*
Medical benefits	−30.57	30.57
Unemployment insurance	−189.71**	189.71**
Universal family allowance	−161.07	161.07
Employment family allowance	−157.73	151.73
Control		
Sex ratio in i's population	237.44	−237.44
Total U.S. immigration from i	0.55***	0.45***

[a] *** Indicates $t \geq 1.96$; ** indicates $1.67 \leq t < 1.96$; * indicates $1.29 \leq t < 1.67$. The actual t-statistics are reported in Appendix Table E1.
[b] Refers to the ratio of the female to the male education variables.

Note that the coefficients on the control variable for total immigration from country i during year t (Table 6.1, last line; $= \Sigma_{g=1}^{2} \text{IMM}_{igt}$) sum across the gender equations to 1.0 and that the coefficients on each other explanatory variable sum to zero. The t-statistics corresponding to Tables 6.1 and 6.2 are reported in Appendix E, Tables E1 and E2.

When pair-wise comparisons are made in Table 6.2 between numerically restricted and exempt immigrants, considerable differences are evident within many of the vectors. This finding highlights the importance of disaggregating the immigration flows. Only the estimated relationships between the female share of migrants and female labor force participation, birth rate, and the Silva program maintain their signs with significance across the groups. We expect exempt immigrants to better reflect the force of economic incentives.

The vector of variables reflecting differential economic opportunity should be relatively more important for economic than for non-economic migrants, and thus better source-country economic opportunities should be associated positively with the female share of migrants. The strongest support of this hypothesis is found in the extent to which the source country is urbanized: enhanced domestic employment and earnings opportunities significantly reduce the flow of economic migrants and therefore increase the share of female migrants, especially those numerically exempt. A significantly positive relationship also exists between the relative size of central government and the

**Table 6.2 Female U.S. Immigrants By Entry Class:
Hausman-Taylor Instrumental Variable Estimates**[a]

Variable	Numerically restricted	Numerically exempt
Diff. econ. opportunity		
Relative per capita income	−16.18	−120.87
Relative growth of GDP	−33.79	131.12
Government revenues	1.18**	1.04
% Urban	−0.44	7.54***
% Female labor force	−3.93*	−22.05***
Migration costs		
Distance from *i* to U.S.A.	−4.71	−57.75
Birth rate	5.25***	6.59*
U.S. military presence	−4.02	78.32***
Relative female education[b]	−7.46	115.44***
English language	−114.04	2063.67***
U.S. college students from *i*	27.60*	−82.48*
Polit. attract. and religion		
Political competitiveness	−5.03*	0.86
Catholic	−28.58	748.73***
Muslim	−123.36*	−228.60
U.S. immigration policy		
Per capita naturalizations	3.49*	−1.41
Lottery visas	−8.53	−88.76***
Silva visas	675.80***	491.95***
Western Hemisphere 1972–76	30.28**	44.90
Asia	1.72	1434.76***
Social programs		
Universal old-age	12.02	103.75
Employment-related old-age	52.31***	−122.67*
Provident fund old-age	53.33*	−66.08
Old-age pension not portable	30.29*	−28.67
Universal sickness	108.52***	−44.04

Variable	Numerically restricted	Numerically exempt
Cash sickness benefits	−54.58*	240.39***
Maternity benefits	14.02	53.16
Medical benefits	19.54	43.87
Unemployment insurance	14.17	151.62**
Universal family allowance	14.27	128.37
Employment family allowance	−7.80	149.09*
Control		
Sex ratio in i's population	38.77	−109.58
Total numerically restricted (or exempt)	0.51***	0.45***

[a] *** Indicates $t \geq 1.96$; ** indicates $1.67 \leq t < 1.96$; * indicates $1.29 \leq t < 1.67$. Actual t-statistics are reported in Appendix Table E2.
[b] Refers to the ratio of the female to the male education variables.

female share in the numerically restricted category, perhaps reflecting lower migration costs associated with leaving a relatively unattractive source country.

In contrast to our expectation, however, higher source-country incomes reduce the share of female migrants (Table 6.1). This finding may reflect economic incentives that are operating in accordance with underlying gender-specific wage differentials. Also contrary to our expectations is a highly significant negative relationship between the female share of migrants and the female percentage of the total labor force. The reason for this finding may be that, as suggested by Mincer (1978, p. 769), "trends toward equalization of labor market experience of men and women may contribute to a decrease in migration rates of married couples." That is, wives who are economically active may reduce family-unit migration, thereby increasing the ratio of economic to non-economic migrants and decreasing the female share of international migrants. Furthermore, the source countries where the female percentage of labor force is high also may provide better relative economic opportunities for females (as compared with males).[6]

The influence of distance from the United States is negative for females (positive for males) in the regression for all male and female

U.S. immigrants (Table 6.1). Therefore, this result does not support the hypothesis that distance will discourage male migration, nor does it support the role of distance suggested by Jasso and Rosenzweig (1990) in determining the gender of a spouse who enters the United States via the marriage market. Rather, the evidence suggests that migration costs that are incurred by all migrants, but for which only economic migrants receive offsetting economic returns, will cause the ratio of economic to non-economic migrants to rise. The female share of migrants also may fall with distance if diseconomies are associated with moving families over greater distances (for example, the higher costs of return trips to visit with family members before full family reunification occurs).

Perhaps the most surprising finding concerns the birth rate variable. We hypothesized that higher birth rates (presumably, larger families) would discourage family-unit migration, but a larger share of women are represented in immigration flows from countries with high birth rates. On the other hand, consistent with our hypothesis, as women become more educated relative to men, the female share of immigrants rises.

The influence of U.S. military personnel in the country of origin is positive for females and is highly significant in the equations for all males and females (Table 6.1). Our hypothesis with respect to U.S. military personnel is further substantiated when immigrants are distinguished by entry class. Because spouses of U.S. citizens are numerically exempt and the U.S. military is predominantly male, the influence of U.S. military personnel should be positive for numerically exempt females, which it is. In the regressions for numerically restricted immigrants, the presence of U.S. military personnel does not significantly influence the gender composition of migrants (Table 6.2). There is also evidence of another marriage market. The female share is negatively related to the number of foreign students attending U.S. colleges and universities (Table 6.1). Moreover, the foreign-students variable is marginally significant in the equations for the numerically exempt immigrants (Table 6.2). Thus, the number of immigrant husbands of U.S. citizens is positively associated with the origin country's number of students attending U.S. colleges and universities.

Other influences may be associated with foreign students as well. For instance, we expect that skill losses would be lower from countries that send a relatively large number of students to the United States, so the United States should receive relatively more economic (male) migrants from these countries. Natives from English-speaking nations also should experience greater ease in transferring their occupational skills. However, the evidence does not support these hypotheses. If attending a U.S. university facilitates skill transfer and therefore induces more male economic migrants, this expected effect would be supported by a negative coefficient in the regressions for female restricted immigrants (Table 6.2), but this is not found. The influence of English language is positive and highly significant for females (Table 6.1) and for exempt females (Table 6.2), suggesting that language serves a crucial role in facilitating social and cultural assimilation (which appears to be of particular importance to female migrants). Social and cultural assimilation also may be facilitated by religious institutions, and the evidence is strong that larger shares of female migrants come from nations where Catholicism is the primary religion. On the other hand, Muslim nations provide relatively fewer female immigrants, especially in the numerically restricted class.

We are surprised to find that naturalized U.S. citizens do not have more influence on the gender composition of migrants. We hypothesized that such U.S. citizens would be relatively more important for potential non-economic migrants and that the law ought to favor women. Our evidence supports this hypothesis only for the numerically restricted class (through which unmarried adult sons and daughters of U.S. citizens, as well as brothers and sisters of U.S. citizens at least 21 years of age, and their spouses and children, are allowed to enter the United States).

For restricted immigrants, a higher share of female migrants entered the United States from the Western Hemisphere nations during the 1972–76 period. Because Western Hemisphere nations were not subject to the preference quota system until after 1976, and because the preference quota system is heavily oriented toward family reunification, one might have expected relatively more economic (males) in the migration flows that occurred prior to the change in law. In another instance, for all immigrants (Table 6.1) and for numerically exempt immigrants, a significantly higher share of Asian migrants are women. This finding may be a result of pre-1965 discrimination in U.S. immigration policy, with our sample period being a period of catching up, in which family members (perhaps primarily female) are reunited with the first wave of immigrants that arrived after the changes in immigration law. This finding also may reflect some combination of the importance of intervening opportunities for natives from Asian nations and/ or relatively lower wages for women in Asian nations.[7] The large number of U.S. military personnel in Asia during the sample period also may have a positive influence on the relative share of female migrants. Although we did not attach an expectation to the effects of either program, we note that, while the lottery system for allocating visas resulted in relatively fewer female migrants, the Silva program visas resulted in a significantly larger share of female migrants.

Several of the social programs have a significant influence on the gender composition of immigrant flows. For instance, as expected, countries with unemployment insurance programs send relatively more females to the United States. Old-age pension programs appear to have more influence on the gender of numerically restricted immigrants than on the exempt. For numerically restricted immigrants, as expected, old-age programs that are employment-related reduce the flow of economically active individuals, who are primarily male. For the numerically exempt, some evidence exists of the opposite effect, possibly because once the benefits are provided, these individuals have the wealth necessary to cover the costs of relocation.

The results shown in Table 6.1 support the hypothesis that employment-related sickness programs induce relatively more females to migrate to the United States. We argued that employment-related cash benefits for illnesses should reduce the flow of economic migrants, and the evidence for all males and females supports this position. However, between numerically restricted and exempt immigrants, a number of striking differences are found. For instance, whereas the presence of employment-related sickness programs is associated with a higher share of females in the flow of exempt immigrants (as expected), universal sickness programs also are associated with a higher share of females among the numerically restricted immigrants (which was not expected). We do not know the precise reason for these differences. In addition, we are not clear about why the availability of maternity benefits (Table 6.1) or employment-related family allowance programs (Table 6.2, numerically exempt) positively influence the share of migrants that is female. Although this evidence is not strong, we had expected the opposite, since each of these programs should serve to retard the flow of family-unit migration.

SUMMARY

We are somewhat surprised that the factors associated with economic opportunities do not provide more support for our hypotheses regarding gender composition, especially the findings for the numerically exempt class. On the other hand, the factors associated with migration costs have considerable influence on the gender composition of U.S. immigrants, and, with the exception of the birth rate variable, the findings are not unexpected. One implication of this evidence is that, if the level of education of females worldwide continues to rise relative to that of males, the female share of U.S. immigrants also should rise. English-language familiarity is a strong factor in female immigration to the United States. The evidence also supports the hypothesis that gender sorting occurs within the operation of marriage markets and that this sorting provides a means of entry for foreign-born spouses of U.S. citizens. One such market appears to be linked to foreign students at U.S. schools, increasing the entry of foreign-born males. On the other hand, more foreign-born wives come from nations hosting relatively large numbers of U.S. military personnel.

Our evidence suggests that the culture of Muslim nations tends to restrict the movement of potential female migrants, but this relationship is not particularly strong. On the other hand, especially for exempt females, the Catholic Church is a positive factor. U.S. immigration policy also has a significant influence on gender composition, although this influence is probably an unintended side-effect. For example, the recent lottery programs had a definite male tilt.

Regarding social programs in the source country, the findings for numerically exempt immigrants provide more support of our hypotheses than those for the restricted class. However, except for employment-related sickness programs and unemployment insurance, the overall influence of the various social programs on gender share is not very strong. In particular, the findings do not support our hypotheses concerning the influence of universal program coverage or specific programs designed to provide maternity and family allowance benefits.

Notes

1. Evidence concerning gender wage differentials is very limited. For example, considering female to male hourly earnings in manufacturing in 17 advanced industrialized countries, Blau and Ferber found "no uniform patterns emerge from an examination of the data . . . except that women are always paid less than men" (1992, p. 314). However, their data indicate that, in comparison with the other 16 industrialized nations in three time periods (i.e., 1973, 1982, and 1988), the ratio of women's to men's hourly earnings is lower in the United States than in the other country in 37 of 48 comparisons.

2. In stating this expectation, we assume that the gender wage differential does not vary across countries, but as noted earlier, we have reason to believe that this differential does vary. For a sample of 36 countries in 1990, the United Nations (1995, Table 5.20, p. 128) provides data on average female wages in manufacturing as a percentage of a comparable measure for males. Comparing the United States with the other 20 countries classified as "developed" indicates that female wages relative to male wages are higher in the United States in only 2 of 20 comparisons. However, in comparison with the other 15 nondeveloped countries, relative female wages in the United States are higher in 7 of the 15. This evidence may suggest that, where a higher level of development or higher per capita income exists in the source country, the wage differential between the United States and country i is lower for females than males. If this is the case, then relative income may be negatively related with the share of female migrants.

3. Tyree and Donato (1985) argued that, where the "status" of females is especially low, they do not have sufficient control over their fates for emigration to be a viable option. Tyree and Donato also observe particularly high male-to-female ratios for immigrants from Muslim countries.

4. An alternative to the specification described here is to employ actual shares as the dependent variables. In this case, for any given country/year the dependent variables of the system would sum to 1.0. Moreover, if the right-hand-side independent variables contain the same number of countries/years for each data partition on the left-hand-side of the regression, the constant term would sum to 1.0 and the coefficients of each independent variable would sum to zero. Greenwood, McDowell, and Waldman (1996) employed this methodology to study the occupational composition of a class of male U.S. immigrants.

    We do not adopt this approach here because to "balance" the model requires that entire countries be dropped from the data set. As immigrant groups are more and more finely identified, zeros begin to appear in the data. For example, if in a given year no females 20 and over from Tanzania reported an occupation, all observations on Tanzania would have to be dropped from the analysis of occupational composition (because the shares would be undefined due to division by zero). In fact, if the strict share methodology were followed, the occupational runs reported below for certain entry classes would contain only 37 countries. This lack of decomposability leads to sufficient lack of comparability for us to dismiss this approach.

5. $\chi^2 = 20.19$ rejects the random effects estimator.

6.   Borjas and Bronars (1991) provided an analysis of the types of families that are likely to migrate and of the types of individuals who are likely to characterize links in the immigration chain.

7.   Data from the United Nations (1995, Table 5.20, p. 128) indicate that female wages relative to male wages are particularly low in Asian nations, where females average only 63.6 percent of male wages, compared with 76.5 percent in non-Asian countries. This gender wage differential should serve to further stimulate a higher share of female migrants from Asian nations.

7 The Age Composition of U.S. Immigrants

The age composition of U.S. immigrants is important for several reasons. First, the age at which immigrants enter the United States is a determinant of the benefits that will be derived by the United States from the presence of the immigrants. The estimated present value of immigrants' income earned in the U.S. economy has been suggested as a measure of the immigrants' value (or gross benefit) to the economy (McDowell and Singell 1993). Other things being equal, immigrants who migrate at younger ages will also enter the U.S. labor force at a younger age, and thus they provide greater benefits to the economy.

Evidence also strongly suggests that the age at migration is an important determinant of how well immigrants do once they enter the U.S. labor force (Smith 1991; Friedberg 1993; McDowell and Singell 1993). Immigrants who enter at a younger age appear to assimilate more rapidly into the economy. Thus, the younger the age at which immigration occurs, the more similar will be the career earnings profiles of the foreign-born and native-born workers. Such similarity in earnings profiles is in marked contrast to the situation that is often ascribed to immigrants, where, when compared with native-born workers of similar characteristics, the immigrants suffer an earnings disadvantage during their initial years in the U.S. labor force (Chiswick 1978).

Younger immigrants also tend to become more proficient in English-language skills during their post-entry years than immigrants who enter at older ages (Jasso and Rosenzweig 1990; Chiswick and Miller 1992; Chiswick 1993). Apparently, either learning new language skills is easier (i.e., less costly) for younger individuals or, given the longer period over which to derive the benefits from human capital investments, younger immigrants have a greater incentive to invest in English-language skills. Greater proficiency in English further augments the immigrants' labor force productivity and also facilitates their more general social and cultural assimilation.

The age composition of immigrants is also important because, together with gender composition, it can influence the overall U.S. fertility rate in subsequent years. When immigration is concentrated in the childbearing years, the United States may experience subsequent augmentation in population growth rates. Moreover, relevant to the social security system, the age composition of newly entering immigrants may alter the extent of general population aging and thus affect the overall U.S. worker-to-dependent ratio (Arthur and Espenshade 1988). In addition to the demographic implications, the age composition of immigrants may influence the costs that they impose on the U.S. economy, including, for younger immigrants and families, the costs on social service providers such as the public school system, and for older immigrants, the costs of social services such as health care.[1]

In this chapter, we discuss factors that influence the age composition of immigrant flows. Our model of age composition is tied to the concept of the marginal migrant. In the context of the model, the marginal migrant is the individual for whom expected U.S. utility minus home-country utility just equals migration costs. By focusing on the marginal migrant, we are able to generate hypotheses concerning how various factors influence the age composition of immigrant flows.

THE AGE COMPOSITION MODEL

The general form of the age-composition model follows that of Eq. 5.1. In addition to the variables noted in Chapter 5, the age composition equation includes a control variable that reflects the median age of the source country's population in year t. The median age of source country populations varies widely, from a low of 14.6 years to a high of 38.3 years. The inclusion of this variable provides at least a crude control for the age of the population at risk to migrate. Relative to the gender composition equation (Chapter 6), median age now replaces the population sex ratio as the basic control variable; also in the age equation, the general education level (which is measured in gender-specific terms in the gender-specific model) is used as the measure of educational attainment.

The Concept of the Marginal Migrant

To understand who (i.e., younger versus older) among the source country's indigenous population choose to emigrate, we use the concept of the marginal migrant. In general, individuals will decide to move to the United States when the expected benefits from doing so exceed the expected foregone home-country benefits by an amount that is greater than the costs of migration. For the marginal migrant, the returns (total U.S. benefits accruing from migration minus foregone home-country benefits) must equal migration costs; thus, the net migration benefit is equal to zero.

To illustrate the concept of the marginal migrant, we consider a simplified characterization of country i's indigenous population in which we allow members of the indigenous population to differ in age, while assuming that all individuals are endowed with a given level of occupational skills. We make this assumption about occupational skills in order to focus on the age at which migration occurs.[2] In this simplified form, the equilibrium condition for the marginal migrant may be expressed as

Eq. 7.1 $\quad \sum_{t=\alpha}^{T} (w_j - w_i) K^* (1+r)^{-(T-t)} = C_i$,

where
    α is the age of migration,
    T is the age of the immigrant at death,
    w_j and w_i are the respective U.S. and country-of-origin wage per
        unit of occupational skill,
    K^* is the index of the occupational skill, and
    r is a discount rate.

The left side of Eq. 7.1 therefore represents the discounted total returns accruing to the marginal migrant who moves from country i to j at age α; the right side represents the total migration costs (C_i) incurred by an individual who migrates from country i. Total migration costs include direct entry costs, skill losses associated with less-than-perfect international skill transferability, and the foregone relative attractiveness of the country of origin.[3]

For the marginal migrant who is age α, the decision to migrate is one of indifference, since the expected benefits from migration are exactly offset by the migration costs. However, within country i's population, other individuals who also possess the skill level K^* will find emigration beneficial if they are younger than age α, and individuals older than α would incur negative net benefits from migration and thus would not find migration beneficial. Therefore, given the age α at which net benefits are zero, this equilibrium condition determines the ages at which individuals will find migration beneficial, and hence determines the age composition of immigrants. The younger the age of the marginal migrant, the younger the overall age composition of migrants from country i to the United States.

In this model, the age at migration is considered to be the choice variable. The marginal migrant is presumed to be capable of adjusting to any factors that would alter either the returns on or the costs of migration ("adjusting" means choosing to migrate at a younger or at an older age). Hence, the general age composition of migrants from country i will be responsive to factors related to relative economic advantage between i and the United States as well as to the total migration costs.

Figure 7.1 diagrammatically shows these relationships. For those for whom migration is profitable, the return on migration declines with age, because those who migrate at older ages eliminate the returns that are discounted least. Given costs of migration from country i to country j of C_{ij} and an expected differential return, $R_i(\alpha)$, that is a function of age at migration, the marginal migrant would move at age α_0. If costs were higher, such as $C_{ij}{}'$, the marginal migrant would move at an earlier age, α_1; for example, $C_{ij}{}'$ could refer to migration from a more distant country, from a politically more desirable country (where the opportunity cost of departing is greater), or from a non-English-speaking country. In each case, the costs of transferring accumulated occupational skills to the United States would be higher, and the marginal migrant would move at an earlier age. (In Figure 7.1, we have assumed that costs are independent of age, but this assumption easily could be relaxed.) If expected returns to the marginal migrant were higher at every age, as shown by $R_i{}'(\alpha)$ in Figure 7.1, the marginal migrant would be older (α_2). This could be the case, for example, for

Figure 7.1 Age of Migration

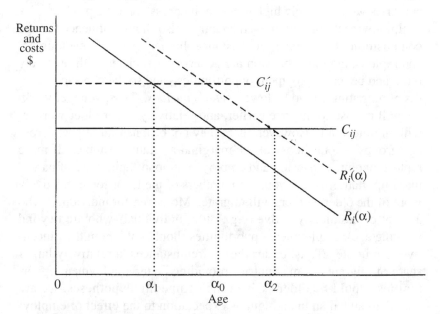

more highly educated individuals or for individuals in lower-income source countries.

Clearly, this model could be complicated considerably by relaxing various assumptions that were explicitly or implicitly made in developing it.[4] For example, the accumulated stock of human capital (K) could be made a function of age, as could the costs of migration. However, the model is sufficient to allow us to specify hypotheses concerning the variables included in the model of migrant age composition.

Hypotheses

To illustrate the types of hypotheses that can be based on the concept of the marginal migrant, we consider the expected effects of the factors in the differential economic opportunity vector. Other things being equal, higher country-of-origin wages per unit of human capital will decrease the returns to migration. In response, the marginal migrant must adjust by moving at a younger age in order to raise returns so that net benefits again equal zero. Therefore, if relative per capita income is a proxy for the country-of-origin wages relative to those of the United States, younger migrants should come from source countries with relatively higher per capita gross domestic product.

Employment opportunities in country i also should influence the age composition of migrants. For instance, higher levels of development and rapid economic expansion are generally associated with relatively more and better employment opportunities, and so the expected benefits of migrating would be lower, *ceteris paribus*. Thus, younger workers will choose to migrate earlier, and relatively fewer older workers will migrate at all. However, there may not be a neutral impact across age groups, as our theory of the marginal migrant presumes. If more rapid economic expansion and employment opportunities are of particular importance for the younger members of the labor force, relatively more of the older workers will migrate. Moreover, for individuals who are not economically active (e.g., older individuals who are beyond working age), employment opportunities should not inhibit their incentive to migrate. Thus, under these circumstances, a relatively larger share of migrants from countries providing better employment opportunities should be older. Given the competing hypotheses, we are unable to attach an unambiguous expectation to the effect of employment opportunities on immigrant age composition.

The marginal migrant also will adjust to differences in the direct costs of migration. If higher migration costs are not linked to any age-specific cost differences, then they would cause the marginal migrant to adjust by migrating at a younger age. However, the direct costs of migration may not be spread evenly throughout all age groups. For instance, the presence of U.S. military personnel reduces the costs of migration primarily through the marriage market, where potential wives of U.S. servicemen would benefit most. The parents of the foreign-born spouses also may ultimately benefit from this connection, but the presence of U.S. military personnel does not provide an obvious advantage for other potential migrants. High birth rates may also act differentially, being particularly relevant in the migration decisions of younger individuals and their families; high birth rates and larger families thus should reduce the flow of relatively younger individuals.

Less-than-perfect international transferability of skills also imposes costs on migrants. Where skill-transfer costs are higher, the greater expected skill losses should cause the marginal migrant to migrate at a younger age. Therefore, since migrants from English-speaking nations should experience lower skill losses, economic migrants from such nations should be relatively older than migrants from other nations. Moreover, relatively more older non-economic migrants should come from English-speaking countries because language skills are important for social and cultural assimilation and, if they do not possess English-language skills upon entry, older immigrants are less likely to become proficient in English. Prospective migrants (especially non-economic migrants) from countries where Catholicism is the primary religion should face lower adjustment costs in terms of social and cultural assimilation, and immigrants from these nations should be relatively older.

Among U.S. immigration policy factors, the number of prior immigrants from country i who have become U.S. citizens is of particular relevance in determining the age composition of migrants. Because of the lower direct entry costs for potential immigrants, the age of immigrants should be associated with the number of U.S. citizens who originated from a given country of origin, especially in the numerically exempt class (spouses and parents of U.S. citizens); however, the precise overall effect is unclear, because spouses tend to be younger and parents tend to be older.[5]

In the vector of social programs, old-age pension programs that transfer wealth from working-age individuals to older individuals would be expected to discourage older persons from moving while encouraging younger persons to move. However, not all pension programs constitute an income transfer—provident fund systems are a good example—and even if a transfer is involved, the net effect is not necessarily to reduce the age composition of migrants. If benefit payments are internationally transferable, the added income from the pension program may induce relatively more older individuals to migrate. Furthermore, younger workers may anticipate that the present value of their future old-age benefits outweighs the current costs being imposed on them and decide not to migrate. Therefore, the overall impact of employment-related old-age programs on the age composition of migrants is ambiguous.

Other features of old-age pension programs may cause a differential impact on particular age groups. For instance, whether financed indirectly through income taxes or directly through employee and/or employer contributions, universal pension programs transfer income from the younger to the older, retired population. Under these circumstances, workers are less likely to anticipate that their benefits will outweigh their current costs, and therefore, such programs are expected to induce a relatively larger flow of young migrants.

By similar reasoning, universal sickness programs also should encourage the migration of younger individuals. However, specific features of medical, cash sickness, and maternity benefits present a more complicated picture. Women of child-bearing age should be discouraged from leaving countries with such programs both because of the maternity benefits that accrue to themselves and because of the medical benefits that accrue to their children; their husbands also should be discouraged from emigrating. Likewise, older persons should be less likely to leave countries with sickness and medical benefits. Cash sickness benefits should be relevant only to persons who are working-age individuals, so these benefits should encourage the flow of the oldest age group of potential migrants, which includes individuals who are not economically active.

Unemployment insurance generally constitutes a transfer from older working age groups with typically lower unemployment rates to younger age groups with typically higher unemployment rates. As a consequence, we expect the presence of unemployment insurance to discourage the migration of younger persons and to encourage the migration of older persons. Finally, family allowance programs should discourage migration of individuals in the 20–34 age class and their families.

ESTIMATION OF THE AGE COMPOSITION EQUATIONS

The statistical methodology used to estimate the age-composition equation is essentially the same as that for estimating the gender composition of immigrant except for the focus on age shares rather than gender shares. In our age analysis, we do not present the results for all age groups; we focus on only the shares of immigrants aged 20–34 and those aged 55 and older, which are the two extremes of the migration-age spectrum. Individuals aged 20–34 are most likely to be international migrants and are more likely to be economically active, and therefore they are more responsive to basic economic incentives. Individuals aged 55 and older are often out of the labor force.

Because we present the results for only two age groups, our interpretation of the coefficients in the regressions is slightly different than for the gender regressions. In the gender equation, the coefficient on the control total (e.g., total immigration of individuals aged 20 or older, regardless of gender) must sum to 1.0 across all gender groups. However, in this chapter we essentially present two separate models, one focused on persons 20–34 relative to those 35 and older and the second focused on persons 55 and older relative to those 20–54. Within each set, the adding-up property holds. However, the two age groups that occupy our attention (20–34 and 55 and older) are not estimated as parts of the same system of equations.

A practical reason for examining only two age groups at a time is that the generalized least squares feature of the Hausman-Taylor methodology, as well as its instrumental variables feature, destroy the adding-up property for all cases except the special case of a two-group decomposition.[6] Although multiplying each equation of the system by a weight generally negates the adding-up property that is inherent in data, that this is not true for two-equation systems.[7]

EMPIRICAL FINDINGS

All Immigrants

Table 7.1 reports coefficients and significance levels for all immigrants (i.e., males and females combined) aged 20–34 and aged 55 and older, where the totals are aggregated across the restricted and exempt classes. (The corresponding t-statistics are provided in Appendix Table F1).

In the economic opportunities vector, we find strong support for our hypotheses concerning how these variables will influence the age composition of migrants. For instance, higher relative per-capita incomes lower the returns to migration for individuals at every age, and consequently, individuals who choose to migrate do so at a relatively younger age. A significantly larger number of migrants aged 55 and

Table 7.1 Age Composition of Immigrants: Hausman-Taylor Instrumental Variable Estimates[a]

Variable	Aged 20–34	Aged 55 and older
Diff. econ. opportunity		
Relative per capita income	364.94***	–226.84**
Relative growth of GDP	–848.92*	867.05***
Government revenues	7.08***	–5.57***
% Urban	–19.81***	17.42***
% Female in labor force	62.70***	–50.59***
Migration costs		
Distance to U.S.A.	–350.96***	150.42*
Birth rate	–7.92	–2.22
U.S. military presence	12.74	22.87
Education	–10.01***	6.50***
English language	–860.70	2077.68***
U.S. college students	25.45	–6.15
Polit. attract. and religion		
Political competitiveness	20.05	6.86
Catholic	415.03	540.61
Muslim	–175.22	126.86
U.S. immigration policy		
Per capita naturalizations	16.87*	–10.82*
Lottery visas	245.85***	–132.18***
Silva visas	3097.98***	–2062.75***
Western Hemisphere 1972–76	–424.99***	301.31***
Asia	1284.38*	294.69
Social programs		
Universal old-age	251.30*	–91.92
Employment-related old-age	–242.68**	31.24
Provident fund old-age	208.12	–278.36***
Old-age pension not portable	–127.55	58.06
Universal sickness	–28.43	40.82
Cash sickness benefits	–472.01***	386.07***

Variable	Aged 20–34	Aged 55 and older
Maternity benefits	177.26**	−82.46
Medical benefits	−145.53*	143.87**
Unemployment insurance	−212.27*	164.30*
Universal family allowance	−39.88	52.48
Employment family allowance	−165.22	165.34
Control		
Median age in i	−77.21***	35.07***
Total migrants from i aged 20 and over	0.44***	0.16***

[a] *** Indicates $t \geq 1.96$; ** indicates $1.67 \leq t < 1.96$; * indicates $1.29 \leq t < 1.67$. Table F1 reports the corresponding t-statistics.

older, and significantly smaller number of migrants aged 20–34, come from source countries with higher levels of development (as reflected by the degree of urbanization) and with more rapid growth of GDP. The influence of relative government size is positive (negative) and highly significant for the share of migrants aged 20–34 (aged 55 and older). Thus, in countries where government revenues are large, the flow of younger migrants is stimulated and that of older individuals is lessened (apparently because of government benefits to older individuals for which they are less likely to bear a proportionate share of the tax burden).

We have considerably less evidence that either migration costs or political/religious considerations significantly influence the age at which migration occurs, with two exceptions. English language has a particularly large and significant influence on the number of individuals aged 55 and older who migrate to the United States: per year, over 2,000 additional individuals aged 55 and older migrate from an English-speaking nation relative to a non-English-speaking nation. This finding suggests that familiarity with language plays a particularly critical role in facilitating the social and cultural assimilation of older migrants. Second, the education level in the source country is significant; more highly educated individuals should be better able to adapt to their new situation, and the lower adjustment costs should thus induce relatively older persons to move, which is what the evidence indicates.

On the other hand, contrary to our expectations, fewer migrants aged 20–34 come from nations that are more distant from the United States; one possible explanation is that more potential intervening opportunities attract relatively young economic migrants to locations other than the United States.

Factors associated with U.S. immigration policy significantly influence the age composition of migrants. While we did not develop an hypothesis regarding either the lottery visas or the Silva program, the evidence clearly indicates that each program resulted in significantly fewer migrants aged 55 and older and more migrants aged 20–34. The Silva program had a particularly large effect, with over 3,000 additional migrants aged 20–34 from Mexico during both 1978 and 1981. The differential treatment of migrants from the Western Hemisphere during 1972–1976 had the opposite effect: the lower immigration barriers appear to have increased the relative age of migrants.

Old-age pension programs appear to have some influence on the age structure of migrants, but contrary to our expectation, they do not significantly discourage the flow of older migrants. Younger persons are only slightly influenced by old-age programs, but (as expected) they have a higher propensity to migrate if pensions are universally provided. Other specific features of employment-related programs have very different effects. For instance, whereas employment-related old age programs that are of the social insurance variety significantly reduce the number of migrants aged 20–34, provident funds reduce the flow of migrants aged 55 and older. A key difference in these programs may be the waiting period before any benefits can be received.[8] Social insurance programs generally provide benefits only at a specified retirement age, but provident funds can often be received at an earlier age, thus, providing the opportunity to accumulate assets and allow persons to emigrate before the age of 55.

Within health-related programs, we do not find the anticipated effect that universal programs retard the flow of older migrants, but cash sickness benefits available only to economically active individuals do reduce the flow of younger migrants, as expected. Also as expected, countries with unemployment social insurance programs send relatively fewer (more) young (older) migrants to the United States, though the significance of the effect is not high. Contrary to our hypothesis, significantly more migrants aged 20–34 come from nations where maternity benefits are provided, and the evidence does not indicate that family allowance programs retard the flow of young individuals and their families. Finally, that medical benefits positively influence the number of migrants aged 55 and older is somewhat surprising.

Immigrants By Gender

Table 7.2 presents separate results for male and female immigrants by age; corresponding *t*-statistics are presented in Appendix Table F2. Certain factors have similar effects on the age composition of both genders; these effects are most apparent for those aged 55 and older and, in particular, in the differential economic opportunity vector. Significantly more older male and female migrants come from source countries characterized by high levels of development and rapid growth of GDP, and larger government revenues (and their associated benefits and taxes) tend to retard the flow of older migrants, regardless of gender. These effects are expected. Also as expected, employment-related sickness benefits that are specifically geared toward the economically active positively influence the flow of older migrants. English-language skills also are particularly important in facilitating the migration of persons aged 55 and older, whereas both the lottery and Silva programs resulted in significantly fewer older migrants of both genders.

For immigrants aged 20–34, the most obvious similarities across the genders concern the influence of U.S. immigration policy, in particular, the lottery program and the differential treatment of Western Hemisphere natives. In other areas, however, the differences across gender are striking. For instance, evidence supporting the hypothesis that higher source country incomes tend to decrease the relative age of migrants is found primarily for males, but the other factors in the differential economic opportunity vector (except for female labor force participation) are only significant in the regressions for females.[9] Moreover, factors associated with migration costs appear to be much stronger forces in shaping the age composition of female migrants. Certain U.S. immigration policy variables also influence the number of female, but not the number of male, migrants. For instance, prior immigrants who have become U.S. citizens, the Silva program, and

Table 7.2 Age Composition of Immigrants by Gender: Hausman-Taylor Instrumental Variable Estimates[a]

Variable	Aged 20–34		Aged 55 and older	
	Male	Female	Male	Female
Diff. econ. opportunity				
Relative per capita income	193.75**	93.85	−108.23**	−80.76*
Relative growth of GDP	−275.91	−611.37***	377.00***	490.64***
Government revenues	2.78*	4.57***	−2.38***	−3.34***
% Urban	−2.27	−19.29***	4.49***	12.81***
% Female in labor force	35.96***	24.14***	−26.73***	−20.27***
Migration costs				
Distance to U.S.A.	−85.84*	−228.16***	40.44	103.60*
Birth rate	−8.10*	7.66**	0.29	−5.45**
U.S. military presence	−27.89	39.17*	20.66	−3.47
Education	2.81	−10.33***	0.96	4.17***
English language	−389.03	−1135.49	807.09***	1336.74***
U.S. college students	23.30	−2.09	−16.74	−0.80
Polit. attract. and religion				
Political competitiveness	8.81	6.89	4.04	3.27
Catholic	260.25	−206.05	154.65	446.78
Muslim	388.23	−988.44	−221.02	520.76
U.S. immigration policy				
Per capita naturalizations	−0.86	14.20***	−2.14	−8.25***
Lottery visas	145.06***	100.07***	−74.77***	−50.55**
Silva visas	5.27	2972.35***	−382.48***	−1830.96***
Western Hemisphere 1972–76	−161.08***	−227.20***	115.33***	172.27***
Asia	18.71	1088.95**	332.89*	−106.99
Social programs				
Universal old-age	152.22*	130.79*	−62.19	−48.94
Employment-related old-age	−150.50	−154.55***	29.07	11.56
Provident fund old-age	48.69	179.46***	−114.39**	−167.66***
Old-age pension not portable	−36.18	−92.49***	13.53	46.99
Universal sickness	26.93	−8.65	−5.30	28.89
Cash sickness benefits	−156.74*	−273.34***	170.02***	192.92***

Variable	Aged 20-34		Aged 55 and older	
	Male	Female	Male	Female
Maternity benefits	81.51*	114.14***	–31.31	–62.50**
Medical benefits	–5.97	–90.89**	38.24	91.40***
Unemployment insurance	–122.05	–63.49	73.02*	68.67
Universal family allowance	–87.40	–7.66	22.99	36.85
Employment family allowance	–132.90	–62.68	71.08	92.92*
Control				
Median age in i	–43.77***	–41.97***	15.90***	21.55***
Total sex-specific immigration from i^c	0.52***	0.39***	0.10***	0.21***

[a] *** Indicates $t \geq 1.96$; ** indicates $1.67 \leq t < 1.96$; * indicates $1.29 \leq t < 1.67$. Table F2 reports the corresponding t-statistics.

[b] In the gender-specific regressions, the education control variable is measured specific to the respective gender.

[c] In the gender-specific regressions, the control total variable is measured specific to the respective gender.

being from an Asian nation all positively affected the number of female immigrants aged 20–34, while not significantly influencing the males.

For social programs, pair-wise comparisons across the gender regressions also indicate considerable differences. For males aged 20–34, few social programs appear to have any effect even at the lowest level of significance. However, several social program variables have a highly significant influence on the number of female migrants aged 20–34. For example, employment-related old-age programs significantly reduce the number of young female migrants, but if the program is of the provident funds variety, significantly more young females migrate. On the other hand, if pension benefits are not internationally transferable, the number of young female migrants is reduced, which is unanticipated. The availability of maternity benefits positively influences the number of female migrants aged 20–34, another unanticipated result. More consistent with our hypotheses, the availability of other health-related programs (i.e., sickness and medical) significantly influence the number of young female migrants, but these effects are either not significant or only marginally significant for males. The reason for the differences in results across gender is not totally clear.

Male and Female Immigrants By Entry Class

Tables 7.3 and 7.4 present age-composition results for numerically restricted and numerically exempt immigrants; corresponding t-statistics are found in Appendix Tables F3 and F4. As noted in the context of gender composition, differences are evident within many of the vectors when comparing between the numerically restricted and exempt classes. However, when we compare the effects of specific factors on the age composition of male versus female immigrants, differences across genders appear to lessen once the data are disaggregated by entry class.

For numerically restricted immigrants, the factors included in the differential economic opportunity vector do not play a strong role in determining the age composition of either gender. Although providing some evidence consistent with our hypotheses, the findings concerning the factors listed under "migration costs" also are not found to be particularly robust or highly significant.[10] Apparently (as with the gender composition model), even though we have attempted to control for U.S. policy-related considerations, immigration restrictions blunt most of the expected effects of these economic incentives.

Political and religious considerations have some effect on the age structure of numerically restricted immigrants. The effect is most apparent for religion (Table 7.3), where significantly fewer males and females aged 55 and older come from nations where Catholicism is the primary religion, which is not what we anticipated. To an even greater extent, U.S. immigration policy-related factors affect the age of numerically restricted migrants. For example, whereas the lottery program significantly reduced the relative age of migrants, the Silva program and the differential treatment of the Western Hemisphere generally increased their relative age. Moreover, significantly fewer restricted male and female immigrants aged 55 and older came from Asian nations, *ceteris paribus*. The one factor for which a clear difference is evident across genders is the influence of U.S. citizens.[11] Significantly fewer females aged 55 and older and more females aged 20–34 came from nations from which more natives became U.S. citizens. Within the class of numerically restricted immigrants, adult daughters and sisters who are less than age 35 are apparently the primary beneficiaries of the lower entry costs associated with U.S. citizenship.

Many of the social programs considered play a significant role in affecting the age of restricted migrants, and the effects are generally consistent across genders. For example, universal-coverage programs that are likely to be important to older persons (i.e., universal old-age and sickness programs) induce relatively more migrants aged 20–34 (Table 7.3). On the other hand, universal programs serving the interests of younger individuals and their families (i.e., universal family allowances) induce more individuals aged 55 and older of both genders to migrate. Moreover, for both males and females, employment-related old-age pension programs tend to increase the relative age of migrants, as do employment-related sickness benefits, which we expected. Although the direction of the relationship is not expected, the impact of maternity benefits also is consistent across genders.

Although social programs importantly affect the age of numerically restricted immigrants, such is not the case generally for numerically exempt immigrants (Table 7.4). Instead, the factors in the economic opportunities vector serve as primary determinants of the age composition of the exempt group. This is especially true for older male and female migrants and for female migrants aged 20–34. For numerically exempt males aged 20–34, only relative income and female labor force participation are significant. The effect of relative income is as expected. Although we did not predict the effect of female labor force participation on the age of male migrants, this positive relationship could have been caused by the added competition faced by males for jobs in markets where females represent a relatively large percentage of the labor force. For the other variables, as the findings relate to both male and female migrants aged 55 and older and female migrants aged 20–34, the signs on all the coefficients are in the expected direction and the level of significance is high, thus providing strong support for our hypotheses concerning the influence of economic opportunities in shaping the age composition of both male and female numerically exempt immigrants, who we expect to better reflect the forces of economic incentives.

The influence of migration costs on exempt immigrants is similar to that for numerically restricted migrants: migration costs are not primary determinants of age composition, particularly for males. A notable exception is the influence of English-language skills in shaping a relatively older flow of exempt immigrants. The presence of U.S. mili-

Table 7.3 Age Composition of Numerically Restricted Immigrants: Hausman-Taylor Instrumental Variable Estimates[a]

Variable	Aged 20–34		Aged 55 and older	
	Males	Females	Males	Females
Diff. econ. opportunity				
Relative per capita income	19.65	49.96	−12.26	−17.36
Relative growth of GDP	−112.88	−141.95	49.77*	−0.09
Government revenues	0.84	1.53*	−0.26	−0.15
% Urban	−1.58	−3.85***	0.53*	0.39
% Female in labor force	2.28	9.78***	−3.90***	−1.54*
Migration costs				
Distance to U.S.A.	−15.91	−35.26*	12.09***	8.32*
Birth rate	1.10	1.23	1.10**	2.38***
U.S. military presence	−8.42	−1.11	2.63	0.38
Education[b]	0.92	−4.48***	0.10	−0.03
English language	−0.83	−64.97	−64.18	−130.14***
U.S. college students	23.76	26.82	9.59*	25.58***
Polit. attract. and religion				
Political competitiveness	5.17	3.25	−0.94	−2.17*
Catholic	169.52**	202.56	−80.29***	−105.40***
Muslim	52.83	100.23	−69.55*	−78.92*
U.S. immigration policy				
Per capita naturalizations	4.19	6.33**	−0.83	−5.17***
Lottery visas	73.70***	83.43***	−13.59***	−9.42*
Silva visas	−754.89***	85.66	110.16***	124.93***
Western Hemisphere 1972–76	−23.93	−62.17***	30.70***	47.05***
Asia	102.27	181.26	−65.80**	−80.79***
Social programs				
Universal old-age	114.89***	136.91***	−13.96	−7.09
Employment-related old-age	−110.68***	−146.65***	32.29***	24.65***
Provident fund old-age	26.38	42.66	2.73	20.44*
Old-age pension not portable	−47.75*	−33.99	4.10	−0.38
Universal sickness	144.17***	126.31***	0.13	−5.14

Variable	Aged 20–34		Aged 55 and older	
	Males	Females	Males	Females
Cash sickness benefits	−135.28***	−180.35***	23.85**	48.40***
Maternity benefits	41.72*	70.35***	−12.75**	−32.39***
Medical benefits	31.90	17.85	11.57*	30.19
Unemployment insurance	32.92	26.88	13.78	24.38**
Universal family allowance	−6.86	42.39	18.94*	31.69**
Employment family allowance	10.56	28.56	13.72	24.24*
Control				
Median age in i	−6.81	−7.24	1.67	−1.82
Total numerically restricted from i^c	0.62***	0.62***	0.06***	0.06***

[a] *** Indicates $t \geq 1.96$; ** indicates $1.67 \leq t < 1.96$; * indicates $1.29 \leq t < 1.67$. Table F3 reports the corresponding t-statistics.

[b] In the gender-specific regressions, the education control variable is measured specific to the respective gender.

[c] In the gender-specific regressions, the control total variable is measured specific to the respective gender.

tary personnel positively affects the entry of females aged 20–34. However, the reason that birth rate is associated with a larger number of female migrants aged 20–34 is unclear. Moreover, while the relationship is expected, we are uncertain of the reason that nations with more highly educated females send relatively older female migrants, while the age of male migrants is not affected by education.

U.S. immigration policy and political/religious considerations also influence the age of numerically exempt immigrants. For instance, as with numerically restricted immigrants, the lottery generally decreased the relative age of exempt immigrants, whereas the differential treatment of Western Hemisphere natives during 1972–1976 increased their relative age.[12] However, unlike restricted migrants, numerically exempt males from Asian nations tend to be older than other migrants, *ceteris paribus*. This finding may be due to the presence of intervening opportunities that attract the younger economic migrants. More older male and female exempt migrants came from nations with unattractive political environments and from nations where Catholicism is the primary religion. Both findings are as anticipated.

Table 7.4 Age Composition of Numerically Exempt Immigrants: Hausman-Taylor Instrumental Variable Estimates[a]

	Aged 20–34		Aged 55 and older	
Variable	Males	Females	Males	Females
Diff. econ. opportunity				
Relative per capita income	140.82*	74.48*	−95.54**	−73.17
Relative growth of GDP	−163.69	−579.23***	347.59***	615.27***
Government revenues	1.76	2.83***	−2.20***	−3.19***
% Urban	1.60	−8.92***	3.17**	9.92***
% Female in labor force	32.37***	23.98***	−23.91***	−25.51***
Migration costs				
Distance to U.S.A.	−14.96	−69.26	10.44	37.33
Birth rate	−4.91	8.67***	−1.51	−7.04***
U.S. military presence	−33.69	32.07**	19.08	−2.08
Education[b]	0.43	−4.77***	1.27	2.97**
English language	−757.00***	−1337.99***	968.11***	1687.24***
U.S. college students	25.89	−19.07	−28.90	−10.87
Polit. attract. and religion				
Political competitiveness	−3.07	−8.44*	7.68*	11.52***
Catholic	−147.90	−481.59*	273.68*	600.60*
Muslim	254.17	−553.45	−186.36	358.89
U.S. immigration policy				
Per capita naturalizations	−9.60*	−2.55	−0.04	1.27
Lottery visas	83.48***	35.62*	−61.70***	−31.49
Silva visas	−100.69	−26.29	−35.21	12.95
Western Hemisphere 1972–76	−90.59***	−87.06***	70.76***	92.08***
Asia	−417.51**	90.83	521.18***	375.70
Social programs				
Universal old-age	23.64	14.69	−43.11	−24.24
Employment-related old-age	15.14	33.67	−3.36	6.66
Provident fund old-age	33.39	118.85***	117.81***	−160.42***
Old-age pension not portable	27.50	−4.88	−2.01	7.85
Universal sickness	−65.01	−9.44	−28.91	−31.69

Variable	Aged 20–34		Aged 55 and Older	
	Males	Females	Males	Females
Cash sickness benefits	29.18	−32.67	138.63***	118.87***
Maternity benefits	32.84	7.88	−11.50	2.61
Medical benefits	22.09	−8.03	9.71	23.59
Unemployment insurance	−129.68*	−47.41	56.30	49.76
Universal family allowance	−97.17	0.24	1.87	11.11
Employment family allowance	−143.71*	−35.37	53.50	62.53
Control				
Median age in i	−35.28***	−29.59***	15.00***	24.16***
Total exempt from i^c	0.57***	0.45***	0.10***	0.22***

[a] *** Indicates $t \geq 1.96$; ** indicates $1.67 \leq t < 1.96$; * indicates $1.29 \leq t < 1.67$. Table F4 reports the corresponding t-statistics.

[b] In the gender-specific regressions, the education control variable is measured specific to the respective gender.

[c] In the gender-specific regressions, the control total variable is measured specific to the respective gender.

SUMMARY

This chapter has attempted to model the age composition of U.S. immigrants in a fashion that we believe is unique, and with the inclusion of a vector of social programs variables. By using INS microdata to identify and cross-classify various groups, we have been able to distinguish the age composition of numerically restricted and numerically exempt U.S. immigrants, by gender.

Our analysis has found that the economic opportunity variables are generally strong and work in the expected directions. For example, higher source-country incomes relative to the United States result in more younger and less older immigrants. This finding is particularly interesting because these same factors do not play an especially significant role in explaining the rate of U.S. immigration. Migration costs and political/religious forces are not particularly important determinants of age composition, in spite of the fact that certain of these costs and forces are consistently important in explaining the rate of immigration from the various source countries. One general conclusion from these observations is that whereas the rate model identifies certain forces that are critical in shaping the volume of movement from various source countries, it conceals forces that are important determinants of age composition.

Another general conclusion is that U.S. immigration policy, perhaps in indirect or unintended ways, has influenced the age composition of immigrants. A larger number of prior immigrants who have become U.S. citizens lowers the direct entry costs for potential immigrants. These lower costs have primarily served to facilitate the entry of young, adult, numerically restricted female immigrants, suggesting that adult daughters and sisters less than age 35 are the primary beneficiaries. Moreover, whereas both the lottery and Silva programs resulted in significantly fewer migrants aged 55 and older and more migrants aged 20–34, the differential treatment of potential migrants from the Western Hemisphere nations had the opposite effect. The sensitivity of migrant age composition to such factors should be kept in mind by policymakers in their attempts to formulate optimal immigration policies.

Because we feel that this chapter breaks new ground in the study of immigrant age composition, we are less concerned than we might otherwise be that a number of variables, particularly social program variables, have unanticipated effects for which we do not have good explanations. Nevertheless, many social program variables prove to be significant determinants of age composition. As far as we know, this study is the first to show that source-country social programs play any role in determining the age structure of migrants to the United States.

Notes

1. Simon (1984) has noted that the largest single category of transfer payments or services received by immigrant families is that for schooling costs of children aged 5–17.
2. This assumption is relaxed in the next chapter that focuses on the skill composition of immigrants.
3. The concept of relative attractiveness incorporates the idea that nonmonetary characteristics associated with country i and the United States may enter the decision maker's utility function and therefore influence the decision to migrate. If we assume that these characteristics are included in a vector x, the foregone relative

attractiveness of the country of origin could be expressed as $(x_i - x_j)$, where the subscript j represents the United States. Therefore, more highly valued nonmonetary characteristics associated with the country of origin imply higher migration costs. Alternatively, if x_j is actually higher than x_i, this concept may be better interpreted as an opportunity cost of not migrating which, of course, would be lower the higher x_i. Moreover, if x_j is higher than x_i, the individual will choose to migrate only if the added value attached to the nonmonetary characteristics (plus any net gains in earnings if he or she is economically active) exceeds the "other" costs (i.e., direct entry costs and possible skill losses).

4. Measuring the benefits of migration solely in terms of earnings differentials essentially presumes that individuals are all economically active which, of course, is not realistic. Individuals may choose not to be economically active because of their age (e.g., retirement from work) or for other reasons, perhaps related to gender differences in the propensity to work in the formal labor market. For such individuals, employment opportunities would play a less important role in the decision of whether to migrate, though for spouses of economically active marriage partners such considerations still play a critical role. Rather, for individuals who are not economically active, the decision of whether to migrate would entail a more direct comparison of the other migration costs incurred and the change in the value of the nonmonetary characteristics associated with the move.

5. This effect on age composition may be clearer for the numerically restricted immigrant class, where unmarried adult sons and daughters as well as brothers and sisters of U.S. citizens 21 years old and over may enter.

6. This "problem" results in at least three options. First, we could live without the adding up property and argue that this property now holds only approximately. Because we view the adding-up property as inherent to the estimation of a system of share equations, we reject this option. Second, we could use a simple econometric technique like one- or two-way fixed effects. However, Appendix C makes a strong case for the Hausman-Taylor approach over these alternatives. Finally, we could estimate a series of two-equation systems that satisfy the adding-up property. This last option is preferable to the use of a still more sophisticated approach suggested by Berndt and Savin (1975) that requires a number of additional simplifying assumptions.

7. Consider a two-equation system that includes an adding-up property:

Eq. F1 $y = \alpha_1 T + \alpha_2 x + \varepsilon_1$, and

Eq. F2 $T - y = \beta_1 T + \beta_2 x + \varepsilon_2$

where T is the "control total," y is a component of T, x is a vector of explanatory variables, and ε_1 and ε_2 are error terms. Now subtract T from both sides of Eq. F2 to yield

Eq. F3 $-y = (\beta_1 - 1)T + \beta_2 x + \varepsilon_2$.

If we multiply Eq. F3 through by -1, we obtain

Eq. F4 $y = (1 - \beta_1)T - \beta_2 x - \varepsilon_2 .$

Even if we multiply all terms in Eq. F1 and F2 by a weight (w), the following conditions hold in the two-equation system:

Eq. F5 $\alpha_1 = 1 - \beta_1;$ and $\alpha_2 = -\beta_2$

8. Another difference is that provident funds programs are generally associated with developing countries, whereas employment-related social insurance old-age programs are more frequently found in developed nations with at least a relatively high degree of industrialization.

9. For potential female migrants, higher rates of female labor force participation may reflect generally better earnings opportunities for female workers, and therefore relatively more young female migrants should come from source countries where the female percentage of total labor force is relatively high.

10. The evidence indicating that, for both males and females, birth rate is positive and significant for immigrants aged 55 and older is consistent with our hypotheses. However, the findings that more immigrants aged 55 and older come from nations that are more distant from the United States and that fewer women aged 55 and older come from English-speaking nations are not expected.

11. Note also that, whereas both the Silva program and the differential treatment of Western Hemisphere natives during 1972–1976 have a significantly positive effect on both males and females aged 55 and older, a significantly negative effect occurs on migrants aged 20–34 only for males with the Silva program and only for females from the Western Hemisphere during 1972–1976. We suspect that information related to specific policy-related features of these programs may explain these differences.

12. We do not understand why the lottery and Silva programs influence exempt immigrants, because these variables reflect admission programs that affected restricted immigrants. Exempt immigration could be affected in later years after the restricted immigrants acquire U.S. citizenship, but how the exempt category would be influenced in the years of the programs is not clear.

8 The Skill Composition of U.S. Immigration

A strong focus of current debates regarding U.S. immigration policy is the issue of whether a decline has occurred in the quality of U.S. immigrants (e.g., Borjas 1985 and 1987b) or not (e.g., Chiswick 1986). Recent literature seems to indicate that the quality of immigrant skills has in fact declined (Borjas 1995) relative to those of native-born Americans.

The skill composition of immigrants has many potential effects on the U.S. economy. The supply of highly skilled immigrant workers is often stressed as critically important to maintaining a vibrant and competitive U.S. work force in an economy that is increasingly becoming more globalized. Moreover, in an era of rapid technological change, high-skilled workers are necessary to maintain productivity at the frontiers of technological developments.

Skill levels have many other potential influences, including many of the influences discussed earlier in the context of the age composition of migrants. High-skilled workers are more economically productive than low-skilled workers and therefore add more to overall U.S. productivity. Moreover, their higher incomes contribute more to the private sector in terms of consumption expenditures and to the public sector in the form of tax payments. High-skilled workers also are less likely to experience periods of unemployment and thus are less likely to impose a net burden on the U.S. economy. Furthermore, by virtue of their education and innate abilities, high-skilled workers are likely to be more proficient in English or to learn English-language skills more quickly, and therefore they are able to assimilate more rapidly in the U.S. economy. Given the linkage between skill level and income/education levels, the skill composition of immigrants also may have links to the dependency ratio within immigrant families and may affect the overall U.S. fertility rate in subsequent years. Moreover, crime rates are related to income and education levels. Therefore, the skill level of migrants may affect the extent to which immigrants impose a net cost on the U.S. society.

THE SKILL COMPOSITION MODEL

The Marginal Migrant Once Again

The general form of the skill composition model follows that of Equation 5.1, and we again use the concept of the marginal migrant. In our prior discussion in the context of age composition, we assumed that all members of the indigenous population were endowed with a given amount of human capital. Clearly, in order to discuss skill composition, this assumption must now be relaxed. We here assume that, over time, potential immigrants accumulate occupational skills through formal schooling and occupational experience. Individuals differ in terms of the rate at which these occupational skills are accumulated (e.g., different innate abilities). As a consequence, within any particular age group of country i's indigenous population (e.g., those individuals aged $a*$), individuals possess different skill levels. While we presume that the skill levels of the indigenous population are a continuous spectrum from low to high, for convenience we categorize members of the population as being either low- or high-skilled workers.

In its modified form, the equilibrium condition for the marginal migrant in age group a* now may be expressed as:

$$\text{Eq. 8.1} \quad \sum_{t=a*}^{T}(w_j - w_i)K**(1 + r)^{-(T-t)} = C_i \, ,$$

where
  $a*$ is age at migration for a specific age group,
  T is the age of the immigrant at death,
  w_j and w_i are the respective U.S. and country-of-origin wage per unit of occupational skill,
  $K**$ is the index of the marginal migrants occupational skill, and
  r is a discount rate.

The left side of Eq. 8.1 therefore represents the discounted total returns accruing to the marginal migrant who possesses skill level $K**$ and moves from i to j at age $a*$. The right side of Eq. 8.1 represents the total migration costs incurred by an individual who migrates from country i. Once again, these total migration costs (C_i) include direct entry costs, skill losses associated with less-than-perfect international skill transferability, and the foregone relative attractiveness of the country of origin.

For the marginal migrant in age group a^*, the decision to migrate is one of indifference, since the expected benefits from migration are exactly offset by the migration costs. However, within country i's indigenous population, other individuals who are also aged a^* will find it beneficial to migrate if they possess a skill level that is higher than K^{**}, since such individuals would receive net positive benefits from migrating. Therefore, within the group of individuals of age a^*, given the skill level K^{**} at which net benefits are zero, the marginal migrant equilibrium condition determines the skill levels at which other members of the indigenous population would find migration beneficial and hence determines the skill composition of immigrants. The higher the skill level of the marginal migrant, the more highly skilled the overall skill composition of migrants.

Since we are now focusing on a particular age group (a^*), the skill level of the marginal migrant is now considered to be the choice variable. Once again, the marginal migrant is presumed to be capable of adjusting to any factors that would alter either the returns to or the costs of migration ("adjusting" here means choosing to migrate at a higher or lower skill level).[1] Such an adjustment would be expected if, for example, migration costs were higher; the marginal migrant will adjust by moving at a higher skill level and, by doing so, increase the returns to migration in order to offset the higher costs. Hence, the overall skill composition of migrants from country i will be responsive to factors related to relative economic advantage between i and the United States, as well as to the total migration costs incurred by those who choose to migrate from i to the United States.

Figure 8.1 illustrates these relationships. The return on migration increases with the skill level of the potential migrant, because those who migrate at a higher skill level receive the same wage per unit of occupational skill but over more units of skill than the low-skilled individual. Given costs of migration from country i to country j of C_{ij} and the expected differential return, $R_i(K)$, that is a function of the skill level possessed at migration, the marginal migrant aged a^* would

Figure 8.1 Skill Level at Migration

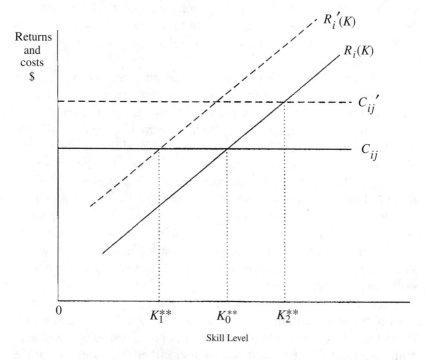

move at skill level $K_0{}^{**}$. If costs were higher, however, such as C_{ij}', the marginal migrant would move at a higher skill level, $K_2{}^{**}$. For example, C_{ij}' could refer to migration from a more distant country or from a non-English-speaking country. If the expected returns on migration were higher at every skill level, such as shown by $R_i'(K)$—for example, for individuals in lower-income source countries—the marginal migrant would possess a lower skill level ($K_1{}^{**}$). Other things being equal, any factors that would result in higher returns or lower costs to individuals who migrate would induce relatively fewer of the high-skilled individuals to become international migrants.

One important feature of Eq. 8.1 should be noted. This equation specifies the equilibrium condition for the marginal migrant (i.e., net benefits to migration equal zero) for only the a^* age group. In a more complicated form of the model, a similar condition may be specified for the marginal migrant in all other age groups. Other things being equal, the only difference in the specifications for the other age groups is that the indexed skill level of the marginal migrant in younger (older) age groups would be associated with a lower (higher) skill level than K^{**}. However, the adjustments made to differences in the returns and/or the costs of migration would be the same within each age group. Therefore, within each age group, the skill level of migrants would be responsive to factors related to relative economic advantage between country i and the United States, as well as to the total migration costs incurred by those who choose to migrate. Hence, if individuals are allowed (conceptually) to adjust within all age groups, any factors that are associated with lower returns to individuals who migrate would induce a relatively more skilled flow of international migrants. Similarly, the higher the costs imposed on migrants, the more highly skilled the international migrants.

Hypotheses

Consider the expected effects of the factors included in the differential economic opportunity vector, other things being equal. Higher country-of-origin wages per unit of human capital will decrease the returns to migration at all skill levels, so migrants should possess a relatively higher average skill level if they come from source countries with relatively higher per capita gross domestic product.[2] Djajic (1989) also notes that a lower wage differential will induce migration of individuals with a higher average skill level.

Other factors may influence relative earnings as well. For instance, high government revenues are likely to be associated with higher taxes, which will tend to increase the relative after-tax wage differential. However, given their progressive nature, these taxes should fall disproportionately on the higher-income (highly skilled) individuals, lowering the net wage of the higher income workers relatively more than that of the lower-income workers.[3] Thus, high government revenues should induce relatively more high-skilled individuals to migrate.

Higher levels of development and more rapid short-term expansion of country i's economy are both generally associated with enhanced employment opportunities, meaning the expected benefits from migrating are generally lower, *ceteris paribus*. Thus, relatively more high-skilled workers would choose to migrate. However, if the level of development is particularly relevant in determining the employment opportunities for the more highly skilled individuals, a negative relationship may exist. Rapid economic expansion and the associated enhanced employment opportunities may be of particular importance for the economic prospects of the low-skilled workers, which would tend to reinforce our hypothesis that relatively more high-skilled workers would migrate. However, while this is certainly plausible, the ultimate impact of growth in real per capita GDP depends on how relative wages within the source country are affected. If the relative employment and wage opportunities of high-skilled workers improve with short-term expansion, then the average skill composition of migrants would be inversely related to the rate of economic expansion. Since little evidence exists concerning the relationship between short-term growth and relative employment or wage opportunities, we do not predict the sign concerning the relationship between economic growth and the skill composition of migrants.

The marginal migrant also will adjust to differences in the direct costs of migration. For example, greater distance from the United States would impose higher direct entry costs on all migrants, so migrants from more distant countries should have relatively higher average skill levels. Less-than-perfect international transferability of skills also imposes costs, and greater expected skill losses should cause the marginal migrant to adjust by migrating at a higher skill level. However, others (e.g., McManus, Gould, and Welch 1983) assert that whereas direct migration costs (e.g., distance) do not vary with skill level, the negative effects of losses associated with less-than-perfect international skill transferability should be proportionately greater in the more skilled occupations. Therefore, other things being equal, migrants from English-speaking nations should be relatively more skilled than migrants from non-English speaking nations.

We expect migrants to be relatively more skilled if they come from source countries that have more highly educated indigenous populations. Furthermore, given per capita income, an increase in the relative number of highly educated individuals should decrease the wages of high-skilled relative to low-skilled occupations in country i, thereby affecting the relative propensies of high- versus low-skilled individuals to migrate. Acquiring an education at a U.S. university should reduce skill losses for those who immigrate to the United States, by increasing the probability that their knowledge will be easily transferred to U.S. occupations and by creating a better flow of information back to country i concerning U.S. opportunities. Consequently, larger numbers of students from country i should increase the skill level of migrants from i.

The less politically attractive the country of origin, the lower the opportunity costs of departing; therefore, *ceteris paribus*, migrants from politically less attractive countries should be less skilled. However, evidence suggests that as political and civil rights are deprived, professionals respond vigorously by emigrating (Huang 1987).

The number of prior immigrants from country i who have become U.S. citizens should also be relevant in determining the skill composition of migrants. Because migration costs are lower for persons who have citizen relatives in the United States, the average skill composition should be higher for countries having a low number of naturalized citizens. In addition, to the extent that the differential treatment of Western Hemisphere natives during 1972–1976 represents a lower immigration barrier (i.e., fewer restrictions), the average skill level should also be lower.

The anticipated effect of social programs on skill composition is not straightforward, and consequently our reasoning is somewhat indirect. To the extent that a social program entails a transfer from higher income (high-skilled) to lower income (low-skilled) individuals, we expect the program to increase the relative share of high-skilled migrants, because those bearing the greatest burden are generally the least likely to benefit from the program. Thus, countries with programs that provide universal coverage should have relatively more high-skilled migrants in their immigration flows.

Likewise, unemployment insurance constitutes a transfer from high-skilled workers to low-skilled workers, who typically have higher unemployment rates; consequently, we expect unemployment insurance to discourage the migration of low-skilled workers and to encourage the migration of the high-skilled. Because the number of children in a family is likely to be inversely related to the family's income, family allowance programs should be relatively more important in reducing the flow of lower-income (low-skilled) migrants. Fixed payments per child would increase the income of the low-income family relatively more (as a percentage of unaugmented base income); hence, we expect employment-related family allowance programs to encourage more highly skilled migrants.

Not all social programs constitute an income transfer, however. For instance, employment-related old-age pension programs and cash sickness programs present a complex situation in which both costs and benefits are most often roughly proportional to income levels. Therefore, without additional information concerning specific programs, we are unable to ascertain precisely how they would affect the skill composition of migrants. However, some sickness-related programs may transfer wealth from high-skilled to low-skilled workers and therefore should increase the relative skill level of migrants.

ESTIMATION OF THE SKILL COMPOSITION EQUATION

The statistical methodology used to estimate the skill-composition relationships is essentially the same as that used for the gender and age composition of immigrant flows. Because our empirical analysis is designed to study the composition of occupational skills, we limit our analysis to immigrants who are aged 20–64. (Immigrants over the age of 64 are excluded because they are not likely to be economic migrants who possess skills that will be used in the U.S. labor market.) Moreover, by necessity, our empirical analysis is limited to only those immigrants aged 20–64 who declare an occupation upon their admittance as permanent resident aliens. For these immigrants, a separate analysis of skill shares is performed for each of three age groups: all immigrants aged 20–64; immigrants aged 20–34; and immigrants aged 35–64. The shares of migrants in two skill classes are considered: 1) high-skilled, which includes all individuals who declare an occupation in one of the professional, technical, and kindred (PTK) occupational categories, as well as managers, officials, and proprietors (except farm); and 2) low-skilled, which includes all other individuals who declare an occupation. Tables 4.13 and 4.14 provide an overall picture of these groups broken out by gender and entry class.

Since within each group the two skill classes together equal the sum of all individuals examined, the interpretation of the coefficients in the regressions is similar to that used with the gender regressions. Thus, the coefficient on the control total (e.g., total immigration of individuals aged 20–64) must sum to 1.0 across the two skill groups. The interpretation of the other independent variables is the same as in Chapters 6 and 7 in the sense that these coefficients are interpreted as a change in the absolute number of immigrants in a particular skill group and the coefficients sum to zero across the skill classes. Within all groups analyzed, the results for the high- and low-skilled classes are essentially mirror images, and therefore we present the results only for the high-skilled group. Moreover, the explanatory variables include a measure of the percentage of individuals who do not declare an occupation. This variable is measured specific to the age (and gender) group under consideration and is included to partially correct for selectivity into the group of immigrants who declare an occupation. The variable is treated as endogenous, or correlated with unobserved country-specific effects, and thus falls into the x_2 vector (as described in Appendix C).

EMPIRICAL FINDINGS

All Immigrants

For highly skilled immigrants, Table 8.1 reports coefficients and significance levels for all immigrants aged 20–64, those aged 20–34, and those aged 35–64, where the totals are aggregated across gender and entry classes (i.e., numerically restricted and numerically exempt). Under the economic opportunities vector, we hypothesized that migrants will possess a relatively higher skill level if they come from higher-income source countries. Borjas (1987b), in particular, has argued that if income distributions are more unequal in the home country than in the United States, then individuals who migrate will be drawn from the lower tail of the home country's income distribution (i.e., lower skill levels). If the extent of source-country income inequality is negatively related to the country's average income level, this consideration of income inequality should reinforce our expectation. However, contrary to expectations, source-country income levels do not significantly affect skill composition.

Table 8.1 Highly Skilled Immigrants by Age: Hausman-Taylor Instrumental Variable Estimates[a]

Variable	Total	Aged 20–34	Aged 35–64
Diff. econ. opportunity			
Relative per capita income	40.43	73.27	–5.16
Relative growth of GDP	–599.43***	–564.32***	73.51
Government revenues	1.89	2.06*	–0.44
% Urban	–10.23***	–3.39	–3.00**
% Female in labor force	21.85***	34.74***	–11.68***
Migration costs			
Distance to U.S.A.	–293.40***	–171.52***	–72.88***
Birth rate	5.42	6.81**	0.49
U.S. military presence	30.61	20.28	18.58*
Education	–9.70***	–9.62***	0.56
English language	2721.00***	1724.09***	1050.23***
U.S. college students	–49.35	13.50	–43.49*
Polit. attract. and religion			
Political competitiveness	4.16	–1.35	0.94
Catholic	1284.60***	991.52***	316.10**
Muslim	340.84	666.05*	–162.62
U.S. immigration policy			
Per capita naturalizations	–2.28	–5.72	–0.57
Lottery visas	76.80**	68.12***	19.39
Silva visas	–358.94**	–597.58***	–250.85***
Western Hemisphere 1972–76	–212.84***	–150.99***	–15.21
Asia	2456.86***	1430.92***	842.17***
Social programs			
Universal old-age	92.96	130.61**	6.51
Employment-related old-age	–146.52***	–119.43***	–47.81*
Provident fund old-age	164.50**	219.34***	–50.67
Old-age pension not portable	–102.50**	–95.89***	6.17
Universal sickness	–82.31	–36.94	–7.36
Cash sickness benefits	12.98	–80.12	149.83***

Variable	Total	Aged 20–34	Aged 35–64
Maternity benefits	48.66	59.75*	–7.51
Medical benefits	65.84	74.78*	34.69
Unemployment insurance	–27.22	–10.39	35.34
Universal family allowance	143.35*	179.05***	31.95
Employment family allowance	14.68	54.89	15.79
Control			
% No occupation[b]	–284.73***	–102.99*	25.80
Total U.S. immigration from i[c]	0.08***	0.12***	0.10***

[a] *** Indicates $t \geq 1.96$; ** indicates $1.67 \leq t < 1.96$; * indicates $1.29 \leq t < 1.67$. Corresponding t-statistics are reported in Appendix Table G1.

[b] The control for the percentage of immigrants that does not declare an occupation is measured specific to the group examined (i.e., total, aged 20–34, and aged 35–64).

[c] The control total is measured specific to the group examined (i.e., total, aged 20–34, and aged 35–64).

The findings for the other economic opportunity variables provide only mixed support for our hypotheses, and these findings are sensitive to the actual age group considered. We hypothesized that relatively more high-skilled migrants would come from source countries that provide enhanced employment opportunities, which would lower the earnings differential, but, to the extent that higher levels of development and more rapid short-term growth are associated with enhanced employment opportunities, the evidence suggests that the propensity of high-skilled workers to migrate is reduced by such opportunities. For level of development or degree of urbanization, this finding may not be surprising, but we do not understand why this would be the case only for those individuals aged 35–64. Apparently, more rapid short-term expansion of the economy also improves the wage and employment opportunities of high-skilled relative to low-skilled workers, especially among migrants aged 20–34.

The impact of the relative size of government is positive and marginally significant for the high-skill share of migrants aged 20–34. The findings concerning the relationship between female labor force participation and the skill level of migrants are sensitive to the age group considered. Among migrants aged 20–34, a higher percentage of females in the labor force is associated with a significantly larger number of high-skilled migrants; however, among the migrants aged 35–64, the opposite is found. This may reflect the fact that in countries where female labor force participation is relatively high, a generally higher skill level exists among the population, thus resulting in the migration of relatively more high-skilled workers. However, this argument does not explain why the high-skilled share is lower for the migrants aged 35–64.

The results indicate that English-speaking nations send relatively more high-skilled migrants to the United States: other things being equal, over 2,700 additional high-skilled workers annually migrate to the United States from these countries. This finding is expected. On the other hand, the findings indicating that fewer high-skilled workers come from nations with relatively highly educated populations is surprising. This evidence may indicate that, in these countries, the labor market provides more favorable returns to human capital.

Because greater distance from the United States imposes higher direct entry costs on all migrants, we anticipated that, in order to overcome these higher costs, migrants would tend to be relatively more skilled. The findings strongly suggest the opposite. Greater distance from the United States could entail more potential intervening opportunities that serve to attract the relatively skilled migrants to locations other than the United States, but the exact reason for this finding is not clear.

Our findings indicate that high birth rates differentially affect members of the indigenous population, depending on their skill (income) level. If births within families are inversely related to family incomes, then higher migration costs would be particularly imposing on the migration decisions of lower income (low-skilled) individuals and their families. The evidence suggests that these higher costs do fall disproportionately on the low-skilled workers, especially among the group aged 20–34 where young children are most likely to be present.

We did not attach a prior to the religion variables. Our results indicate that a particularly large number of skilled migrants come from nations where Catholicism is the primary religion. For reasons that are not altogether clear, Catholicism increases the high-skilled component of U.S. immigration for both age groups, and it is especially important for the group aged 20–34. The Muslim variable is positive and marginally significant for this same age group.

The family reunification provisions of U.S. immigration law have long been suspected as one cause of declining skill composition of U.S. immigration. The results shown in Table 8.1 fail to support this position. Although the signs on the naturalization variable are negative, as anticipated, the coefficients are not statistically significant. Given the level of skill aggregation used in this study and given these findings, we must look elsewhere for the cause of declining immigrant quality.

The differential treatment of Western Hemisphere natives during the 1972–1976 period resulted in significantly fewer high-skilled workers among the total migrants and particularly among those aged 20–34. Thus, lower immigration barriers appear to decrease the relative skill level of migrants. Although we did not attach a prior to either lottery or Silva programs, both programs resulted in significant changes in the number of high-skilled migrants: the Silva program resulted in fewer high-skilled migrants, and the lottery visas in more. These lottery findings are similar to those of Barrett (1996), who observed that lottery winners were more highly skilled than family immigrants. Thus, these results illustrate that, whether intentional or not, U.S. policy does influence the skill composition of U.S. immigrants.

In terms of magnitude, the control for Asian nations indicates a particularly large effect, with approximately 2,500 additional high-skilled migrants coming from Asian nations, *ceteris paribus*. The earnings differential between high- and low-skilled workers may be relatively low in Asian nations, thus inducing relatively more high-skilled workers to migrate. Alternatively, potential migrants from Asia may encounter intervening opportunities that provide relatively better alternatives for the low-skilled. However, we noted above that intervening opportunities may provide the opposite set of incentives for potential migrants from more distant non-Asian nations.

Of the social programs considered, those that appear to have the greatest influence on the skill composition of migrants involve universal coverage and generally are related to old-age pension programs. As expected, the presence of universal old-age programs provides a significant incentive for an increased flow of younger (aged 20–34) high-skilled workers. Employment-related pension programs also significantly influence the skill composition of migrants. Whereas the presence of old-age social insurance programs reduces the number of high-skilled migrants, provident funds programs tend to increase their number. Moreover, if the pensions are not internationally transferable, the number of high-skilled migrants is reduced. These results are not unexpected. Employment-related pension programs that are of the social insurance variety often entail a cost to the insured individual that is equal to some fixed percentage of his or her earnings and, in turn, the benefits derived from such programs generally take the form of payments that equal some percentage of the average or highest earnings during some specified period. Apparently, where social programs provide benefits that are positively related to income levels, the higher-income, high-skilled workers find such programs to be relatively attractive inducements to stay at home. High-skilled workers also are less likely to migrate and leave their pensions behind, which would be necessary under situations where the pensions are not transferable. On the other hand, provident funds programs provide the opportunity for individuals to save an amount that would be sufficient to cover relocation expenses. Therefore, such programs may be positively associated with the skill level of migrants because the high-skilled (higher-income) individuals would be able to accumulate these savings more quickly. Thus, within a given age group of potential migrants, the highly skilled are more likely to migrate than less-skilled individuals if provident funds are available.

Universal family allowance programs also provide a significant incentive for an increased number of high-skilled migrants aged 20–34. However, our more direct measure of coverage within health-related programs does not provide evidence of the anticipated effect that universally provided sickness programs increase the flow of high-skilled migrants. The findings concerning certain features of sickness programs provide some support for the expected relationships, however. For instance, among the group of migrants aged 20–34, the availability of maternity and medical benefits positively influence the number of high-skilled migrants, though the level of significance is not high. We would expect these programs to generally increase the skill level of migrants, since the primary beneficiaries (women) tend to have lower skills. Among migrants aged 35–64, programs that provide cash sickness benefits also increase the relative share of the highly skilled, perhaps again reflecting that the availability of such programs is particularly important to women.

Immigrants By Gender

Table 8.2 presents the findings for total male and total female immigrants classified as highly skilled, as well as for the gender-specific subgroups aged 20–34 and 35–64, where within each of these groups the immigrants are aggregated across entry classes.

In general, most factors have similar effects on the skill composition of both males and females. The similarities are most apparent in the pair-wise comparisons of the factors included in the economic opportunity and migration costs vectors. For educational attainment and distance from the United States, the only substantive differences across gender are for the subgroup aged 35–64, where (as expected) countries with higher education levels send more high-skilled (female but not male) migrants, and nations more distant from the United States send fewer high-skilled (male but not female) migrants. Concerning relative economic growth and English-language skills, the findings concerning the effects on skill composition are essentially the same in both the male and female regressions. Thus, the incentives created by economic expansion and language skills do not appear to entail any gender tilting. The relationship between female labor force participation rates and the skill composition of migrants also is essentially identical across genders.

Certain factors in these vectors have a different effect on females than males, but the most notable differences are expected. For example, high birth rates should impose a relatively higher migration cost on potential low-skilled migrants; the fact that the evidence supports this hypothesis for females but not males is consistent with the notion that child rearing costs fall more heavily on the female marriage partner. The finding that the presence of U.S. military personnel has a significant influence on the composition of female but not male migrants is also not surprising, since this variable should reflect the operation of a marriage market that focuses on the wives of U.S. servicemen.[4] Contrary to the evidence, however, we expected U.S. military personnel to represent lower cost of entry and therefore to have a negative effect on the skill level of female migrants. The observed effect could be due to

Table 8.2 Highly Skilled Immigrants by Gender: Hausman-Taylor Instrumental Variable Estimates[a]

Variable	Males				Females			
	Total	Aged 20–34	Aged 35–64	Total		Aged 20–34	Aged 35–64	
Diff. econ. opportunity								
Relative per capita income	39.31	54.70	1.50		11.02	19.81		1.37
Relative growth of GDP	–272.28*	–341.43***	102.23		–248.05**	–193.46**		–6.24
Government revenues	0.77	1.07	–0.31		0.86	0.69		–0.20
% Urban	–4.06**	0.14	–2.41***		–3.48***	–1.21		–0.31
% Female in labor force	17.12***	22.59***	–5.55***		5.18*	10.88***		–6.24***
Migration costs								
Distance to U.S.A.	–194.35***	–113.41***	–60.82***		–85.50***	–43.13***		–9.82
Birth rate	0.87	2.48	–0.72		5.37***	5.49***		1.35
U.S. military presence	14.56	8.96	10.14		21.41*	15.09*		7.56
Education[b]	–3.48***	–2.89***	–0.71		–2.61***	–4.04***		1.60***
English language	1835.57***	1313.00***	629.61***		1164.51***	613.62***		452.87***
U.S. college students	–28.60	2.89	–26.30*		–11.09	20.61		–17.05
Polit. attract. and religion								
Political competitiveness	11.90***	3.97	4.78**		–6.58*	–5.13*		–3.64**
Catholic	761.32***	670.13***	133.81		649.43***	412.41***		183.56***
Muslim	429.82	634.87***	–110.71		130.98	184.37		–28.85

(continued)

U.S. immigration policy

Per capita naturalizations	-2.03	-2.65	-1.09	-2.28	-5.02***	0.27
Lottery visas	68.54***	50.30***	24.88***	10.10	16.49	-4.27
Silva visas	-97.35	-173.04***	-138.61***	-464.41***	-702.48***	-136.42***
Western Hemisphere 1972–76	-115.01***	-85.36***	-11.54	-72.77***	-33.60***	2.62
Asia	1499.97***	872.11***	564.48***	908.34***	516.54***	272.82***

Social programs

Universal old-age	45.62	91.80**	-18.27	80.13*	67.01**	24.39
Employment-related old-age	-101.85***	-82.22***	-27.57	-55.63*	-38.81*	-8.28
Provident fund old-age	84.97*	120.84***	-37.98	80.64*	89.18***	-7.62
Old-age pension not portable	-53.75*	-57.90***	7.56	-42.32*	-30.40*	-0.20
Universal sickness	-65.49*	-23.49	-19.06	4.75	3.19	14.55
Cash sickness benefits	15.51	-54.73	93.05***	17.35	-0.23	56.48***
Maternity benefits	-3.59	28.60	-24.55*	49.39**	25.64*	17.60
Medical benefits	40.43	37.72	26.46*	34.89	48.64***	9.12
Unemployment insurance	-34.87	-11.83	8.83	34.88	32.73	34.35*
Universal family allowance	85.55	105.15**	22.34	80.33*	99.74***	20.16
Employment family allowance	9.75	32.76	11.99	21.84	45.80	11.03

172

Table 8.2 (continued)

Variable	Males			Females		
	Total	Aged 20–34	Aged 35–64	Total	Aged 20–34	Aged 35–64
Control						
% No occupation[c]	–149.97***	–85.88**	2.31	–56.65*	–9.26	3.41
Total U.S. immigration from t^d	0.07***	0.09***	0.09***	0.14***	0.24***	0.16***

[a] *** Indicates $t \geq 1.96$; ** indicates $1.67 \leq t < 1.96$; * indicates $1.29 \leq t < 1.67$. Corresponding t-statistics are reported in Appendix Table G2.

[b] In the gender-specific regressions, the education control is measured specific to the respective gender.

[c] The control for the percentage of immigrants that does not declare an occupation is measured specific to the group examined (i.e., male total, aged 20–34, aged 35–64; female total, aged 20–34, and aged 35–64).

[d] The control total is measured specific to the group examined (i.e., see note c).

marriage sorting that pairs better-educated females in source countries with U.S. military personnel.

Like the findings presented earlier concerning all immigrants, significantly more of both male and female high-skilled migrants come from nations where Catholicism is the primary religion, but gender-specific differences are evident in the other factors of this vector. For example, significantly more high-skilled male migrants aged 20–34 come from Muslim nations. Apparently, high-skilled males are able to exercise their choice to migrate, but the same may not be true of potential female migrants for whom social customs inhibit movement (Tyree and Donato 1985). Unattractive political environments have very different impacts on the skill composition of male and female migrants: a larger share of male migrants from politically less attractive nations is highly skilled, but a smaller share of female migrants is, perhaps reflecting different emigration restrictions. For males, this evidence also may suggest that general economic opportunities for high-skilled workers are relatively less desirable in countries that are politically less attractive. For female workers, either the supply of potential high-skilled migrants is low (e.g., suppressed opportunities to acquire the skills necessary to become a high-skilled migrant) or, compared to their low-skilled counterparts, the economic opportunities are relatively good.

For many of the factors in the U.S. immigration policy vector, the findings are similar for both males and females and are essentially the same as the findings discussed earlier in the context of all immigrants (i.e., males and females aggregated). However, whereas the findings for all immigrants do not support our hypotheses concerning naturalized U.S. citizens, among females aged 20–34, significantly fewer high-skilled migrants come from nations with a relatively high number of natives who have become U.S. citizens, which is as anticipated. The effect of the lottery program also suggests a very different impact on males than females. The lottery visas are associated with a significantly larger number of high-skilled male migrants, but this program had little effect on the skill composition of female migrants. Apparently (perhaps because their numbers were relatively large among the nonimmigrants already present in the United States at the time the lottery program was initiated), high-skilled male workers were in a better position than other potential migrants to take advantage of the lottery visas.

In the social programs vector, we hypothesized that universal benefits would provide incentives for relatively more high-skilled workers to migrate, which is supported by evidence for both males and females for universal old-age and family allowance programs. The effects on skill composition of various other features of old-age pension programs do not appear to generally differ by gender, though the significance of the findings is higher in the male regressions. However, certain social programs exert a different influence on males than on females. For instance, the availability of unemployment insurance increases the number of high-skilled female migrants aged 35–64, which is expected, but the same is not true for males.

Other notable differences in the findings for male versus female migrants relate to variables associated with sickness programs. Potential female migrants appear to be more sensitive than males to the availability of sickness-related programs; in particular, maternity and medical benefits primarily affect the skill composition of female migrants, which is not surprising. Concerning medical programs, apparently the higher income (high-skilled) workers bear a disproportionate share of the costs for such programs, thus inducing an increase in the skill level of female migrants. Moreover, if birth rates are inversely related to income levels, then maternity programs should increase the skill level of female migrants, since the low-skilled (low-income) female workers benefit most from the provision of such benefits. Programs providing cash sickness benefits, which are generally tied to some percentage of the insured workers earnings, increase the high-skilled share of both male and female migrants aged 35–64; such benefits appear to be viewed by both genders as lowering the perceived earnings differential between the country of origin and the United States, thus inducing relatively more high-skilled workers to migrate.

Male and Female Immigrants By Entry Class

Table 8.3 presents the findings for both male and female numerically restricted and exempt immigrants classified as highly skilled and aged 20–64. In large part, the findings for the numerically restricted class of immigrants are similar to those found when the data were not disaggregated by entry class. However, some differences are apparent, particularly within many of the vectors when pair-wise comparisons are made between numerically restricted and exempt immigrants.

Earlier, within the context of gender and age composition, we found that economic incentives served better in forming the composition of numerically exempt immigrants. With respect to skill composition, this does not appear to be the case; at least in terms of the number of significant relationships, the skill composition of numerically restricted immigrants seems to be more influenced by economic opportunities. Moreover, in terms of directional influence, the differences across entry class are readily apparent. For instance, whereas the extent of female labor force participation and the relative size of government both positively influence the number of high-skilled migrants within the numerically restricted class, these same factors negatively influence the number of high-skilled migrants in the exempt class. Our hypotheses are more generally supported by the evidence relating to restricted immigrants.

In terms of migration costs, whereas similarities are apparent concerning the effects of distance and English-language skills, differences across entry classes are again noteworthy. On the one hand, we are not surprised that the presence of U.S. military personnel affects the composition of exempt but not restricted immigrants. On the other hand, we do not understand why (as expected) relatively more high-skilled female numerically restricted workers migrate from countries with high birth rates, but the same relationship is not found among exempt migrants. Perhaps numerically restricted female immigrants more frequently move within the context of a family unit, where family size and its associated costs would be particularly relevant to migration decisions.

The difference across entry class in terms of the effect of education also is quite striking. For exempt migrants, as expected, more high-skilled migrants come from nations where the level of educational attainment is relatively high. However, the evidence points more toward a brain-drain phenomenon for the numerically restricted immigrants. Apparently, within this class, the heavy orientation toward family maintenance considerations serves to retard the entry of potential high-skilled migrants from nations with high levels of education, perhaps because these nations have fewer recently formed family linkages with the United States.

Table 8.3 Highly Skilled Immigrants by Entry Class: Hausman-Taylor Instrumental Variable Estimates[a]

Variable	Numerically restricted		Numerically exempt	
	Males	Females	Males	Females
Diff. econ. opportunity				
Relative per capita income	77.52*	30.57	−29.15	1.43
Relative growth of GDP	−369.93***	−252.42***	47.60	22.18
Government revenues	1.86**	1.08**	−0.87***	−0.62
% Urban	−0.95	−0.99	−1.03	−0.22
% Female in labor force	26.25***	11.22***	−6.13***	−8.05***
Migration costs				
Distance to U.S.A.	−138.24***	−21.06	−31.98*	−0.59
Birth rate	−2.72	6.43***	1.17	1.36
U.S. military presence	6.42	10.34	10.49*	15.55*
Education[b]	−4.03***	−3.55***	0.80*	1.72**
English language	1609.82***	383.20**	333.32**	434.56***
U.S. college students	−4.64	30.63*	−29.71***	−25.74
Polit. attract. and religion				
Political competitiveness	3.10	−6.22**	4.06**	−6.22**
Catholic	835.27***	338.00***	14.15	125.78*
Muslim	808.31***	175.54	−142.04	−68.50
U.S. immigration policy				
Per capita naturalizations	−1.50	−3.01*	−1.95	−2.69
Lottery visas	64.14***	27.34**	−0.06	−21.65*
Silva visas	−1425.81***	−1608.63***	83.61**	107.85*
Western Hemisphere 1972–76	−126.61***	−25.73*	28.54***	35.15***
Asia	1055.99***	421.96***	293.91***	224.11**
Social programs				
Universal old-age	38.51	53.00*	−18.00	24.29
Employment-related old-age	−81.50***	−14.35	−5.64	−9.80
Provident fund old-age	104.32**	100.41***	−56.59***	−30.28
Old-age pension not portable	−34.90	−18.44	14.60	0.17
Universal sickness	24.85	50.64**	−29.54*	−0.24

Variable	Numerically restricted		Numerically exempt	
	Males	Females	Males	Females
Cash sickness benefits	−97.75**	−49.67*	93.41***	105.86***
Maternity benefits	−26.13	0.56	−7.71	20.65
Medical benefits	49.32*	31.73*	5.28	25.08
Unemployment insurance	−49.52	40.28	7.17	51.41*
Universal family allowance	94.31*	106.46***	2.93	42.38
Employment family allowance	20.41	47.35	5.25	38.85
Control				
% No occupation[c]	−174.09***	−21.55	−26.34*	−16.32
Total U.S. immigration from i^d	0.17***	0.33***	0.05***	0.17***

[a] *** Indicates $t \geq 1.96$; ** indicates $1.67 \leq t < 1.96$; * indicates $1.29 \leq t < 1.67$. Corresponding t-statistics are reported in Appendix Table G3.

[b] In the gender-specific regressions, the education control is measured specific to the respective gender.

[c] The control for the percentage of immigrants that do not declare an occupation is measured specific to the group examined (i.e., male numerically restricted, numerically exempt; female numerically restricted, numerically exempt).

[d] The control total is measured specific to the group examined (i.e., see note c).

Within the numerically exempt class, the influence of foreign students should exert itself through the operation of a marriage market, in which we anticipated that the composition of males would be more influenced than that of females. The evidence is consistent with this interpretation. However, for restricted migrants, the marriage market would not appear relevant for explaining why significantly more high-skilled female (but not more male) migrants come from nations where relatively large numbers of the population attend a U.S. college or university. Rather, the explanation may be that acquiring a U.S. education provides potential independent migrants with an opportunity to take an initial first step toward an ultimate goal of more permanent immigration to the United States. Various potential cultural and social constraints may make this alternative relatively more attractive to females than males.

The findings concerning political and religious considerations are much the same as found previously when the data were disaggregated by entry class. However, whereas source-country political conditions appear to be more likely to affect the composition of exempt migrants, the effects of religious considerations are more pronounced for restricted migrants. This difference is not unexpected, since within families religious considerations are a matter of importance, and for the potential numerically restricted migrants a heavy emphasis is placed on family reunification. On the other hand, individuals seeking freedom from political repression are not necessarily linked so closely to religious considerations.

As found earlier, significantly more high-skilled migrants come from Asian nations, regardless of gender or entry class. The potential exists for naturalized U.S. citizens to affect the composition of both numerically restricted and exempt immigrants, but an effect is found only for restricted female migrants, where (as expected) fewer high-skilled migrants are associated with lower entry costs. With the other U.S. policy controls, the effects were expected to be more pronounced for numerically restricted than exempt migrants, which is the case with lottery visas, where significantly more of both male and female high-skilled migrants are found to enter under this program. Moreover, the findings relating to the Silva program and the Western Hemisphere treatment (1972–1976) indicate, as expected, that fewer high-skilled numerically restricted migrants are associated with lower immigration barriers. However, that these factors have such a strong association with the skill composition of exempt migrants is somewhat surprising. Opening the door to allow relatively more low-skilled migrants to enter through the numerically restricted class has apparently caused high-skilled migrants to turn to other avenues of entry which, in this case, is manifested in the exempt class of migrants.

The factors included in the vector of social programs appear to have more influence in shaping the skill composition of restricted than exempt migrants. The skill composition of restricted female migrants appears to be particularly sensitive to the provision of programs relating to sickness and family allowances, as well as program coverage. For instance, the evidence relating to female migrants supports our expectation that universal old-age, sickness, and family allowance programs all provide incentives that increase the number of high-skilled migrants. Moreover, as expected, programs providing health-care or medical benefits increase the number of high-skilled female migrants, and (to a lesser extent) cash sickness benefits tend to decrease that number. Whereas the skill composition of male restricted migrants is also influenced by the availability of these programs, old-age pension programs have a greater influence on the composition of male than female migrants. For countries with employment-related social insurance old-age pension programs, the flow of migrants includes significantly fewer high-skilled male migrants.

The social programs that influence the composition of exempt migrants also do so in a manner that appears quite different from that found for restricted migrants. For instance, the evidence indicates that unemployment insurance increases the number of high-skilled exempt migrants, but no such evidence is found for restricted migrants. Further, the availability of cash sickness benefits is negatively related to the skill level of restricted migrants but is positively related to skill level of the exempt. The impact of provident funds old-age programs also differs across entry class, suggesting that the opportunity to save resources necessary to cover relocation costs may be less critical in the decisions of exempt migrants. The reasons for differential impact of the sickness-related programs are not immediately obvious.

SUMMARY

Economic opportunities are more influential in determining the skill composition of numerically restricted migrants relative to those exempt. The evidence relating to exempt migrants is, in large part, contrary to our expectations. On the other hand, the findings for numerically restricted migrants, as well as the evidence from data that are not disaggregated by entry class, are generally as expected. These findings have several implications. For example, as the level of development increases around the world, source countries will increasingly provide employment and earnings opportunities that are particularly attractive to high-skilled workers. Economic expansion also appears to improve the job-related opportunities of high-skilled workers. Thus, from countries experiencing increasing development and economic expansion, the skill composition of migrants to the United States will be relatively lower. On the other hand, as the relative extent of female participation in formal labor markets increases, the skill level of U.S. migrants may increase because the relative number of potential high-skilled migrants is increasing. Moreover, to the extent that government sectors around the world become larger in terms of their share of gross domestic product, the number of high-skilled workers moving to the United States should increase.

Migration costs also significantly influence skill composition; in particular, English-language familiarity is of considerable importance, regardless of gender or entry class. Certain other cost factors have effects that are gender-specific, but these differences are generally quite understandable.

Like our findings relating to the other composition models, political and religious considerations and U.S. immigration policy play major roles in forming skill composition. The findings relating to the social program variables also provide support for many of our hypotheses and, as with economic opportunities, these influences are more apparent with numerically restricted than numerically exempt migrants. Moreover, interesting differences exist across males and females for certain types of programs. The skill composition of female migrants is particularly sensitive to program coverage and the availability of sickness and family allowance programs.

Notes

1. Given that w_i and w_j measure the wage rate per unit of occupational skill, a level of skills that is higher than K^{**} would imply a larger discounted value of benefits (Eq. 8.1).
2. Of course, this presumes that the differentials in return are not skill specific. If the earnings differentials between country i and the United States are larger for low- than high-skilled workers, this expectation may be reversed.
3. Moreover, if government revenues provide some measure of the extent of transfer activity in country i, such transfers are likely to benefit most the low-income (low-skilled) individuals, thus further increasing the relative incentive for high-income (high-skilled) workers to migrate.
4. In Chapter 7, we also found that certain factors associated with migration costs (i.e., birth rate, U.S. military, education, and distance) have gender-specific differences: these factors appeared to be much stronger in shaping the age composition of female migrants than of male migrants.

9 Summary and Conclusions

In this study, we attempt to model the gender, age, and skill composition of legal U.S. immigration. Our empirical work is based on fairly simple and intuitive human capital models relating to the rate of legal immigration from various countries to the United States, as well as to the gender, age, and skill composition of the immigrants. The models emphasize the differential economic advantages and costs of migrating, including the costs of transferring accumulated occupational skills. We hypothesized that the gender composition of immigrant flows should vary across source countries depending upon source-country characteristics that serve to place females in the pool of potential economic migrants. The proportion of immigrants that is female also should be determined by factors that influence the ratio of economic to non-economic/tied migrants. To study age and skill composition, we introduce the concept of the marginal migrant, a hypothetical individual for whom the costs and benefits of migrating just balance. Conceptually, the marginal migrant is able to adjust to changes in any benefit or cost associated with migration, so that for a given skill level, he or she would become younger or older and for a given age would become more skilled or less skilled. The concept of the marginal migrant yields testable hypotheses concerning the age and skill composition of U.S. immigration.

Legal U.S. immigration is emphasized in this study for both substantive and practical reasons. The substantive reason is that U.S. authorities have control over legal immigration and can influence immigrant composition in terms of gender, age, and skills (though they have rarely exercised this ability). Moreover, the composition of migration has not been widely modeled, so this study has some interest and policy relevance of its own, particularly in terms of the influence of social programs in source countries. The practical reason is that the data used in the study refer only to legal immigrants. The annual data were drawn from the Immigration and Naturalization Service Public Use Tapes, which provide a record on every legal resident alien admitted into the United States beginning in 1972. Our focus is on the period 1972–1991, because a new immigration policy regime began in Fiscal Year 1992.

The empirical results of the study, which were obtained by the demanding Hausman-Taylor instrumental variable approach, yield two broad conclusions.

- Source-country characteristics significantly shape the rate and composition of U.S. immigration. The importance of these characteristics holds across the board in the sense that, for the rate of immigration and/or for some components of migrant composition, each variable proves to be significant (although very few variables are significant for every feature of immigration studied here). To the extent that source-country characteristics help shape the rate and/or composition of migration to the United States, the U.S. government at best has only limited control.

- U.S. immigration policy also importantly shapes the rate of immigration, as well as the immigrants' characteristics. Many effects of U.S. policy, especially regarding immigrant composition, are probably unintended. The importance of policy is reflected directly by various policy variables in the models and by the distinction between numerically restricted and numerically exempt immigrants.

This chapter consists of two major sections. The first recaps the importance of the various variables in explaining the rate and composition of migration to the United States. The second is oriented toward the implications of this research for U.S. immigration policy.

FACTORS THAT INFLUENCE U.S. IMMIGRATION— SOURCE-COUNTRY CHARACTERISTICS

Differential Economic Opportunities

From the economist's perspective, differential economic opportunities are expected to play a key role, if not the key role, among the determinants of U.S. immigration and its composition. Differential economic opportunities in large part explain migration from various

European countries to the United States during the nineteenth and early twentieth centuries. Such opportunities also explain more recent migration to the United States (Greenwood and McDowell 1991). However, in the modern era, emigration restrictions and immigration barriers impede the free international flow of labor and blunt the force of economic incentives. Such constraints present investigators with difficulties and probably conceal the true effects of variables that reflect economic opportunities and significance.

In this study, we have attempted to account for institutional impediments to U.S. immigration in two ways. First, our models include a vector of variables whose presence is intended to control for different treatment by U.S. authorities of countries or regions at different times. Second, we distinguish between immigrants who are numerically restricted versus those who are numerically exempt under U.S. law. Restricted immigrants clearly confront entry barriers, whereas exempt immigrants possess the required family ties to enter the United States if and when they wish. Consequently, economic incentives ought to be more clearly reflected by exempt immigrants.

As noted in Chapter 5, per capita GDP in source countries relative to that of the United States is not statistically significant as a determinant of the overall rate of U.S. immigration. This result is somewhat surprising given that similar measures were important explanatory variables in roughly comparable studies, including our own earlier work (Greenwood and McDowell 1991). The current result is clearly due in part to the econometric technique adopted for this study, the Hausman-Taylor instrumental variable approach. We stand by our current findings: in the aggregate, per capita GDP in source countries relative to that of the United States does not appear to influence the rate of migration to the United States. However, for those persons for whom U.S. immigration is an institutionally unconstrained option, the force of differential earnings opportunities is more apparent: the rate of such migration is higher if the source country has lower per capita GDP. This finding emphasizes the importance of accounting for institutional restrictions and specifically distinguishing numerically exempt immigrants.

Relative per capita GDP does not perform well in the gender equations, where its t-value never exceeds 1.67. We anticipated that by especially discouraging potential economic migrants (and therefore males), higher values of this variable would be negative in the regression for males and correspondingly positive in that for females. One possible explanation for its lack of significance is that the variable fails to appropriately distinguish gender-specific returns. A better variable would be the ratio of female to male earnings in source countries versus the same measure for the United States, which would better reflect the relative position of females in the source country. Unfortunately, data on female wages or earnings are nonexistent for most countries in our sample, but the available data for the manufacturing sectors of a few advanced, industrial nations are illustrative (Table 9.1).

The data in Table 9.1 have been calculated from information presented in Blau and Ferber (1992, Table 10.4). The evidence is clear that, relative to the United States, the remuneration of females compared to males in various countries around the world varies greatly. Females do relatively better in most European countries than in the United States, but if Japan is a reasonable proxy for other Asian nations, they do relatively worse in Asia. Although this richness of information is missing from our models, the strong positive influence of the Asia dummy variable on female immigrants (especially those who are exempt from numerical restrictions; see Table 6.2) is precisely what would be expected from the information provided in Table 9.1.

In our model of age composition, we argue that the age of the marginal migrant ought to increase (decrease) as relative per capita GDP decreases (increases), because for source countries with smaller wage differentials relative to the United States, the marginal migrant must be younger in order to enjoy the smaller differential return over a longer period of time to just cover the cost of migrating. In the age composition equations, relative income plays the expected role: a one-percentage-point increase in relative per capita GDP causes about 365 more immigrants aged 20–34 and about 227 fewer immigrants aged 55 and over to annually enter the United States from country i (see Table 7.1). Moreover, the magnitude of the effects is larger and generally more significant for males than for females, which also is anticipated, because relatively more males are likely to be economic migrants.

**Table 9.1 The Ratio of Female to Male Hourly
Earnings in Manufacturing Relative to
the Same Measure for the United States**

Country[a]	1973	1988
Australia	1.12	1.13
Belgium	1.11	1.06
Denmark	1.33	1.20
Finland	1.16	1.10
France	1.24	1.13
Germany, FR	1.15	1.04
Greece	1.06	1.11
Ireland	0.97	0.98
Japan	0.87	0.69
Luxembourg	0.90	0.83
Netherlands	1.22	1.07
New Zealand	1.07	1.06
Norway	1.24	1.20
Sweden	1.36	1.28
Switzerland	1.06	0.96
United Kingdom	0.98	0.97

SOURCE: Calculated from Blau and Ferber (1992), Table 10.4.
[a] See Blau and Ferber for details concerning the measures for
specific countries.

Short-term growth of job opportunities, as reflected in country i's
rate of growth of GDP relative to that of the United States, encourages
higher rates of migration to the United States (see Table 5.1). On the
surface, this finding may be surprising, but other considerations perhaps soften this surprise. First, more rapid growth may allow potential
migrants in country i to accumulate the assets needed to cover the costs
of an international move. Second, and perhaps more importantly,
short-term growth is likely to be of most benefit to young persons who

have recently entered the labor force or are about to enter it (see Table 7.1), particularly females (see Table 7.2). Thus, higher values of the relative growth variable ought to discourage the emigration of the young while at the same time encouraging that of older potential migrants. The empirical results indicate that the effects of this variable are as anticipated, but the effect appears to have a more significant influence on older persons than on younger persons, which in itself could increase migration rather than decrease it.

The effect of relative growth of GDP is strongest for exempt females, for whom the variable has a particularly sizable influence on the oldest age group (see Table 7.4). Because the exempt group in general consists mostly of spouses and parents of U.S. citizens, the financing argument takes on added relevance. Older exempt females are likely to consist mainly of mothers of U.S. citizens. By affecting the assets of older females or those of their children in source countries, migration to the United States becomes a viable option for reuniting with other children who moved there previously.

With respect to skill composition, considerable differences are evident between the empirical results for restricted and exempt immigrants (see Table 8.3). Short-term growth in source countries relative to the United States strongly discourages the migration of numerically restricted persons with the highest skills. On the other hand, the skill composition of numerically exempt immigrants is unaffected. This result suggests that economic growth in source countries differentially benefits those with better skills and higher incomes, thus tilting skill composition of U.S. immigrants toward the less skilled, especially those who are younger (see Table 8.2). (If migration from Mexico to the United States follows the same pattern, any growth induced by the North American Free Trade Agreement could have the result of increasing the rate of movement to the United States while at the same time decreasing the skill composition.)[1]

High government revenues as a percentage of GDP (and hence presumably high taxes in source countries) boost the rate of migration to the United States, as well as influencing age and skill composition. The effects on age composition tend to operate almost exclusively through the numerically exempt class (young spouses and older parents of U.S. citizens). These results make sense: high government revenues (high taxes on workers) encourage the migration of more young persons (especially females) and discourage the migration of older persons, both males and females (see Table 7.4). The effect is that when the appropriate family ties to parents exist, the parents move to the United States only when their expected receipt of transfers in the source country is low.

Generally, the urbanization variable works as anticipated. The rate of immigration to the United States from more highly urbanized societies is clearly lower (see Table 5.1). Moreover, relatively more females come from such societies, presumably because urban employment opportunities for women attract them into the labor force, where they expand the pool of potential economic migrants (see Table 6.1). The positive effect of percent urban is particularly important for numerically exempt females (see Table 6.2), and especially for older exempt females (see Table 7.4), although the effect is also of some importance for older exempt males. Urban job opportunities are likely to be of most importance to young persons, and the empirical results bear this out for young females, especially those who are exempt (see Table 7.4). Historically, urban areas have provided opportunities for the most highly skilled workers; thus, that relatively few highly skilled persons, especially older male workers, migrate from more highly urbanized countries is not surprising (see Table 8.2). Indirectly, this finding also may suggest a "brain drain" from less-developed, less-urbanized countries to the United States.

Female labor force participation in source countries reduces female migration and tilts the gender composition toward males (see Table 6.1), particularly for the exempt class (see Table 6.2). Our theory of the marginal migrant suggests that both lower differential returns and higher costs will cause an increase in the skill composition of U.S. immigrants. Since greater female labor force participation presumably reflects better earnings opportunities and generally higher skill levels, females from countries with high levels of female participation ought to be more skilled. Moreover, the costs of migrating are higher for numerically restricted immigrants, which should reinforce the higher expected skill level for this group. Female labor force participation behaves in the expected fashion for restricted immigrants, but it does not for the exempt group (see Table 8.3). Although the lower migration costs for exempt migrants may result in quantitative differences for the two groups, the qualitative differences are difficult to understand. The results are consistent for both males and females.

Migration Costs

Distance proxies both the monetary and nonmonetary costs of migration, each of which should rise with greater distance from the United States. On average, per 1000-mile increase in distance from the United States, immigration falls by 300 persons per million population of the origin country, other things being equal (see Table 5.1). This drop off with distance is about twice as sharp for numerically restricted as for numerically exempt immigrants, whose transportation expenses in many cases may be subsidized by their citizen relatives. Moreover, distance plays a role in shaping the composition of immigration to the United States: in other words, the costs represented by distance help determine who migrates. Writing during the last century, Ravenstein (1885) observed that females were overrepresented in short-distance moves. This observation is reinforced by our findings, which suggest that contemporary movement to the United States consists of significantly more males if the migration originates in more distant countries (see Table 6.1).

Our theory of the marginal migrant predicts that immigrants from more distant countries will consist of relatively more young persons, because to offset the higher costs of moving requires that the marginal migrant move at an earlier age. The empirical results reject this hypothesis. Relatively few young persons (20 to 34 years of age), especially young females, move to the United States from more distant countries (see Table 7.2); relatively more older persons (55 years old and over), especially numerically restricted males (see Table 7.3), move from more distant countries.

U.S. military presence clearly influences the composition of U.S. immigration, especially gender composition. Female migration is boosted, specifically for the numerically exempt (see Table 6.2), and especially for young exempt females (see Table 7.4), reflecting the working of the marriage market. Although the evidence is not strong, it does point toward more highly skilled exempt young women (and men) from source countries with U.S. military presence (see Table 8.3).

As female educational opportunities (relative to male opportunities) rise in potential source countries, the female share of U.S. immigrants increases as anticipated, especially for the exempt class (see Table 6.2). Our theory of the marginal migrant predicts that older persons will move from countries with higher levels of education. The empirical results are consistent with this prediction and are due mainly to fewer young exempt females and more older exempt females coming from such countries (see Table 7.4). Contrary to the predicted direction of the effect, fewer highly skilled immigrants, especially young males and females, originate in countries with high general levels of educational attainment (see Table 8.2). This finding is consistent with a drain of talent from countries with generally lower levels of education.

Familiarity with the English language should facilitate the transfer of occupational skills and education to the United States, as well as facilitate social and cultural assimilation. However, the rate of immigration from English-speaking countries is not significantly higher than from other countries; yet, the English variable is an important determinant of the composition of the flows.[2] The share of female immigrants, especially numerically exempt females, is significantly higher from English-speaking countries (see Table 6.2), which suggests that social and cultural assimilation are particularly important in female migration.

Our theory of the marginal migrant predicts that older migrants will originate in English-speaking countries because they will experience lower skill losses than migrants from other countries. Moreover, because their returns to learning English are generally lower, older persons have a lesser incentive to migrate from non-English-speaking countries because they will find social and cultural assimilation harder. The empirical results indicate that higher shares of older immigrants, both female and male, come from English-speaking countries (see Table 7.2), and this observation is particularly true for the numerically exempt class (see Table 7.4). Immigrant workers from English-speaking nations also are more highly skilled.

Political Attractiveness and Religion

Political conditions in source countries importantly influence U.S. immigration. The rate of migration to the United States is significantly higher from countries with less competitive political systems (see Table 5.1). This effect is especially strong for older, numerically exempt females (see Table 7.4). Moreover, countries with such political cal systems provide the United States with significantly more highly skilled males but significantly fewer highly skilled females (see Table 8.2); this may be due to more limited opportunities for females in these countries to attain high levels of education and generally to access highly skilled occupations.

Religions in source countries affect the composition of immigration to the United States. More numerically exempt females originate in countries that are heavily Catholic (see Table 6.2). Countries that are predominantly Catholic also are the sources of more highly skilled immigrants, particularly young males and females, as well as older females (see Tables 8.1 and 8.2). Countries that are predominantly Muslim are the source of more highly skilled young males who enter the United States as numerically restricted (see Table 8.3).

Source-Country Social Programs

To determine the impact of various social programs on the volume and composition of immigration, it is necessary to ascertain the program's net cost-benefit impact on the indigenous population. In terms of volume, the primary concern is with social program impacts on the young workers, who are otherwise more likely to migrate than other individuals. Thus, other things being equal, to the extent that young workers receive net benefits from a program, their propensity to migrate should be reduced, and the overall rate of migration should be lower. Unemployment insurance is an example of a program from which young workers are most likely to benefit and, as shown in Table 5.1, the existence of unemployment insurance systems in source countries significantly reduces the rate of migration to the United States.

Compositional effects also should be determined by the extent to which a wealth transfer occurs as a result of a program's presence. The members of the indigenous population who receive net gains (losses) should be less (more) likely to migrate. For example, unemployment insurance affects primarily the economically active. Because men are more likely to be economically active than women, unemployment insurance should more directly reduce male migration, and shift immigration flows toward a relatively higher share of female migrants (see Table 6.1). Unemployment insurance also generally constitutes a transfer from individuals typically having lower unemployment rates to those having higher unemployment rates. Therefore, countries with unemployment insurance should show an effect of encouraging the flow of older individuals; the evidence concerning the effects of unemployment insurance on age composition is particularly strong in the findings for female migrants (see Table 7.3). This result may suggest that the variation in unemployment rates across age classes is more pronounced for females than males.

Provident funds may affect migration by providing old-age benefits that are portable (often immediately available to those who permanently emigrate). Thus, our finding that fewer older individuals migrate from countries having provident funds (see Table 7.2) may indicate that if potential migrants can take their pension benefits, they are more likely to migrate and reunite with their families at an earlier age. An added incentive may be that, if they did not emigrate, these individuals would have to wait longer before they receive their benefits at retirement. The evidence also indicates that more numerically exempt females aged 20–34 migrate from these countries (see Table 7.4). Since these young females are most likely spouses of U.S. citizens, provident funds appear to facilitate their flow by providing relatively liquid assets that can be transferred internationally.

The availability of provident funds also tends to stimulate the flow of young male and female high-skilled workers (see Table 8.2), especially in the numerically restricted class (see Table 8.3). Here, provident funds may provide an opportunity to accumulate the assets necessary to cover the costs of relocation. Given the general nature of such funds (i.e., fixed percentage of earnings going into compulsory savings that is matched by employers), these savings will more quickly accumulate for the young high-skilled workers, who are more likely to migrate than low-skilled workers.

Employment-related old-age programs have the potential to result in a transfer of wealth from younger workers to older retired individuals, but the rate of migration does not appear to be affected by such programs (see Table 5.1), and therefore such transfers may not exist to the extent that is commonly believed. Employment-related old-age programs do affect the composition of immigrants, however, increasing the female share of restricted migrants (see Table 6.2). Moreover, these programs discourage (encourage) the flow of younger (older) male and female restricted migrants (see Table 7.3). These effects on composition are very similar to those found for programs that provide cash-sickness benefits to individuals unable to work. This similarity is perhaps linked to the fact that, in these employment-related programs, the costs imposed on workers and the benefits received both tend to rise or fall in accordance with an individual's income level.

The empirical results support our view: whereas cash-sickness benefits increase the flow of older high-skilled workers, employment-related old-age programs discourage the migration of younger high-skilled workers (see Table 8.2). With numerically exempt migrants, employment-related old-age programs have little effect on gender, age, or skill composition, but cash-sickness benefits affect the compositional aspects of these migrants.

Universal old-age pension and universal sickness benefit programs are expected to transfer wealth from the younger, economically active population to the older inactive population. While neither of these programs significantly influences the overall immigration rate (see Table 5.1), each program is critical in terms of composition. Both programs increase the number of young, numerically restricted male and female migrants (see Table 7.3). Moreover, universal old-age programs increase the number of young male and female high-skilled migrants (see Table 8.2), and universal sickness programs increase the flow of highly skilled, numerically restricted female migrants (see Table 8.3). This impact on skill share is expected, since universal programs supported by taxes would be expected to fall disproportionately on the high-skilled (high-income) workers.

Universal programs of family allowances for families with children are expected to transfer benefits to younger families, particularly those that have low-skilled (low-income) family heads or heads who are not economically active. The evidence provides support for our hypothesis in the sense that such programs encourage the migration of young high-skilled workers (see Table 8.1). Moreover, the age of female numerically restricted migrants is relatively older for migrants from countries with these programs (see Table 7.3). That the age effect is apparent primarily for females is probably because the program's benefits are primarily family-related rather than employment-related.

Other programs providing family-related benefits include maternity benefits, employment-related family allowances, and possibly programs providing medical benefits. In general, employment-related family allowance programs have little effect on either the volume or composition of immigrants, but maternity and medical programs increase the number of high-skilled female migrants (see Table 8.2). Given the nature of these benefits, we expected that the composition of females would be more influenced than that of males. While the evidence concerning skill composition supports our hypotheses, the findings relating to age composition do not. For instance, the reason or reasons that more young individuals, particularly young females (see Table 7.2), come from countries providing maternity benefits is not immediately clear.

General Comments

In general, the empirical results of this study are quite strong in terms of anticipated signs and significant coefficients, but in many equations specific variables do not perform as anticipated. Because much of the original research described above is new in terms of models and econometric procedures, we are not overly concerned with the surprises we have received. We hope that many of these issues will be addressed in future research and that concepts such as that of the marginal migrant will be further refined.

FACTORS THAT INFLUENCE U.S. IMMIGRATION— U.S. POLICY

The importance of U.S. immigration policy is certainly reflected in our results. After the 1965 changes in U.S. immigration law were fully implemented, family reunification became the primary policy focus. One major aspect of family reunification is that immediate relatives (spouses, children, and parents) of U.S. citizens 21 years of age and older are exempt from numerical limits, but other relatives enter as restricted. Through 1991, at least 80 percent of the numerically restricted visas went to relatives. Of the remaining 20 percent, spouses and children of individuals who qualified under the occupational preferences also counted against these preferences.

With all of the potential for family ties to play a role in admittances, we are not surprised to find that the more (naturalized) U.S. citizens who were born in country i, the greater the rate of migration from i to the United States (see Table 5.1).[3] Although the naturalization variable has a very strong influence in the immigration-rate equation, it plays only a limited role in shaping immigrant composition. Among the numerically restricted immigrants, the family ties proxied by the naturalization variable increase young females and decrease older females (see Table 7.3). This is the expected pattern, because the restricted category is inherently oriented toward younger persons more than the exempt category, which includes parents of U.S. citizens. Most effects of naturalization work through skill composition, but these effects are not dominant. Family connections to U.S. citizens reduce the skill level of young females (see Table 8.2). However, in general, while increasing the number of immigrants in any given year, the family-ties variable does not appear to greatly influence the composition of those entering. This is an important finding for policy purposes.

Between 1946 and 1994, programs such as the NP-5 program (for countries adversely affected by the 1965 immigration program) and the OP-1 program (for natives of underrepresented countries) added "irregular" immigrants to those admitted through the normal system. The NP-5 and OP-1 admittances are included in our lottery variable. The lottery program not only increased the rate of immigration, specifically of numerically restricted immigrants (see Table 5.1), but it also skewed immigration toward males (see Table 6.1). Even after controlling for numerous forces that influence migration to the United States, the model reflects the favoring of males during episodes of irregular immigration. The lottery program increased the number of young migrants (but especially males), while decreasing the share of older migrants (see Table 7.2). This program also increased the skill composition of young male immigration (see Table 8.2). In general, then, the NP-5 and OP-1 programs reflected in the lottery variable favored young, highly skilled males.

Our model results indicate that Asia is the source of relatively many female immigrants to the United States, other factors held constant (see Table 6.1) . This observation is especially true for exempt females (see

Table 6.2) and for young females (see Table 7.2). It is also true for older exempt males. Moreover, relatively many highly skilled males and females, both young and old (but especially young males), originate in Asian countries. We have argued that with respect to females, the Asian dummy variable may reflect lower wage rates (relative to males) in Asian countries. Although we have no data reflecting wage differences by skill level, this variable could also reflect a lower wage gap between more and less highly skilled workers in Asian countries.

POLICY OPTIONS

To this point, we have discussed actual U.S. policy regarding immigrant admittances. However, many other policy options are open to U.S. lawmakers that, if implemented, would almost certainly influence the source-country, gender, age, and skill composition of U.S. immigration. In this section, we discuss certain of these options and their implications.

Legal Immigration

The extreme positions with respect to legal immigration are to bar it altogether or to place no (or few) restrictions on it. The United States never has barred immigration completely, not even for a short period, and thus the first position does not appear to be likely. On the other hand, the United States has had periods during which few restrictions were imposed. Until 1882 (when the Chinese were barred), most individuals were free to enter the United States; until 1921, all were basically free to enter with the exception of the Chinese and persons from the Asian "barred zone." Although this open policy has proponents today, it too is unrealistic.

Some have proposed taxing immigrants, especially highly skilled and educated individuals who were trained at public expense in poor countries (and therefore presumably had their education expenses subsidized), but such a policy would be seen as discriminatory in the United States. U.S. immigrants pay certain processing fees that are somewhat controversial in their own right. The idea of taxing immigrants in general has not been well received in the United States, because many of the immigrants are poor and such taxes could be considerable burdens. The U.S. Congress recently considered taxing the employers of certain highly trained and educated immigrants, but employer groups vehemently protested such a policy and its consideration quickly ceased. Taxing employers would have the effect of reducing job opportunities for highly educated immigrants.

Most countries have settled on quotas as a means of controlling legal entry for permanent residence. The quotas may be fixed or flexible, and they frequently involve selection criteria, as with the U.S. preference categories, or the points systems used in Canada and Australia. Binding quotas also clearly impose costs on potential immigrants, who must wait for their number to come up, and thus quotas discourage migration or deflect it to other alternative destinations. Many countries have humanitarian concerns and establish separate quotas to accommodate refugees. Auctioning a fixed number of immigration permits to the highest bidders also has been proposed as a means of allocating U.S. entry visas, but such a policy option is highly unlikely to be adopted. However, visa allocations set aside for entrepreneurs and investors in countries like the United States and Canada provide a means of entry for those who possess considerable wealth.

Illegal Migration

The United States clearly has a problem with illegal immigration, but it is not the only country with such a problem. However, what sets the United States somewhat apart is that it is a high-income country with an extensive land border with Mexico, a relatively poor country where job prospects have not been good.

Guestworker programs are one option for dealing with illegal migration, but such programs in Western Europe and the United States (Bracero program) have proven to be as much a cause as a solution. After the programs are discontinued, employment demand remains, along with a plentiful supply of potential migrants, and the guestworkers have various ties to the host country that give them access to the employment opportunities. Currently, the United States maintains various nonimmigrant temporary worker programs to satisfy seasonal employment needs.

For many years, the United States practiced a policy of benign neglect along its border with Mexico. Although many illegal aliens were apprehended for entering without documents, many made it through the border area where U.S. Border Patrol resources were concentrated. Significantly tightening the border required far more expenditures than Congress was prepared to provide. U.S. employers and landowners were clear beneficiaries of the flow of illegal migrants, so their lobbies worked against the imposition of tighter controls. The consequence of the policy of benign neglect was that the estimated number of individuals residing illegally more or less permanently in the United States grew into the millions.

Congress responded with the Immigration Reform and Control Act of 1986 (IRCA), which provided for the eventual legalization of about 2.7 million persons. IRCA also provided for fines against employers who knowingly hired illegal migrants, but employer fines were not difficult to avoid and were not sufficiently high to be effective. Presently, an estimated 5.0 million illegal aliens reside in the United States, approximately 2.0 percent of the nation's population.

The United States currently is pursuing two types of policies that may affect the flows of both legal and illegal migrants. In the short run, welfare reform legislation that bars illegal aliens (as well as certain legal aliens) from using various federal public service programs may affect the flows. However, Mexicans appear to enter the United States for jobs and higher wages, and they do not appear to be particularly heavy users of welfare programs when they enter or for some years thereafter. Thus, this legislation may not be especially helpful in discouraging illegal migration from Mexico.

Although the North American Free Trade Agreement (NAFTA) was not passed to discourage illegal migration, in the long run it could have such an effect. In the short run, it may cause even more illegal migration from Mexico (Martin 1993), because much illegal migration originates in rural Mexico, where agricultural practices are frequently primitive. The agricultural sector of Mexico will be hard-hit by competition engendered by NAFTA, which will release even more labor from rural Mexico. Several years may be required for the Mexican economy to feel the positive impacts of NAFTA and thus for NAFTA to discourage migration to the United States.

Finally, individuals born in the United States, even to illegal alien mothers, are U.S. citizens. This fact may provide an incentive for migration to the United States. Congress is considering various changes in citizenship requirements.

Compositional Consequences of U.S. and Canadian Policies

The United States and Canada are two of the world's major immigrant-receiving nations. Their immigration histories are similar: each experienced "mass" immigration during the laissez-faire period of the late nineteenth and early twentieth centuries; each was populated mainly by persons of European ancestry; and, until the 1960s, each had exclusionary policies against persons of Asian ancestry. When they opened their doors to Asian immigrants at about the same time, migration from Asia soon displaced that from Europe as a major source for each country. However, while the United States maintained a policy oriented toward family reunification, Canada adopted a policy that stressed domestic economic conditions and the likelihood that the immigrant would assimilate into the Canadian economy and society.

Historically, immigration has played a relatively far more important role in Canada than in the United States. During the 1950s and 1960s, when legal U.S. immigration was attracting little attention from policymakers or the public, Canadian immigration accounted for 9.8 and 7.1 persons per 100 population, respectively; corresponding figures for the United States are 1.5 and 1.7. During the 1970s and 1980s, when the Canadian figures were 6.3 and 5.2, U.S. immigration amounted to 2.1 and 3.1 persons per 100, respectively.

Although the Immigration Act of 1990 has moved the United States toward slightly more emphasis on employment considerations, U.S. entry requirements remain strongly oriented toward family ties. In 1993, 63.9 percent of the legal immigrants who entered the United States did so based on family relationships, and only 5.9 percent (of nonlegalizations) entered as a result of the skills or education they possessed. However, in spite of its points program and the selective nature of its admittance system, in 1993 Canada accepted 62.4 percent of its immigrants based on family ties, almost the same percentage as the United States.

Tables 9.2 and 9.3 provide comparative details on U.S. and Canadian immigrants. The Canadian system recognizes the importance of age and gives points to prospective immigrants based on age. In spite of its preferences, Canada attracts only a slightly higher percentage of persons 20 to 39 years old (48.9 percent of all immigrants during 1981–1993) than the United States (47.0 percent) (Table 9.2). Although the percentage of immigrants of age 50 and over has been trending up for the United States and down for Canada, for the entire period the percentages are similar (13.0 percent for the United States, 14.1 percent for Canada).

Because human capital accumulates with increased age (i.e., experience), age and skills are somewhat correlated. The Canadian admittance system appears to allow for more selectivity on account of skills than does the U.S. system. However, over the 1982–1993 period (and excluding IRCA legalizations from the U.S. data) the percentage of each country's immigrants who were presumably highly skilled (professional, technical, and kindred workers, as well as managers and proprietors) differed very little (11.2 percent for the United States and 10.4 percent for Canada). With the new U.S. law in effect during 1992 and 1993, the U.S. data show a slight upward break in the series (Table 9.3).

Thus, in spite of having admittance programs that on their surface appear considerably different, and in spite of having a somewhat different source-country composition of their immigrants, the United States and Canada have remarkably similar immigrant composition in broad terms.

IMPLICATIONS FOR U.S. IMMIGRATION POLICY

Aspects of the New Law

Effective October 1, 1991, U.S. immigration law changed considerably. These changes were the result of the Immigration Act of 1990 which, while retaining the basic principles of earlier legislation, provided the most comprehensive change in legal immigration since 1965. Our data relate to the old law, but this change does not negate nor reduce in any important way the relevance of the U.S. data we have

Table 9.2 Age Composition of U.S. and Canadian Immigration, 1982–1993 (%)

Year	Age 20–39		Age 50 and over	
	U.S.A.[a]	Canada	U.S.A.[a]	Canada
1993	44.2	47.5	13.9	13.9
1992	43.6	50.4	14.1	13.6
1991	44.4	52.2	15.4	13.3
1990	45.5	49.8	14.7	12.0
1989	47.2	49.6	13.6	11.2
1988	48.5	46.7	13.7	12.5
1987	48.9	50.5	13.0	12.8
1986	49.0	50.1	12.8	15.6
1985	50.1	47.6	11.8	18.1
1984	49.2	47.0	11.4	19.9
1983	49.6	45.7	10.8	20.6
1982	47.5	47.4	11.3	17.4
1981	46.8	45.4	11.2	17.8
1981–93	47.0	48.9	13.0	14.1

[a] Does not include legalizations under the Immigration Reform and Control Act of 1986.

Table 9.3 Percentage of U.S. and Canadian Immigrants Classified as Skilled,[a] 1982–1993

Year	U.S.A.	Canada
1993	12.4	8.9
1992	12.7	7.5
1991	10.9	8.9
1990	11.5	11.4
1989	11.0	12.1
1988	10.1	12.9
1987	10.7	12.1
1986	10.5	10.0
1985	10.9	9.4
1984	10.8	8.7
1983	10.5	10.3
1982	10.9	15.2
1982–93	11.2	10.4

[a] Refers to professional, technical, and kindred workers and managers and proprietors. U.S. figures exclude IRCA legalizations.

analyzed, because the new law has so many similarities to the earlier law.

Several changes made by the 1990 act are of particular relevance. Under the previous law, the annual allocation of numerically restricted visas was only 270,000. The 1990 act established a "flexible" world-wide cap on family-based, employment-based, and diversity immigrant visas. Beginning in fiscal year 1995 (after a "transition" period during which the annual quota was set at 700,000), the worldwide limit is 675,000. Separate ceilings are set for each of the immigrant catego-ries: for diversity visas, 55,000; for employment-based visas, 140,000; and for family-sponsored visas, 480,000. While immediate relatives of U.S. citizens remain exempt from numerical limitations, the number of spouses, minor children, and parents of U.S. citizens are subtracted from the overall numbers available for family sponsorship. However, under no circumstances can the number of numerically restricted fam-ily-sponsored visas be less than 226,000. Therefore, if the number of immediate relatives of U.S. citizens exceeds 254,000 (i.e , 480,000–226,000), the flexible worldwide cap of 675,000 may be pierced.

In addition to setting a higher overall limit on admissions, the 1990 act altered per-country limitations; previously, the per-country quota was 20,000 visas per year. The 1990 act provides that family-based and employment-based visas made available to citizens of a single independent foreign state may not exceed 7 percent of the total avail-able. Given the minimum of 226,000 family-sponsored and 140,000 employment-based allocations, the per-country ceiling for an indepen-dent country is thus raised to 25,620. Additional flexibility is provided by the fact that the 7 percent limit is not subdivided between family-sponsored and employment-based allocations.

In many respects the new law concerning family-based immigrants is similar to the previous law. Immediate relatives of U.S. citizens remain exempt from numerical limitation. Moreover, the annual floor of 226,000 numerically restricted family-sponsored visas is a relatively small increase over the 216,000 available under the previous law's family-related preference categories. However, the new law's provi-sions should alter the mix of immigrants within the family-sponsored categories. The major change involves spouses, minor children, and unmarried adult children of permanent resident aliens (i.e., second preference). For these immigrants, the new law increases the allotment from 70,200 to at least 114,200. Moreover, at least 77 percent of these visas are designated for spouses and minor children of permanent resident aliens, and three-quarters of these are not subject to per-country limits. The other family-based categories (i.e., first, fourth, and fifth preference) either had their allocation remain essentially unchanged (i.e., fifth) or reduced by the new law.

The new law also accommodates more skill-based immigrants, and it provides for more source-country diversity. Prior to the 1990 act, 54,000 visas were available for occupation-based immigrants. The new law allows up to 140,000 employment-based visas and also places more emphasis on skilled migrants within this category. The so-called "diversity" immigration allocations, made available for the first time by the 1990 act, are designed to facilitate the entry of potential migrants from countries adversely affected by the 1965 law. Effective in 1995, the diversity quota is 55,000 visas to be allocated to natives of countries that have sent fewer than 50,000 immigrants to the United States over the previous five years. No single country may receive more than 7 percent (3,850) of the total. To be eligible for a diversity visa, a prospective immigrant must have at least a high school education or its equivalent and at least two years of work experience in an occupation that requires at least two years of training or experience. Diversity immigrants are therefore a kind of occupational immigrant.

Immigration under the New Law

The present study relies on data that relate to immigration under the 1965 Amendments to the Immigration and Nationality Act. Data relating to present legislation are now available for five years (FY 1992, FY 1993, FY 1994, FY 1995, FY 1996), and the recent data are informative.

Table 9.4 bridges immigration under the old law and immigration under the Immigration Act of 1990. Data in this table are averages for 1990 and 1991 (the last years of the old law), 1992–1994 (the three transition years of the new law), and 1995 and 1996 (the first two years during which the more or less permanent cap and quota numbers were in effect). Between 1990–1991 and 1995–1996, family-based immigration increased by 16.9 percent to 528,551 and employment-based immigration increased by 72.3 percent to 101,418. Immigration not subject to the numerical cap fell by 7.7 percent, and in 1995–1996 accounted for 16.3 percent of total immigration, compared with 21.1 percent in 1990–1991.

Between 1990–1991 and 1995–1996, immigration subject to the numerical cap increased 27.0 percent and 29.4 percent of this increase was due to employment-based immigrants. Between 1992 and 1996, employment-based immigration accounted for 17.3 percent of total immigration under the cap. During 1990–1991, employment-based immigration accounted for only 11.0 percent of the cap total; thus the Immigration Act of 1990 clearly has had the effect of boosting employment-related immigration, which was one of its major objectives. However, professionals with an advanced degree or with advanced ability declined steadily after the first year that the new law was in effect: 58,401 in 1992, 29,468 in 1993, 14,432 in 1994, and 10,475 in 1995 (an exception was in 1996, at 18,462). This pattern suggests a pent-up demand for entry by such individuals that was relieved by the Immigration Act of 1990.

Sorensen et al. (1992) point out that the percentage of employment-based visas received by professionals declined from 50 percent in 1976 to 30 percent in 1988. Moreover, during the same period, the percentage of sixth-preference principals who were certified to work in service jobs increased from 20 to 45. These authors argue that these trends were important factors in the decision of Congress to cap unskilled workers at 10,000 in the Immigration Act of 1990. In turn, this cap has the potential to shift the composition of employment-related visas toward more highly skilled occupations.

Table 9.5 also bridges the old and new laws, but it provides occupational detail for persons 16 to 64 years of age. Consistent with Table 9.4, Table 9.5 shows that executive (and especially professional) immigration increased. However, Table 9.5 shows not only that blue-collar workers increased, but also that they increased as a percentage of the total (from 14.3 percent during 1990–1991 to 15.4 percent during 1994). Professional and executive white-collar workers as a percentage of the total increased only slightly during this period (from 15.0 percent to 16.0 percent).

Table 9.4 Average Immigrant Admissions by Major Category, FYs 1990–1996[a]

Category of Admission	1990–91	1992–94	1995–96
Total	680,058	829,681	813,730
Not subject to the numerical cap (NX)[b]	143,557	150,591	132,521
Refugees and those seeking asylum	118,222	121,938	121,615
Other	25,335	28,653	10,907
Subject to the numerical cap	536,502	679,090	681,209
Family-based immigrants	452,028	513,295	528,551
Immediate relatives of U.S. citizens (NX)	234,392	246,769	260,395
Spouses and children	172,509	185,582	202,855
Parents	61,883	61,187	57,541
Children born abroad to alien residents (NX)	2,317	2,010	1,777
Family-sponsored immigrants	215,319	217,287	266,148
Unmarried sons/daughters of U.S. citizens	15,623	12,829	18,046
Spouses and children of LPRs[c]	X[d]	120,473	163,685
Married sons/daughters of U.S. citizens	26,933	22,590	23,164
Siblings of U.S. citizens	63,857	61,349	61,254
Legalization dependents (NR)[e]	X	47,230	231
Employment-based immigrants (NR)	58,859	128,834	101,418
Priority workers	X	15,874	22,420

Professionals w/ adv. deg. or of adv. ability	X	34,100	14,469
Skilled, professionals, other workers (CSPA)[f]	X	70,738	56,501
Special immigrants	4,520	7,542	7,291
Investors	X	362	738
Professionals or highly skilled (old 3rd)	27,147	113	X
Needed skilled or unskilled workers (old 6th)	27,192	104	X
Diversity programs	25,616	36,961	53,018
Diversity transition (NR)	X	36,145	3,745
Nationals of adversely affected countries (NR)	16,320	522	X
Natives of underrepresented countries (NR)	9,296	294	X

SOURCE: For 1990–1994, U.S. Commission on Immigration Reform (1995), Chart 1; for 1995–1996, U.S. Immigration and Naturalization Service (1997), Tables 4 and 5.

[a] Excludes persons granted legal permanent resident status under the provisions of the Immigration Reform and Control Act of 1986.

[b] NX = numerically exempt.

[c] LPR = legal permanent resident.

[d] X = not applicable.

[e] NR = numerically restricted.

[f] CSPA = Chinese Student Protection Act.

**Table 9.5 Immigrant Admissions of Persons Aged 16 to 64,
by Occupation, 1990–1994**

Occupation	Average 1990–91	Average 1992–93	1994
Total	495,944	616,600	578,647
White-collar workers	111,054	140,708	126,362
Professional	53,132	75,081	66,310
Executive	21,406	29,317	26,185
Sales	12,698	13,525	12,591
Clerical	23,819	22,786	21,276
Blue-collar workers	71,019	85,694	89,019
Skilled craft	25,186	25,820	23,497
Operator, fabricator, laborer	45,833	59,874	65,522
Farming, forestry, fishing	12,805	13,357	12,261
Service	45,722	50,549	48,430
No occupation	222,690	287,606	262,812
Homemaker	81,558	106,404	98,452
Student	75,295	90,284	83,307
Unemployed or retired	68,838	90,919	81,053
Not reported	29,656	38,688	39,763

SOURCE: U.S. Commission on Immigration Reform (1995), Chart 4.

Implications for Immigration under the Act of 1990

Several factors should be kept in mind when applying our data and findings to the situation under the new law. First, immediate relatives of U.S. citizens remain exempt from numerical restriction, and thus our findings concerning numerically exempt immigrants should remain relevant. For instance, relative differential economic opportunities will be particularly important in shaping the age composition of exempt migrants. On the other hand, the new law does have an immediate impact on the number of numerically restricted immigrants. Given the new "flexible" cap, the number of restricted immigrants has risen. Therefore, at least in the near term, the share of total U.S. immigrants who are subject to numerical restriction will be relatively larger than in our sample. Because our findings suggest that the composition of numerically restricted immigrants is more sensitive to the availability of social programs than is true of exempt migrants, one implication is that such programs will play more prominent roles in determining the overall composition of U.S. immigrants under the new law. For instance, trends toward universal program coverage will tend to reduce the age and increase the skill level of U.S. immigrants.[4] Moreover, as employment-related programs such as unemployment insurance and cash-sickness benefits become more available worldwide and as old-age pension programs become more of the social insurance variety and less in the form of provident funds, U.S. immigrants will tend to become older.[5] Another implication is that, if source-country social program availability is more crucial in determining migration decisions, the use of U.S. social programs by those who come to the United States also may be affected. In other words, immigrants under the new law may be more inclined to use U.S. benefits such as unemployment insurance and sickness benefits.

Certain other features of the new law also may have a more direct influence on the composition of immigrants. For instance, increasing the allocation of numerically restricted visas should lower the wait time in the backlog of immigrant visa applications; consequently, the average age of migrants may be lowered. This effect may be only short term, however, as the shorter wait time may have the unintended effect of increasing the number of visa applications.

In addition to increasing the number of numerically restricted visas, the new law alters the mix of visas allocated to specific subgroups within the numerically restricted class. The subgroups most positively affected will be employment-based immigrants and the spouses and minor children of permanent resident aliens. Additional provisions relating to employment-based visas should increase the relative skill level of these employment-based immigrants. Using our data, the understanding of the various forces that will influence the composition of employment-based immigrants under the new law would require a close examination of those immigrants who enter the United States under the previous law's third and sixth preference categories (with, perhaps, the third preference entrants receiving a larger weight than those who enter under the sixth preference). For numerically restricted family-sponsored immigrants, the application of our data to the new law also requires a more detailed examination of the individual preference categories (where, for instance, the second preference category should be separated out for analysis that is distinct from the first, fourth, and fifth preference categories).

Given our analysis, the incorporation of diversity visas should be fairly easy, in the sense that the analysis could be refocused to provide a separate study of a sample that includes only those nations that would qualify for the diversity visas. A comparison of our findings with the findings for this group easily could be made, thus revealing any change in importance of the factors that influence the composition of U.S. immigration. However, for understanding the composition of total immigrants under the new law, the comparison to the old law is more complicated than simply accounting for the additional 55,000 diversity visas. While certain countries will likely benefit from the availability of diversity visas, this benefit is somewhat limited because any single nation is restricted to 3,850 of these visas.

Certain features of the new law will provide potentially even more benefit to previously oversubscribed nations. For instance, the new law provides for a larger per-country quota of 25,620, or an increase of 5,620 over the previous law's quota. Moreover, the number of visas made available for spouses and minor children of permanent resident aliens is substantially increased, and three-quarters of these are not subject to the per-country limits. The removal of the per-country limit was intended to address the increasing backlog of visa applications. Thus, countries that sent large numbers of immigrants under the old law should substantially benefit from these relaxations, and, to the extent that they do, the attempt to diversify the source-country mix of U.S. immigrants will be mitigated.

Rolph (1992, p.32) noted that the legalization program, as well as the lotteries of the late 1980s, "established a strong precedent for programs that provide for entry outside of the worldwide ceiling." She also argues that political forces, including immigrant advocacy groups, the business community, and even states themselves (to gain additional revenue-sharing funds), tend to work in favor of expanding immigration. Although Congress stressed that the legalization program was a one-time occurrence, Rolph's arguments suggest that other such programs indeed may occur again. We noted above that "irregular" immigration tends to be strongly male-dominated. If future special opportunities were to operate like those of the late 1980s, we anticipate that they too would be gender-biased in favor of males.

The empirical results of this study indicate that social programs in source countries influence decisions regarding immigration to the United States. Even if immigrants do not use U.S. social programs in greater proportion than native-born persons, they still use social programs such as Supplemental Security Income (SSI). In August 1996, President Clinton signed a welfare reform bill that restricts the welfare usage of legal immigrants in the United States. Such a program could influence not only the volume of U.S. immigration, but also its composition (especially the age composition).

The Immigration Act of 1990 provided for somewhat higher annual levels of legal immigration, but due to the substantial backlog of immigrant visa requests, the quota ceilings of the 1990 act have been met (except in 1995) and promise to continue to be met. As has occurred previously in world and U.S. history, immigrants have been singled out by many native residents (whether in part rightly or, more frequently, wrongly) as an important source of domestic "problems" such as high crime rates, high unemployment rates (for some), increased welfare utilization, an increased gap between the wages of the most highly educated and the least highly educated, and many more. Whatever the economic and social effects of immigration, they are closely tied to the demographic and economic composition of the immigrants themselves. As a consequence of substantial levels of annual immigration that promise to continue well into the future, many of the issues concerning immigrant composition raised in this monograph will remain before the American people for years to come.

Notes

1. Since much of the migration from Mexico consists of persons in the "other" skill category, this conclusion may be somewhat questionable without further disaggregation of the "other" group.
2. In the immigration-rate regressions, the coefficient most affected by the inclusion of the social program variables is that on the English-language variable, which loses significance in their presence. This result suggests that systematic differences exist in social program availability in English and in non-English speaking countries.

3. Not only are the legal ties themselves improtant, but religious, social, and informational ties also play a role in the naturalization variable. U.S. immigration grew dramatically, from 384,685 in 1972 to 704,005 in 1991, not counting 1,123,162 persons legalized under IRCA. Different immigrant groups have different propensities to naturalize. For example, of the 1982 immigrant cohort, only 11.9 percent of those from Mexico had naturalized through fiscal year 1993 (U.S. Immigration and Naturalization Service 1996, p. 133). On the other hand, by 1993, 68.3 percent of the 1982 cohort from Taiwan and 60.2 percent of that from the Philippines had naturalized. Overall, 37.6 percent of the 1982 cohort had naturalized by 1992. For those countries of birth like Mexico for which naturalization propensities are low, the potential exists for naturalizations to occur, thus forming additional qualifying relationships with U.S. citizens and opening the door to more exempt and restricted immigration in the future. Thus, in the wake of California's Proposition 187, which denied access of illegal aliens and their children to certain social services and public education, an increase occurred in naturalizations of persons born in Mexico. Thus, the link to U.S. citizens provides an on-going and perhaps cumulative effect of migration that certain scholars refer to as the "immigration multiplier." Indeed, various scholars argue that the exempt category of immigration has resulted in a lower skill level of U.S. immigrants.

   Sorensen et al. (1992) examined immigrant categories and occupational outcomes of U.S. immigrants. Their main finding was that immigrants who enter under an employment preference earn more than those who enter under a fmaily preference and are also more likely to be employed as PTK workers and managers than their family-presence counterparts. Their work bears only indirectly on the exempt versus restricted debate, but is relevant nonetheless.

4. Each univeral program studied here became more common over the 1972–1991 period: 1) for old-age programs, an increase from 13 to 15 countries; 2) for sickness programs, an increase from 10 to 14; and 3) for family allowance programs, an increase from 11 to 15.

5. Between 1972 and 1991, unemployment insurance became slightly more common in our 60-country sample (from 26 to 28 countries), cash sickness benefits remained the same (44 countries), and provident fund old-age programs became more common (from 7 to 9).

Appendix A

Supplementary Table for Chapter 4

Table A1 Coefficients of Multiple Determination (R^2) in Gender Regressions Obtained for Individual Countries: 1980, 1981, 1982, and 1983

Country	1980	1981	1982	1983
Africa				
Botswana	$-^a$	NA[b]	NA	–
Burundi	–	NA	NA	NA
Egypt	–	0.46	NA	NA
Kenya	0.48	0.54	0.49	0.46
Liberia	0.35	0.38	0.40	0.43
Malawi	0.63	0.64	0.58	0.49
Mauritius	0.47	0.62	0.62	0.45
Swaziland	0.71	–	0.74	0.79
Tanzania	0.47	0.55	0.45	0.47
Tunisia	0.41	0.48	0.58	0.53
Zimbabwe	0.52	0.42	0.51	0.46
Asia				
India	0.47	0.52	0.49	0.47
Indonesia	0.49	0.53	0.50	0.49
Israel	0.44	0.44	0.44	0.46
Japan	0.62	0.62	0.63	0.62
Korea	0.46	0.46	0.45	0.42
Malaysia	0.48	0.50	0.52	0.54
Pakistan	0.44	0.50	0.48	0.47
Philippines	0.53	0.51	0.51	0.51
Singapore	0.59	0.56	0.54	0.55
Sri Lanka	0.50	0.47	0.52	0.46
Thailand	0.47	0.49	0.51	0.51
Europe				
Austria	0.52	0.50	0.58	0.54
Belgium	0.58	0.60	0.55	0.55
Denmark	0.55	0.52	0.56	0.55
Finland	0.58	0.61	0.58	0.58
France	0.55	0.52	0.52	0.52
Germany	0.61	0.62	0.61	0.61
Greece	0.42	0.44	0.42	0.44
Hungary	0.54	0.59	0.50	0.54

Country	1980	1981	1982	1983
Iceland	0.56	0.39	0.48	0.54
Ireland	0.49	0.44	0.48	0.45
Italy	0.45	0.44	0.44	0.45
Netherlands	0.51	0.50	0.53	0.52
Norway	0.49	0.43	0.48	0.45
Spain	0.44	0.47	0.41	0.45
Sweden	0.53	0.53	0.50	0.54
Switzerland	0.55	0.47	0.52	0.53
United Kingdom	0.50	0.49	0.51	0.50
Yugoslavia	0.51	0.49	0.51	0.47
North and Central America				
Barbados	0.55	0.56	0.54	0.52
Canada	0.51	0.49	0.50	0.49
El Salvador	0.51	0.52	0.49	0.47
Haiti	0.47	0.49	0.47	0.46
Honduras	0.54	0.50	0.51	0.50
Jamaica	0.50	0.50	0.50	0.50
Mexico	0.43	0.46	0.41	0.40
Nicaraqua	0.49	0.51	0.50	0.52
Panama	0.49	0.49	0.48	0.51
Trinidad & Tobago	0.50	0.50	0.51	0.55
Oceania				
Australia	0.54	0.53	0.50	0.50
Fiji	0.47	0.49	0.44	0.47
New Zealand	0.51	0.49	0.50	0.50
South America				
Argentina	0.48	0.50	0.48	0.48
Brazil	0.53	0.51	0.53	0.55
Chile	0.48	0.48	0.46	0.46
Ecuador	0.47	0.48	0.50	0.51
Paraguay	0.56	0.53	0.56	0.43
Uruguay	0.53	0.49	0.51	0.48
Venezuela	0.48	0.46	0.51	0.48

[a] A dash indicates too few observations to estimate. Observations with missing data were dropped for these countries/years.

[b] "NA" indicates no missing information on any record.

Appendix B

Definitions of Variables

Dependent variable	**Definition**
Rate of migration from country i to U.S.A.	The rate of U.S. immigration from country i during year t, where the rate is defined as the ratio of total immigration from i during t to the population of i during t; in econometric discussions, this variable is referred to as m_{it}.

Independent variables

1. Differential economic opportunity

Relative per capita income	Per capita gross domestic product (GDP) in country i during year t relative to a comparable measure for the U.S.A. during t, measured in U.S. dollars (IMF, *International Financial Statistics: Yearbook*).
Relative growth of GDP	The rate of growth of GDP in i measured in constant prices and averaged over the previous three years relative to a comparable measure for the U.S.A. (IMF, *International Financial Statistics: Yearbook*).
Government revenues	Country i's central government revenues in year t, expressed as a percentage of GDP during t (IMF, *International Financial Statistics: Yearbook*).
% Urban	The percentage of country i's population that resides in an urban area (UN, *Demographic Yearbook*).
% Female in labor force	Female labor force as a percentage of country i's total labor force (World Bank, *World Tables*).

2. Migration costs

Distance to U.S.A.

Estimated airline mileage from the principal city of country i to the nearest major U.S. city (John S. Swift Co., Inc., no date).

Birth rate

Country i's crude birth rate in year t (UN, *Demographic Yearbook*).

U.S. military presence

The number of U.S. military personnel and civilian military employees in country i during t, expressed relative to i's total population in t (U.S. Department of Defense, *Selected Manpower Statistics*).

Education

The number of students at the third level of education in i expressed as a fraction of i's total population (UNESCO, *Statistical Yearbook*).

English language

A dummy variable equal to 1 if country i's official United Nations language is English, and otherwise equal to zero (Greenfield 1992).

U.S. college students

The number of persons born in country i who attended a U.S. university during t as a proportion of i's total population (UNESCO, *Statistical Yearbook*).

3. Political attractiveness and religion

Political competitiveness

An index of political rights ranging from 1.0 for countries with a fully competitive electoral process to 7.0, indicating least free (Gastil 1987).

Catholic

A dummy variable equal to 1 if country i's primary religion is Catholic (i.e., at least 50 percent of population is Catholic) and otherwise equal to zero (*World Almanac*).

Muslim

A dummy variable equal to 1 if country i's primary religion is Muslim (i.e., at least 50 percent of population is Muslim) and otherwise equal to zero (*World Almanac*).

4. U.S. immigration policy

Per capita naturalizations

The number of naturalizations to U.S. citizenship of persons born in country i, summed over year t and the prior four years, and expressed relative to the population of i during t (U.S. INS, *Annual Reports* and *Statistical Yearbooks*).

Lottery visas

A dummy variable equal to 1 if country i's number of NP-5 (OP-1) admittances is greater than 5 percent of the number of numerically restricted (numerically exempt for OP-1) immigrants for year t who were born in i, and otherwise equal to zero (INS files).

Silva visas

A dummy variable that reflects significant admissions from country i (Mexico) in year t under the Silva program; equal to 1 for Mexico for 1978 and 1981, and otherwise equal to zero.

Western Hemisphere 1972–76

A dummy variable equal to 1 if country i is in the Western Hemisphere and t is 1972, 1973, 1974, 1975, or 1976, and otherwise equal to zero.

Asia

A dummy variable equal to 1 if country i is in Asia (except Israel), and otherwise equal to zero.

5. Social programs

Universal old-age

A dummy variable equal to 1 if country i in year t had an old-age pension program that was universally available for all residents or resident citizens, and otherwise equal to zero.

Employment-related old-age

A dummy variable equal to 1 if country i in year t had an old-age social insurance program available for wage earners, salaried employees, and/or employed persons, and otherwise equal to zero.

Provident fund old-age

A dummy variable equal to 1 if country i in year t had an old-age provident fund system, and otherwise equal to zero.

Old-age pension not portable

A dummy variable equal to 1 if country i in year t had an old-age program and the old-age pension was not payable abroad or was payable abroad only under "limited conditions."

Universal sickness

A dummy variable equal to 1 if country i in year t had a universal medical benefits program, and otherwise equal to zero.

Cash sickness benefits

A dummy variable equal to 1 if country i in year t paid cash sickness benefits when short-term illnesses prevented the insured from going to work, and otherwise equal to zero.

Maternity benefits

A dummy variable equal to 1 if for country i in year t provided maternity benefits, and otherwise equal to zero.

Medical benefits

A dummy variable equal to 1 if country i in year t provided health care, hospital, and pharmaceutical benefits, and otherwise equal to zero.

Unemployment insurance

A dummy variable equal to 1 if country i in year t had an unemployment insurance program, and otherwise equal to zero.

Universal family allowance

A dummy variable equal to 1 if country i in year t had a family allowance program that provided universal benefits to residents with children, and otherwise equal to zero.

Employment family allowance

A dummy variable equal to 1 if country i in year t had an employment-related family allowance program, and otherwise equal to zero.

6. Other

Population of i	A total population of country i during year t.
Sex ratio in i's population	A ratio of males to females in the population of i during year t.
Median age in i	A median age of the population of i during t.
% No occupation	A percentage of a given gender, age, and entry class of immigrants from i that reported no occupation when entering the United States in year t.
Total U.S. immigration from i	Control total for a given model, or the number of immigrants from i in year t who had a specific characteristic.

Appendix C

Econometric Considerations

The use of panel data presents many potential econometric problems, but it also provides valuable econometric opportunities. Here we discuss a number of issues pertinent to the estimation of models based on panel data.[1] As described in Chapter 4, the panels used in this study are immigrant countries of birth, which are followed annually through time from 1972 to 1991. We have full information on the independent variables in our models for 60 countries. The appendix concludes with tables comparing various estimators that are described below. We settled on the use of Hausman-Taylor estimators; these estimators were employed in all regressions that appear in Chapters 5, 6, 7, and 8.

We retain in this section the notation m_{it}, representing the migration from the ith country during period t, but we partition the set of explanatory variables into two groups that cut across the various vectors. In the discussion below, we pay particular attention to the econometric treatment of the time-invariant variables of the model (distance from country i to the United States, whether country i is English speaking or not [a dummy variable], and three additional dummy variables that indicate whether country i is in Asia, is predominately Catholic, or is predominately Muslim). Let $V_{it} = [x'_{it}|z'_{i}]$ where x_{it} is a $K \times 1$ vector of variables that measures characteristics of country i in period t, and z_i is a $G \times 1$ vector of time-invariant variables. The model of migration, then, is

Eq. C1 $m_{it} = \alpha_i + \delta_t + \beta x_{it} + \gamma z_i + \varepsilon_{it}, \quad i = 1,\ldots,60; t = 1,\ldots,20,$

where the β and γ are vectors of unknown parameters, ε_{it} is a random disturbance, and the α_i and δ_t are unobserved country-specific and time-specific variables, respectively.

The ε_{it} are assumed to have zero mean and to be independent across countries. They may be correlated over time according to a first-order autoregressive process (Berndt and Savin 1975). Note that the model allows different cross-sectional and time-specific intercepts. Various assumptions about these are dealt with in the estimation procedures discussed below.

Equation C1 is a straightforward example of a cross section-time series data model (Kmenta 1986), apart from the additional consideration that some exogenous variables do not vary in the time dimension. In the ideal case, Eq. C1 is

221

true for all i and t, that part of migration unaffected by measured covariates does not vary over time or country, and the ε_{it} are white noise. That is, no misspecification of the form of the migration equation exists, either with respect to functional form of the variables or the choice of factors that are thought to influence migration. Migration corrected for the influence of the covariates is the same in each country and for each period (i.e., only one constant is in the model), and the errors are homoskedastic over country and time and are uncorrelated with one another. In this case, the 20 observations for each of the 60 countries may be "stacked" and linear regression applied to the entire 1,200 observations. Nothing is learned from the time series-cross section organization of the data, and nothing disrupts the optimality of linear regression.

The above case is "ideal" only in the sense that no econometric complications are evident. That such a simple representation of reality could capture the complex migration process is unlikely, however. For example, immigration of a given class of migrants could be different for different countries and for different time periods and variables potentially correlated with the time or country effects may be omitted or poorly measured. Part of the advantage of panel data is that it is possible to control for effects unique to time periods or to countries, since repeated observations over time and countries are available.

Time- and Country-Specific Effects

It would seem wise to allow for the possibility that the δ_t of Eq. C1 are indeed different for different time periods (vary with t). This can be done by specifying a model where the time-specific effects are assumed to be either random or fixed.

If it is assumed that the individual time effects are drawings from a normal distribution and that they are uncorrelated with the explanatory variables in the model (i.e., they are random), the effects may be absorbed into the error term, leaving the deterministic part of the equation unchanged, and the random effects model fitted. The force of such an assumption is that the new vector of disturbances (which now includes the random time effects) no longer has a scalar covariance matrix. The reason is that the random time effect does not change for a particular period across countries. Therefore stacking the observations and using linear regression is no longer optimal, and a generalized least squares estimator must be fit to the data.

It may not be reasonable to assume that the individual time effects are uncorrelated with the explanatory variables. If this is the case, fitting the random effects model will produce biased estimates. For example, suppose that government revenues as a percent of GDP have no real effect on the migration of a given class of immigrants. If migration of this group has increased over time and government revenues as a percent of GDP have similarly risen, then assuming a random effects model would attribute to the government revenues variable the effect of the drift over time in the migration of that class. An alternative to the random effects model that alleviates this problem is the fixed effects model, where the data are augmented to include a constant for each period. To estimate this model, Eq. C1 may be represented in group mean-deviated form: Let $\tilde{m}_{it} = m_{it} - \overline{m}_{it}$ and $\tilde{x}_{it} = x_{it} - \overline{x}_t$. The new regression is

Eq. C2 $\qquad \tilde{m}_{it} = \alpha_i^* + \beta\tilde{x}_{it} + \gamma z_i^* + \tilde{\varepsilon}_{it} \qquad i = 1, \ldots, 60; t = 1, \ldots, 20,$

where $z_i^* \equiv z_i - \overline{z}$ and $\alpha_i^* \equiv \alpha_i - \overline{\alpha}$ have zero mean, and $\tilde{\varepsilon}_{it}$ is defined analogously to $\tilde{m}_{it}$ and $\tilde{x}_{it}$. If desired, the time-specific means may be recovered after estimation.

A similar situation occurs with respect to the country-specific effects. That is, suppose that the migration of various immigrant groups across countries is different for reasons that are not attributable to measurable variables. Then the country-specific constants, α_i^*, must be considered in estimating the parameters of the model. This can be done as discussed above for random time effects. It could be assumed that the α_i^* are random variables uncorrelated with the other variables in the model, and the random effects model fit. But there are several reasons to question the assumption that the α_i^* are uncorrelated with other variables in the model, especially the time-invariant variables. For example, more distant countries may have lower levels of migration in every period. In that case, the coefficient of the distance variable would be biased if the model were estimated under the random effects assumption. A second possibility involves misspecification of the time-invariant variables. Exactly which variables are relevant to the migration decision? This is difficult for economic theory to predict. The possibility exists that some important variable will be omitted. If this is the case, and these omitted variables are correlated with the country-specific effects, then the random effects model will again produce biased parameter estimates.

To examine the fixed country effects model, we may proceed analogously to the case of fixed time effects. Assuming the α_i^* are fixed given the values in the sample, Eq. C2 is averaged over *time*, producing

Eq. C3 $\qquad \overline{\tilde{m}} = \alpha_i^* + \beta\overline{\tilde{x}}_i + \gamma z_i^* + \overline{\tilde{\varepsilon}}_i \quad i = 1, \ldots, 60,$

and subtracted from Eq. C2 to produce

Eq. C4 $\tilde{\tilde{m}}_{it} \equiv \tilde{m}_{it} - \bar{\tilde{m}}_i = \beta \tilde{\tilde{x}}_{it} + \tilde{\tilde{\epsilon}}_{it},\ \ i = 1, \ldots, 60;\ t = 1, \ldots, 20,$

where $\tilde{\tilde{x}}_{it}$ and $\tilde{\tilde{\epsilon}}_{it}$ are defined analogously to $\tilde{\tilde{m}}_{it}$. This regression produces unbiased parameter estimates of β, since the country-specific constants have been eliminated. These estimates, $\hat{\beta}_w$, are reported for a single immigrant class in Table C1 in the column headed "Within." Because only the within-time variation in the data is utilized, identification of the coefficients in the vector γ is lost. Note that the term involving γ and z has disappeared in Eq. C4. This situation did not occur when considering time-specific effects since no country-invariant variable is in the data.

To recapitulate, the existence of a panel of data on migration behavior allows controlling for time-specific and country-specific effects. These effects may be treated in a parallel manner, with either the random or the fixed effects model. The fixed effects model requires fewer assumptions than the random effects model, so that it is the model of choice for the time dimension. However, when the same model is applied to the country dimension, some parameter estimates are lost. Thus, the fixed effects model cannot be fit in this case.[2] For the random effects model to produce consistent estimates requires the assumption of no correlation between the random effects and the explanatory variables. Since it is unlikely that this condition will be true in the data, an alternative technique, that of instrumental variables, is proposed.

If this white noise assumption concerning the random time effects is not made *a priori*, then the within estimates of β may be retained and the coefficient estimates of γ recovered by an instrumental variables (IV) approach of Hausman and Taylor (1981).[3] Conventional IV estimation is often plagued by the problem of finding convincing instruments for the endogenous variables. This is a problem because usually no reason is evident to exclude from the model any variables correlated with m and x, given the imprecise nature of economic models and data. This is not the case here, however, due to the structure of the data and the nature of the variables for which instruments are needed. The data have two dimensions: a cross-sectional dimension (countries) and a time dimension (years). The variables that need instruments vary only in the former dimension. Hence, if it can be assumed that some of the variables in x are uncorrelated with the α_i, then they may be used in two ways because of their variation across both country and time: 1) using deviations from country means, they produce unbiased estimates of the β's (Eq. C4), and 2) using the country means themselves, they serve to identify the endogenous variables in z. Therefore, the instruments are already "in" the model, eliminating the objection to IV estimation mentioned above.

To calculate the IV estimates of γ, partition x and z so that $x = (x_1 | x_2)$ and $z = (z_1 | z_2)$, where it is assumed that the k_1 elements of x_1 and the g_1 elements of z_1 are uncorrelated with the country effects, whereas this is not true for the $k_2 \times 1$ and $g_2 \times 1$ (respectively) vectors x_2 and z_2.[4] First, $\hat{\beta}_w x_{it}$ is subtracted from both sides of Eq. C2 to produce

Eq. C5 $\quad \tilde{m}_{it} - \hat{\beta}_w x_{it} = \alpha_i^* + \gamma z_i^* + \tilde{\varepsilon}_{it}$

where $\tilde{\varepsilon}_{it}$ is now to be interpreted as $\tilde{\varepsilon}_{it} + (\beta - \hat{\beta}_w)\tilde{x}_{it}$. Then, the left side of Eq. C5, is averaged over t, and the variables in z_2 are regressed on z_1 and the time-averaged variables in x_1. This procedure gives consistent estimates of γ regardless of the endogeneity of the α_i.

Although these estimates are consistent, they are not fully efficient, since the covariance structure of the random term, $\alpha_i^* + \tilde{\varepsilon}_{it}$, has been ignored. This omission is the same as ignoring the random effects in the random effects model and simply fitting least squares to the data, as discussed at the beginning of this section. To produce fully efficient estimates, the components of the disturbance variance must first be estimated. This is possible, since β is consistently estimated from the within regression and γ is consistently estimated from the IV regression. With these estimates in hand, m, x, and the instruments for z may be transformed and generalized least squares performed. This will produce consistent, efficient estimates of all parameters under any hypothesis regarding correlation. Hausman-Taylor Instrumental Variable estimates are reported in the fourth column of Table C1; the corresponding t-statistics are in Table C2.

Notes

1. We are grateful to Donald Waldman for this section, which mainly is drawn from Greenwood, McDowell, and Waldman (1996).
2. The intercountry variation may also be utilized by noticing that Eq. C3 contains all the parameters of the original model. A random effects estimation of this equation is known as the "Between" estimator. However, as with the least squares and generalized least squares estimators and unlike the Within estimator, Between estimators are consistent only if the time effects are white noise.
3. For related work, see Amemiya and MaCurdy (1986), and Breusch, Mizon, and Schmidt (1989).
4. The method of partitioning variables into those potentially correlated with unobserved country-specific effects and those that are exogenous is discussed in Chapter 5 under "Empirical Findings."

Table C1 Alternative Estimates of the Rate of U.S. Immigration, 1972–1991[a]

Variable	Random effects (GLS)	One-way fixed-effects, time	One-way fixed-effects, countries (Within)	Hausman-Taylor IV
Diff. econ. opportunity				
Relative per capita income (x_1)	−0.474***	−0.815***	−0.014	−0.016
Relative growth of GDP (x_1)	0.884***	0.541	0.542**	0.603**
Government revenues (x_2)	0.507***	0.053	0.293*	0.288*
% Urban (x_1)	−1.114***	−0.496***	−2.049***	−1.707***
% Female in labor force (x_2)	0.892***	1.599***	−1.208*	−1.304**
Migration costs				
Distance to U.S.A. (z_1)	−0.259***	−0.156***	–	−0.324***
Birth rate (x_2)	−1.964***	−1.409***	−2.603***	−2.550***
U.S. military presence (x_2)	−0.010	−0.034***	0.078***	0.074***
Education (x_2)	−0.468**	−0.775***	0.270	0.298
English language (z_2)	0.656***	0.333***	–	2.100***
U.S. college students (x_2)	−0.025	0.267***	−0.316***	−0.307***
Polit. attract. and religion				
Political competitiveness (x_2)	0.011	−0.065***	0.033***	0.034***
Catholic (z_1)	−0.191***	−0.119***	–	0.274
Muslim (z_1)	0.020	0.221***	–	0.282

U.S. immigration policy

Per capita naturalizations (x_2)	0.085***	0.189***	0.057***	0.056***
Lottery visas (x_1)	0.101***	0.084	0.070*	0.073*
Silva visas (x_1)	0.179	0.344	0.158	0.160
Western Hemisphere 1972–76 (x_1)	−0.121***	0.219***	−0.267***	−0.260***
Asia (z_1)	0.450***	0.157	–	0.637***
Control				
Population of i (x_1)	−0.125***	−0.071***	−0.098*	−0.152***
Constant (z_1)	–	0.950***	–	–

[a] *** Indicates $t \geq 1.96$; ** indicates $1.67 \leq t < 1.96$; * indicates $1.29 \leq t < 1.67$. Table C2 reports the corresponding t-statistics.

Table C2 Alternative Estimates of the Rate of U.S. Immigration, 1972–1991: t-Statistics

Variable	Random effects (GLS)	One-way fixed-effects, time	One-way fixed-effects, countries (Within)	Hausman-Taylor IV
Diff. econ. opportunity				
Relative per capita income (x_1)	-5.025	-9.821	-0.133	-0.158
Relative growth of GDP (x_1)	2.491	1.244	1.704	1.910
Government revenues (x_2)	2.750	0.349	1.540	1.518
% Urban (x_1)	-6.073	-4.457	-4.921	-4.909
% Female in labor force (x_2)	2.464	7.541	-1.567	-1.718
Migration costs				
Distance to U.S.A. (z_1)	-16.072	-15.980	–	-6.170
Birth rate (x_2)	-5.816	-6.344	-5.308	-5.231
U.S. military presence (x_2)	-0.758	-4.321	2.489	2.425
Education (x_2)	-1.770	-3.509	0.985	1.097
English language (z_2)	8.547	8.302	–	2.926
U.S. college students (x_2)	-0.412	4.045	-5.328	-5.183
Polit. attract. and religion				
Political competitiveness (x_2)	1.036	-6.161	3.425	3.525
Catholic (z_1)	-2.392	-2.884	–	0.743
Muslim (z_1)	0.153	3.173	–	0.575

U.S. immigration policy

Per capita naturalizations (x_2)	10.981	19.656	8.234	8.163
Lottery visas (x_1)	0.715	1.000	0.731	0.740
Silva visas (x_1)	1.961	1.194	1.560	1.615
Western Hemisphere 1972–76 (x_1)	–2.375	3.212	–5.931	–5.778
Asia (z_1)	4.249	2.686	–	2.035
Control				
Population of i (x_1)	–3.819	–4.002	–1.295	–2.418
Constant (z_1)	–	2.060	–	–

Note:

1. Within - between test of no endogeneity:
   H0: individual effects are uncorrelated with the regressors; $\chi^2(5) = 442.6 \rightarrow$ reject null.
2. Test of random effects:
   H0: individual effects are uncorrelated with the regressors; $\chi^2(5) = 56.52 \rightarrow$ reject null.
3. Test of exogeneity of Hausman-Taylor instruments:
   H0: instruments are not endogenous; $\chi^2(5) = 0.81 \rightarrow$ do not reject null.

Appendix D

Supplementary Tables for
Chapter 5

Table D1 Means and Standard Deviations of Econometric Variables

Variable[a]	Mean	Std. Dev.
Rate of migration from i to U.S.A. (10^{-3})	0.387	0.941
Population in i (10^5)	341.355	932.555
Relative per capita income	0.336	0.356
Relative growth of GDP	1.013	0.039
Government revenues (10^2)	0.256	0.117
% Urban	0.547	0.251
% Female in labor force	0.327	0.094
Distance to U.S.A. (10^3)	5.036	2.577
Birth rate	26.675	12.730
U.S. military presence	0.528	2.246
Education in (10^{-1})[b]	0.139	0.103
English language	0.350	0.477
U.S. college students (10^{-3})	0.230	0.369
Political competitiveness	3.143	2.097
Catholic	0.367	0.482
Muslim	0.083	0.277
Per capita naturalizations	0.969	2.338
Lottery visas	0.078	0.269
Silva visas	0.002	0.041
Western Hemisphere 1972–76	0.071	0.257
Asia	0.167	0.373
Universal old-age	0.221	0.415
Employment-related old-age	0.660	0.474
Provident fund old-age	0.142	0.349
Old-age pension not portable	0.172	0.377
Universal sickness	0.210	0.408
Cash sickness benefits	0.719	0.450
Maternity benefits	0.699	0.459
Medical benefits	0.668	0.468
Unemployment insurance	0.482	0.500

Variable	Mean	Std. Dev.
Universal family allowance	0.218	0.413
Employment family allowance	0.245	0.430
Male education per capita (10^{-1})	0.155	0.111
Female education per capita (10^{-1})	0.122	0.103
Relative female education	0.736	0.341
Median age in i	25.258	7.073
Sex ratio in i's population	1.011	0.096

[a] For variables carrying exponents, the reported data should be multiplied by the exponent to give the actual coefficient.

[b] In the regressions of Chapter 5, this variable has been multiplied by 10^2. All other variables are defined as reported in this table.

Table D2 The Rate of Migration to the United States, 1972–1991—Hausman-Taylor Instrumental Variable Estimates: t-Statistics

Variable	No social program variable	All immigrants	Numerically restricted	Numerically exempt
Diff. econ. opportunity				
Relative per capita income (x_1)	−0.158	0.052	0.950	−1.470
Relative growth of GDP (x_1)	1.910	1.424	1.482	0.469
Government revenues (x_2)	1.518	2.198	2.235	0.532
% Urban (x_1)	−4.909	−5.421	−4.279	−2.958
% Female in labor force (x_2)	−1.718	1.076	1.399	−0.464
Migration costs				
Distance to U.S.A. (z_1)	−6.170	−3.888	−3.586	−3.913
Birth rate (x_2)	−5.231	−6.625	−5.215	−4.615
U.S. military presence (x_2)	2.425	1.217	1.404	0.236
Education (x_2)	1.097	1.323	1.892	−0.338
English language (z_2)	2.926	−0.025	0.213	0.334
U.S. college students (x_2)	−5.183	−4.355	−4.618	−0.775
Polit. attract. and religion				
Political competitiveness (x_2)	3.525	3.512	2.851	2.376
Catholic (z_1)	0.743	−0.692	−0.638	0.234
Muslim (z_1)	0.575	0.033	0.185	0.307

U.S. immigration policy

Per capita naturalizations (x_2)	8.163	8.812	5.401	8.815
Lottery visas (x_1)	1.615	1.852	2.604	-0.665
Silva visas (x_1)	0.740	0.759	1.266	-0.683
Western Hemisphere 1972–76 (x_1)	-5.778	-6.143	-5.305	-3.288
Asia (z_1)	2.035	-0.256	-0.555	0.788

Social programs

Universal old-age (x_2)	–	0.090	0.632	-0.349
Employment-related old-age (x_2)	–	-0.670	-0.737	-0.473
Provident fund old-age (x_2)	–	-0.459	-0.121	-0.991
Old-age pension not portable (x_2)	–	-1.487	-1.000	-1.333
Universal sickness (x_2)	–	-0.187	-0.855	1.236
Cash sickness benefits (x_2)	–	-5.734	-3.298	-5.881
Maternity benefits (x_2)	–	3.070	2.945	1.198
Medical benefits (x_2)	–	-1.335	0.672	-3.976
Unemployment insurance (x_2)	–	-9.263	-10.046	-1.178
Universal family allowance (x_2)	–	-1.283	-1.473	0.271
Employment family allowance (x_2)	–	-1.588	-1.509	-0.401

Variable	No social program variable	All immigrants	Numerically restricted	Numerically exempt
Control				
Population of i (x_1)	-2.418	-0.878	-0.175	-1.364
Test of exogeneity of H-T instruments	0.81	1.60	1.62	2.73

Appendix E

Supplementary Tables for
Chapter 6

Table E1 Gender Composition of Total U.S. Immigrants: *t*-Statistics

Variable	Male	Female
Diff. econ. opportunity		
Relative per capita income	1.328	−1.328
Relative growth of GDP	−0.670	0.670
Government revenues	0.060	−0.060
% Urban	−1.587	1.587
% Female in labor force	3.904	−3.904
Migration costs		
Distance to U.S.A.	1.788	−1.788
Birth rate	−2.248	2.248
U.S. military presence	−2.496	2.496
Relative female education[a]	−1.595	1.595
English language	−3.562	3.562
U.S. college students	0.800	−0.800
Polit. attract. and religion		
Political competitiveness	−0.130	0.130
Catholic	−2.087	2.087
Muslim	1.045	−1.045
U.S. immigration policy		
Per capita naturalizations	−1.115	1.115
Lottery visas	1.898	−1.898
Silva visas	−11.291	11.291
Western Hemisphere 1972–76	−1.003	1.003
Asia	−5.040	5.040
Social programs		
Universal old-age	−1.251	1.251
Employment-related old-age	0.800	−0.800
Provident fund old-age	−0.033	0.033
Old-age pension not portable	0.571	−0.571
Universal sickness	0.112	−0.112
Cash sickness benefits	−1.700	1.700

Variable	Male	Female
Maternity benefits	−1.523	1.523
Medical benefits	−0.428	0.428
Unemployment insurance	−1.881	1.881
Universal family allowance	−1.242	1.242
Employment family allowance	−1.265	1.265
Control		
Sex ratio in i	0.958	−0.958
Total U.S. immigration from i	122.851	100.507
Test of exogeneity of H-T instruments	2.08	2.08

[a] Refers to the ratio of the female to the male education variables.

Table E2 Female U.S. Immigrants By Entry Class: *t*-Statistics

Variable	Numerically restricted	Numerically exempt
Diff. econ. opportunity		
Relative per capita income	−0.495	−1.254
Relative growth of GDP	−0.324	0.441
Government revenues	1.811	−0.562
% Urban	−0.484	2.303
% Female in labor force	−1.548	−2.938
Migration costs		
Distance to U.S.A.	−0.492	−1.174
Birth rate	3.219	1.384
U.S. military presence	−0.430	2.658
Relative female education[a]	−0.412	2.241
English language	−1.055	3.927
U.S. college students	1.360	−1.416
Polit. attract. and religion		
Political competitiveness	−1.561	0.094
Catholic	−0.410	2.353
Muslim	−1.356	−0.524
U.S. immigration policy		
Per capita naturalizations	1.499	0.215
Lottery visas	−0.565	−2.066
Silva visas	6.574	2.395
Western Hemisphere 1972–76	1.913	0.997
Asia	0.030	4.823
Social programs		
Universal old-age	0.351	1.037
Employment-related old-age	2.014	−1.646
Provident fund old-age	1.430	−0.622
Old-age pension not portable	1.434	−0.479
Universal sickness	3.832	−0.554
Cash sickness benefits	−1.581	2.436

Variable	Numerically restricted	Numerically exempt
Maternity benefits	0.696	0.933
Medical benefits	0.882	0.688
Unemployment insurance	0.456	1.675
Universal family allowance	0.370	1.107
Employment family allowance	−0.216	1.388
Control		
Sex ratio in i	0.513	−0.494
Total U.S. immigration from i	175.779	103.184
Test of exogeneity of H-T instruments	1.25	2.59

[a] Refers to the ratio of the female to the male education variables.

Appendix F

Supplementary Tables for
Chapter 7

Table F1 Age Composition of Immigrants: *t*-Statistics

Variable	Aged 20–34	Aged 55 and older
Diff. econ. opportunity		
Relative per capita income	2.166	−1.900
Relative growth of GDP	−1.638	2.362
Government revenues	2.265	−2.516
% Urban	−3.149	3.893
% Female in labor force	4.645	−5.290
Migration costs		
Distance to U.S.A.	−2.556	1.516
Birth rate	−0.948	−0.376
U.S. military presence	0.245	0.620
Education	−2.156	1.975
English language	−0.654	2.190
U.S. college students	−0.251	−0.086
Polit. attract. and religion		
Political competitiveness	1.266	0.612
Catholic	0.512	0.925
Muslim	−0.150	0.151
U.S. immigration policy		
Per capita naturalizations	1.498	−1.356
Lottery visas	3.315	−2.517
Silva visas	8.377	−7.876
Western Hemisphere 1972–76	−5.581	5.587
Asia	1.513	0.481
Social programs		
Universal old-age	1.419	−0.732
Employment-related old-age	−1.892	0.344
Provident fund old-age	1.136	−2.146
Old-age pension not portable	−1.239	0.796
Universal sickness	−0.208	0.421
Cash sickness benefits	−2.792	3.225

Variable	Aged 20–34	Aged 55 and older
Maternity benefits	1.820	–1.195
Medical benefits	–1.330	1.856
Unemployment insurance	–1.357	1.483
Universal family allowance	–0.195	0.361
Employment family allowance	–0.879	1.241
Control		
Median age in i	–3.605	2.309
Total migration from i aged 20 and over	62.832	31.980
Test of exogeneity of H-T instruments	3.33	2.33

Table F2 Age Composition of Immigrants by Gender: *t*-Statistics

Variable	Aged 20–34		Aged 55 and older	
	Male	Female	Male	Female
Diff. econ. opportunity				
Relative per capita income	1.797	1.234	−2.007	−1.317
Relative growth of GDP	−0.823	−2.622	1.735	2.606
Government revenues	1.372	3.252	−2.000	−2.939
% Urban	−0.629	−6.334	2.360	5.326
% Female in labor force	4.187	3.925	−5.761	−4.088
Migration costs				
Distance to U.S.A.	−1.557	−2.426	1.481	1.613
Birth rate	−1.500	2.037	0.891	−1.794
U.S. military presence	−0.851	1.648	1.140	−0.181
Education[a]	1.155	−4.838	0.621	2.420
English language	−0.728	−1.278	1.821	2.167
U.S. college students	0.357	−0.046	−0.272	−0.022
Polit. attract. and religion				
Political competitiveness	0.869	0.959	−0.013	0.563
Catholic	0.769	−0.382	0.095	1.196
Muslim	0.802	−1.261	−0.678	0.966
U.S. immigration policy				
Per capita naturalizations	−0.118	2.793	−0.469	−2.009
Lottery visas	3.030	2.998	−3.250	−1.874
Silva visas	0.023	17.273	−4.946	−13.171
Western Hemisphere 1972–76	−3.270	−6.638	4.485	6.230
Asia	0.055	1.875	0.784	−0.270
Social programs				
Universal old-age	1.357	1.627	−1.429	−0.757
Employment-related old-age	−1.282	−2.660	1.660	0.247
Provident fund old-age	0.412	2.175	−1.335	−2.517
Old-age pension not portable	−0.544	−1.994	0.336	1.254
Universal sickness	0.305	−0.141	−0.504	0.581

Variable	Aged 20–34		Aged 55 and older	
	Male	Female	Male	Female
Cash sickness benefits	–1.436	–3.594	2.529	3.140
Maternity benefits	1.293	2.607	–1.289	–1.767
Medical benefits	–0.085	–1.842	0.609	2.293
Unemployment insurance	–1.219	–0.897	1.341	1.203
Universal family allowance	–0.679	–0.082	0.489	0.490
Employment family allowance	–1.118	–0.733	1.230	1.349
Control				
Median age in i	–3.372	–4.259	3.111	2.724
Total sex-specific immigration aged 20 and over from i	67.247	59.234	39.156	38.899
Test of exogeneity of H-T instruments	2.31	2.40	2.75	2.12

[a] In the gender-specific regressions, the education variable is measured specific to the respective gender.

**Table F3 Age Composition of Numerically Restricted Immigrants:
t-Statistics**

Variable	Aged 20–34		Aged 55 and older	
	Males	Females	Males	Females
Diff. econ. opportunity				
Relative per capita income	0.378	0.934	−1.002	−1.248
Relative growth of GDP	−0.675	−0.852	1.305	−0.002
Government revenues	0.833	1.523	−1.114	−0.582
% Urban	−1.127	−2.181	1.319	0.920
% Female in labor force	0.554	2.265	−3.989	−1.378
Migration costs				
Distance to U.S.A.	−1.059	−1.326	2.063	1.464
Birth rate	0.412	0.458	1.801	3.390
U.S. military presence	−0.566	−0.068	0.709	0.090
Education[a]	0.757	−2.962	0.359	−2.157
English language	−0.005	−0.234	−1.047	−2.157
U.S. college students	0.734	0.825	1.293	3.002
Polit. attract. and religion				
Political competitiveness	1.013	0.633	−0.812	−1.608
Catholic	1.689	1.204	−2.156	−2.863
Muslim	0.378	0.427	−1.331	−1.550
U.S. immigration policy				
Per capita naturalizations	1.145	1.739	−0.998	−5.399
Lottery visas	3.066	3.496	−2.496	−1.501
Silva visas	−4.833	0.510	3.045	2.846
Western Hemisphere 1972–76	−0.966	−2.536	5.476	7.300
Asia	1.137	1.112	−1.828	−2.333
Social programs				
Universal old-age	2.130	2.465	−1.097	−0.492
Employment-related old-age	−2.720	−3.576	3.455	2.296
Provident fund old-age	0.448	0.725	0.203	1.325
Old-age pension not portable	−1.425	−1.020	0.539	−0.043
Universal sickness	3.229	2.861	−0.013	−0.442

Variable	Aged 20–34		Aged 55 and older	
	Males	Females	Males	Females
Cash sickness benefits	−2.485	−3.319	1.924	3.393
Maternity benefits	1.312	2.234	−1.774	−3.911
Medical benefits	0.907	0.507	1.446	3.267
Unemployment insurance	0.669	0.539	1.212	1.868
Universal family allowance	−0.111	0.659	1.296	1.901
Employment family allowance	0.183	0.481	1.017	1.570
Control				
Median age in i	−1.164	−1.098	0.455	−1.079
Total aged 20 and over numerically restricted from i[b]	67.479	67.034	27.957	26.341
Test of exogeneity of H-T instruments	2.31	3.67	5.12	4.41

[a] In the gender-specific regressions, the education variable is measured specific to the respective gender.

[b] In the gender-specific regressions, the control total variable is measured specific to the respective gender.

Table F4 Age Composition of Numerically Exempt Immigrants:
t-Statistics

Variable	Aged 20–34		Aged 55 and older	
	Males	Females	Males	Females
Diff. econ. opportunity				
Relative per capita income	1.607	1.380	−1.820	−1.263
Relative growth of GDP	−0.597	−3.499	2.138	3.459
Government revenues	1.063	2.839	−2.239	−2.971
% Urban	0.576	−4.144	1.745	4.348
% Female in labor force	4.642	5.507	−5.708	−5.459
Migration costs				
Distance to U.S.A.	−0.399	−1.078	0.340	0.598
Birth rate	−1.114	3.244	−0.576	−2.452
U.S. military presence	−1.277	1.903	1.189	−0.115
Education[a]	0.216	−3.144	1.078	1.820
English language	−2.139	−2.115	3.410	2.716
U.S. college students	0.485	−0.587	−0.911	−0.311
Polit. attract. and religion				
Political competitiveness	−0.371	−1.660	1.568	2.108
Catholic	−0.642	−1.286	1.497	1.636
Muslim	0.765	−1.029	−0.702	0.684
U.S. immigration policy				
Per capita naturalizations	−1.615	−0.708	−0.013	0.329
Lottery visas	2.129	1.502	−2.658	−1.236
Silva visas	−0.539	−0.235	−0.319	0.108
Western Hemisphere 1972–76	−2.254	−3.596	2.977	3.539
Asia	−1.831	0.231	2.750	0.983
Social programs				
Universal old-age	0.260	0.258	−0.787	−0.397
Employment-related old-age	0.226	0.816	−0.084	0.150
Provident fund old-age	0.346	2.029	−2.055	−2.550
Old-age pension not portable	0.505	−0.148	−0.062	0.222
Universal sickness	−0.902	−0.217	−0.678	−0.677

Variable	Aged 20–34		Aged 55 and older	
	Males	Females	Males	Females
Cash sickness benefits	0.327	–0.605	2.619	2.050
Maternity benefits	0.636	0.253	–0.376	0.078
Medical benefits	0.383	–0.230	0.284	0.629
Unemployment insurance	–1.589	–0.944	1.156	0.923
Universal family allowance	–0.935	0.004	0.030	0.156
Employment family allowance	–1.492	–0.582	0.923	0.960
Control				
Median age in i	–3.410	–4.227	2.345	3.224
Total exempt aged 20 and over from i[b]	82.974	89.533	24.404	40.416
Test of exogeneity of H-T instruments	2.20	1.44	1.58	1.12

[a] In the gender-specific regressions, the education variable is measured specific to the respective gender.
[b] In the gender-specific regressions, the control total variable is measured specific to the respective gender.

Appendix G

Supplementary Tables for Chapter 8

Table G1 Highly Skilled Immigrants by Age: _t_-Statistics

Variable	Total	Aged 20–34	Aged 35–64
Diff. econ. opportunity			
Relative per capita income	0.453	1.000	–0.114
Relative growth of GDP	–2.194	–2.503	0.530
Government revenues	1.137	1.504	–0.519
% Urban	–2.985	–1.239	–1.866
% Female in labor force	3.081	5.955	–3.285
Migration costs			
Distance to U.S.A.	–3.578	–2.983	–2.569
Birth rate	1.258	1.927	0.225
U.S. military presence	1.104	0.893	1.326
Education	–4.052	–4.897	0.463
English language	3.756	3.419	3.975
U.S. college students	–0.939	0.312	–1.621
Polit. attract. and religion			
Political competitiveness	0.495	–0.196	0.219
Catholic	2.752	3.004	1.867
Muslim	0.510	1.412	–0.686
U.S. immigration policy			
Per capita naturalizations	–0.382	–1.165	–0.185
Lottery visas	1.953	2.109	0.963
Silva visas	–1.813	–3.621	–2.563
Western Hemisphere 1972–76	–5.243	–4.484	–0.740
Asia	5.014	4.178	5.005
Social programs			
Universal old-age	0.992	1.706	0.138
Employment-related old-age	–2.125	–2.116	–1.360
Provident fund old-age	1.697	2.757	–1.025
Old-age pension not portable	–1.877	–2.127	0.221
Universal sickness	–1.134	–0.619	–0.198
Cash sickness benefits	0.145	–1.089	3.290

Variable	Total	Aged 20–34	Aged 35–64
Maternity benefits	0.942	1.406	−0.284
Medical benefits	1.132	1.560	1.169
Unemployment insurance	−0.326	−0.152	0.838
Universal family allowance	1.312	2.010	0.582
Employment family allowance	0.147	0.671	0.313
Control			
% No occupation[a]	−3.052	−1.452	0.683
Total U.S. immigration from i[b]	14.567	15.489	20.695
Test of exogeneity of H-T instruments	4.10	3.31	5.65

[a] The control for the percentage of immigrants that does not declare an occupation is measured specific to the group examined (i.e., total, aged 20–34, and aged 35–64).

[b] The control total is measured specific to the group examined (i.e., total, aged 20–34, and aged 35–64).

Table G2 Highly Skilled Immigrants by Gender: *t*-Statistics

Variable	Males			Females		
	Total	Aged 20–34	Aged 35–64	Total	Aged 20–34	Aged 35–64
Diff. econ. opportunity						
Relative per capita income	0.710	1.191	0.054	0.238	0.602	0.061
Relative growth of GDP	-1.613	-2.428	1.192	-1.755	-1.902	-0.090
Government revenues	0.750	1.244	-0.588	0.993	1.116	-0.474
% Urban	-1.920	0.084	-2.343	-2.030	-1.017	-0.421
% Female in labor force	3.961	6.273	-2.512	1.394	4.111	-3.483
Migration costs						
Distance to U.S.A.	-3.961	-3.634	-3.048	-2.502	-2.005	-0.908
Birth rate	0.325	1.116	-0.531	2.396	3.435	1.227
U.S. military presence	0.847	0.630	1.167	1.489	1.476	1.082
Education[a]	-2.883	-2.871	-1.153	-2.060	-4.487	2.573
English language	4.109	4.513	3.338	3.751	3.269	4.356
U.S. college students	-0.880	0.107	-1.593	1.489	1.048	-1.252
Polit. attract. and religion						
Political competitiveness	2.308	0.925	1.824	-1.493	-1.629	-1.668
Catholic	2.691	3.611	1.128	3.263	3.273	2.732
Muslim	1.070	2.440	-0.667	0.466	1.039	-0.313
U.S. immigration policy						
Per capita naturalizations	-0.549	-0.861	-0.582	-0.731	-2.252	0.174
Lottery visas	2.817	2.485	2.008	0.493	1.129	-0.420

Silva visas	-0.802	-1.726	-2.280	-4.489	-8.960	-2.799
Western Hemisphere 1972–76	-4.595	-4.073	-0.909	-3.421	-2.173	0.252
Asia	5.134	4.725	4.767	4.473	4.057	4.294
Social programs						
Universal old-age	0.786	1.918	-0.623	1.659	1.953	1.039
Employment-related old-age	-2.394	-2.326	-1.275	-1.556	-1.524	-0.468
Provident fund old-age	1.417	2.424	-1.248	1.595	2.477	-0.306
Old-age pension not portable	-1.589	-2.053	0.439	-1.487	-1.493	-0.014
Universal sickness	-1.460	-0.629	-0.835	0.126	0.119	0.779
Cash sickness benefits	0.280	-1.188	3.314	0.373	-0.007	2.464
Maternity benefits	-0.112	1.072	-1.506	1.836	1.333	1.319
Medical benefits	1.124	1.262	1.448	1.151	2.245	0.608
Unemployment insurance	-0.678	-0.278	0.339	0.805	1.061	1.620
Universal family allowance	1.269	1.897	0.656	1.425	2.499	0.739
Employment family allowance	0.158	0.642	0.384	0.422	1.244	0.437
Control						
% No occupation[b]	-2.682	-1.950	0.070	-1.416	-0.351	0.224
Total U.S. immigration from i[c]	13.477	13.761	19.195	18.036	22.387	22.560
Test of exogeneity of H-T instruments	3.35	3.04	4.85	5.85	5.83	4.25

[a] In the gender-specific regressions, the education variable is measured specific to the respective gender.
[b] In the gender-specific regressions, this control is measured specific to the respective gender, as well as to the specific age group.
[c] In the gender-specific regressions, the control total variable is measured specific to the respective gender, as well as to the specific age group.

Table G3 Highly Skilled Immigrants by Entry Class: *t*-Statistics

Variable	Numerically restricted		Numerically exempt	
	Males	Females	Males	Females
Diff. econ. opportunity				
Relative per capita income	1.452	0.894	−1.251	0.042
Relative growth of GDP	−2.269	−2.412	0.671	0.205
Government revenues	1.869	1.669	−2.014	−0.942
% Urban	−0.489	−0.807	−1.154	−0.218
% Female in labor force	6.289	4.106	−3.363	−2.956
Migration costs				
Distance to U.S.A.	−3.684	−0.978	−1.499	−0.048
Birth rate	−1.061	3.867	1.036	0.811
U.S. military presence	0.388	0.972	1.451	1.494
Education[a]	−3.450	−3.798	1.571	1.798
English language	4.315	1.929	1.780	3.625
U.S. college students	−0.148	1.500	−2.173	−1.231
Polit. attract. and religion				
Political competitiveness	0.620	−1.893	1.875	−1.856
Catholic	3.671	2.648	0.117	1.567
Muslim	2.581	0.990	−0.815	−0.629
U.S. immigration policy				
Per capita naturalizations	−0.422	−1.297	−1.259	−1.127
Lottery visas	2.729	1.798	−0.006	−1.384
Silva visas	−8.706	−15.580	1.720 ·	1.461
Western Hemisphere 1972–76	−5.231	−1.561	2.722	2.196
Asia	4.758	3.316	2.301	3.185
Social programs				
Universal old-age	0.690	1.481	−0.737	0.682
Employment-related old-age	−1.979	−0.540	−0.316	−0.363
Provident fund old-age	1.800	2.683	−2.245	−0.791
Old-age pension not portable	−1.062	−0.870	1.028	0.008
Universal sickness	0.569	1.799	−1.570	−0.008

Variable	Numerically restricted		Numerically exempt	
	Males	Females	Males	Females
Cash sickness benefits	−1.827	−1.436	4.012	3.005
Maternity benefits	−0.842	0.028	−0.572	1.003
Medical benefits	1.423	1.412	0.350	1.085
Unemployment insurance	−1.001	1.256	0.331	1.593
Universal family allowance	1.460	2.563	0.103	1.035
Employment family allowance	0.344	1.236	0.202	1.018
Control			.	
% No occupation[b]	−2.910	−0.849	−1.332	−0.639
Total U.S. immigration from i[c]	16.054	24.358	23.432	25.021
Test of exogeneity of H-T instruments	2.87	4.58	1.44	4.42

[a] In the gender-specific regressions, the education variable is measured specific to the respective gender.

[b] In the gender-specific regressions, the percent no-occupation variable is specific to the respective gender, as well as immigrant class.

[c] In the gender-specific regressions, the control total is specific to gender and immigrant class.

References

Abrams, Elliot and Franklin S. Abrams. 1975. "Immigration Policy—Who Gets In and Why?" *The Public Interest* 38(Winter): 3–29.

Altonji, Joseph G., and David Card. 1991. "The Effects of Immigration on the Labor Market Outcomes of Less-Skilled Natives." In *Immigration, Trade, and the Labor Market*, John M. Abowd and Richard B. Freeman, eds. Chicago: University of Chicago Press, pp. 201–234.

Amemiya, Takeshi, and T.E. MaCurdy. 1986. "Instrumental-Variable Estimation of an Error-Components Model." *Econometrica* 54(July): 869–881.

Arthur, W. Brian, and Thomas J. Espenshade. 1988. "Immigration Policy and Immigrants Ages." *Population and Development Review* 14(June): 315–326.

Barrett, Alan. 1996. "The Greencard Lottery Winners: Are They More or Less Skilled than Other Immigrants?" *Economics Letters* 52: 331–335.

Barrett, Frank A. 1976. "A Schema for Indirect International Migration." *International Migration Review* 10 (Spring): 3–11.

Barten, Anton P. 1977. "The Systems of Consumer Demand Functions Approach: A Review." *Econometrica* 45(January): 23–51.

Bean, Frank D., B. Lindsay Lowell, and Lowell J. Taylor. 1988. "Undocumented Mexican Immigrants and the Earnings of Other Workers in the United States." *Demography* 25(February): 35–49.

Bernard, William S. 1953. "Economic Effects of Immigration." In *American Dilemma*, B.M. Ziegler, ed. Boston: D.C. Heath and Company, pp. 50–70.

Berndt, Ernst R., and David O. Wood. 1975. "Technology, Prices, and the Derived Demand for Energy." *The Review of Economics and Statistics* 57 (August): 259–268.

Berndt, Ernst R., and N. Eugene Savin. 1975. "Estimation and Hypothesis Testing in Singular Equation Systems with Autoregressive Disturbances." *Econometrica* 43 (September-November): 937–958.

Blau, Francine D., and Marianne A. Ferber. 1992. *The Economics of Women, Men and Work.* Englewood Cliffs, New Jersey: Prentice-Hall.

Borjas, George J. 1985. "Assimilation, Changes in Cohort Quality, and the Earnings of Immigrants." *Journal of Labor Economics* 3(October): 463–489.

_____. 1986a. "The Sensitivity of Labor Demand Functions to Choice of Dependent Variables." *Review of Economics and Statistics* 68(February): 58–66.

_____. 1986b. "The Demographic Determinants of the Demand for Black Labor." In *The Black Youth Employment Crisis*, R. Freeman and H. Holzer, eds. Chicago: University of Chicago Press, pp. 191–232.

_____. 1987a. "Immigration, Minorities, and Labor Market Competition." *Industrial and Labor Relations Review* 40(April): 382–392.

_____. 1987b. "Self-Selection and the Earnings of Immigrants." *American Economic Review* 77(September): 531–553.

_____. 1990. *Friends or Strangers: The Impact of Immigrants on the U.S. Economy.* New York: Basic Books, Inc.

_____. 1992. "National Origin and the Skills of Immigrants in the Postwar Period." In *Immigration and the Work Force: Economic Consequences for the United States and Source Areas*, G.J. Borjas and R.B. Freeman, eds. Chicago: University of Chicago Press, pp. 17–47.

_____. 1995. "Assimilation and Changes in Cohort Quality Revisited: What Happened to Immigrant Earnings in the 1980s?" *Journal of Labor Economics* 13(April): 201–245.

Borjas, George J., and Stephen G. Bronars. 1991. "Immigration and the Family." *Journal of Labor Economics* 9(April): 123–148.

Borjas, George J., Richard B. Freeman, and Lawrence F. Katz. 1992. "On the Labor Market Effects of Immigration and Trade." In *Immigration and the Work Force: Economic Consequences for the United States and Source Areas*, George J. Borjas and Richard B. Freeman, eds. Chicago: University of Chicago Press, 213–244.

Borjas, George J., and Valerie A. Ramey. 1994. "Time-Series Evidence on the Sources of Trends in Wage Inequality." *American Economic Review, Papers and Proceedings* 84(May): 10–16.

Breusch, T., G.E. Mizon, and P. Schmidt. 1989. "Efficient Estimation Using Panel Data." *Econometrica* 57(May): 695–700.

Briggs, Vernon M., Jr. 1975a. "Illegal Aliens: The Need for a More Restrictive Border Policy." *Social Science Quarterly* 56(December): 477–491.

_____. 1975b. "Mexican Workers in the United States Labour Market: A Contemporary Dilemma." *International Labor Review* 112(November): 351–368.

Butcher, Kristin F., and David Card. 1991. "Immigration and Wages: Evidence from the 1980s." *American Economic Review, Papers and Proceedings* 81(May): 292–296.

Card, David. 1990. "The Impact of the Mariel Boatlift on the Miami Labor Market." *Industrial Relations Review* 43(January): 245–257.

Chiswick, Barry R. 1978. "The Effects of Americanization on the Earnings of Foreign-Born Men." *Journal of Political Economy* 85(October): 897–921.

_____. 1982. "The Impact of Immigration on the Level and Distribution of Economic Well-Being." In *The Gateway: U.S. Immigration Issues and Policies*, Barry R. Chiswick, ed. Washington, D.C.: American Enterprise Institute, pp. 289–313.

_____. 1986. "Is the New Immigration Less Skilled Than the Old?" *Journal of Labor Economics* 4(April): 168–192.

_____. 1993. "Soviet Jews in the United States: An Analysis of Their Linguistic and Economic Adjustment." *International Migration Review* 27(Summer): 260–286.

Chiswick, Barry R., and Paul W. Miller. 1992. "Language in the Immigrant Labor Market." In *Immigration, Language, and Ethnicity*, Barry R. Chiswick, ed. Washington, D.C.: The AEI Press, pp. 229–296.

Congressional Research Service, Library of Congress, Ninety-Sixth Congress. 1979. *U.S. Immigration Law and Policy: 1952–1979*, Washington, D.C.: U.S. Government Printing Office.

Congressional Research Service, Library of Congress, Ninety-Sixth Congress. 1980. *History of the Immigration and Naturalization Service*, Washington, D.C.: U.S. Government Printing Office.

Davila, Alberto E., and J. Peter Mattila. 1985. "Do Workers Earn Less along the U.S.-Mexico Border?" *Social Science Quarterly* 66(June): 310–318.

DeFreitas, Gregory. 1988. "Hispanic Immigration and Labor Market Segmentation." *Industrial Relations* 27 (Spring): 195–214.

DeFreitas, Gregory, and Adriana Marshall. 1984. "Immigration and Wage Growth in U.S. Manufacturing in the 1970s." *Industrial Relations Research Association, Proceedings of the Thirty-Sixth Annual Meeting*, December 28–30, 1983, San Francisco, California. Madison, Wisconsin: IRRA, pp. 148–156.

Djajic, Slobodan. 1989. "Skills and the Patterns of Migration: The Rule of Qualitative and Quantitative Restrictions on International Labor Mobility." *International Economic Review* 30(November): 795–809.

Donato, Katherine M. 1992. "Understanding U.S. Immigration: Why Some Countries Send Women and Others Send Men." In *Seeking Common Ground*, Donna Gabaccia, ed. Westport, Connecticut: Praeger Press, pp. 159–134.

Duffield, James A. 1990. *Estimating Farm Labor Elasticities to Analyze the Effects of Immigration Reform*. Staff Report no. AGES 90913, Agriculture and Rural Economy, Economy Division, Economic Research Service, U.S. Department of Agriculture.

Duleep, Harriet Orcutt, and Seth Sanders. 1993. "The Decision to Work by Married Immigrant Women." *Industrial and Labor Relations Review* 46(July): 677–690.

Easterlin, Richard A. 1961. "Influences in European Overseas Emigration before World War I." *Economic Development and Cultural Change* 9(April): 331–351.

Ferenczi, Imre, and Walter F. Willcox. 1929. *International Migrations, Vol, 1: Statistics.* New York: National Bureau of Economic Research.

Filer, Randall K. 1992. "The Effect of Immigrant Arrivals on Migratory Patterns of Native Workers." In *Immigration and the Work Force*, George J. Borjas and Richard B. Freeman, eds. Chicago: University of Chicago Press, pp. 245–269.

Friedberg, Rachael M. 1993. "The Labor Market Assimilation of Immigrants in the United States: The Role of Age at Arrival." Unpublished manuscript, Brown University.

Gallaway, Lowell E., and Richard K. Vedder. 1971. "Emigration from the United Kingdom to the United States: 1860–1913." *Journal of Economic History* 31(December): 885–897.

Gastil, Raymond D. 1987. *Freedom in the World.* New York: Greenwood Press.

Gemery, Henry A. 1994. "Immigrants and Emigrants: International Migration and the US Labor Market in the Great Depression." In *Migration and the International Labor Market, 1850–1939*, Timothy J. Hatton and Jeffrey G. Williamson, eds. London: Routledge, pp. 175–199.

Goldin, Claudia. 1994. "The Political Economy of Immigration Restriction in the United States, 1890 to 1921." In *The Regulated Economy: A Historical Approach to Political Economy*, Claudia Goldin and Gary D. Libecap, eds. Chicago: University of Chicago Press, pp. 223–257.

Gordon, Wendell. 1975. "A Case for a Less Restrictive Border Policy." *Social Science Quarterly* 56(December): 485–491.

Gould, J.D. 1979. "European Inter-Continental Emigration 1815–1914: Patterns and Causes." *The Journal of European Economic History* 8(Winter): 593–679.

Greenfield, Stanley R. (editor). 1992. *Who's Who in the United Nations and Related Agencies.* Detroit: Omnigraphics, Inc.

Greenwood, Michael J. 1983. "The Economics of Mass Migration from Poor to Rich Countries: Leading Issues of Fact and Theory." *American Economic Review, Papers and Proceedings* 73(May): 173–177.

_____. 1994. "Potential Channels of Immigrant Influence on the Economy of the Receiving County." *Papers in Regional Science* 73(3): 211–240

Greenwood, Michael J., and Gary L. Hunt. 1995. "Economic Effects of Immigrants on Native and Foreign-Born Workers: Complementarity, Substitutability, and Other Channels of Influence." *Southern Economic Journal* 61(April): 1076–1097.

Greenwood, Michael J., Gary L. Hunt, and Ulrich Kohli. 1996. "The Short- and Long-Run Factor-Market Consequences of Immigration to the United States." *Journal of Regional Science* 36(February): 43–66.

Greenwood, Michael J., and John M. McDowell. 1991. "Differential Economic Opportunity, Transferability of Skills, and Immigration to the United Sates and Canada." *Review of Economics and Statistics* 73(November): 612–623.

Greenwood, Michael J., John M. McDowell, and Eloise Trabka. 1991. "Conducting Descriptive and Analytical Research with the Immigration and Naturalization Service Public Use Tapes." *Journal of Economic and Social Measurement* 17: 131–153.

Greenwood, Michael J., John M. McDowell, and Donald M. Waldman. 1996. "A Model of the Skill Composition of U.S. Immigration." *Applied Economics* 28(March): 299–308.

Greenwood, Michael J., and Eloise Trabka. 1991. "Temporal and Spatial Patterns of Geographically Indirect Immigration to the United States." *International Migration Review* 25(Spring): 93–112.

Grossman, Jean Baldwin. 1982. "The Substitutability of Natives and Immigrants in Production." *Review of Economics and Statistics* 64(November): 596–603.

_____. 1984. "Illegal Immigrants and Domestic Employment." *Industrial and Labor Relations Review* 37(January): 240–251.

Harper, Elizabeth J., and Roland F. Chase. 1975. *Immigration Laws of the United States*. Indianapolis: Bobbs-Merrill Company, Inc., 3rd ed.

Hartley, William G. 1972. "United States Immigration Policy: The Case of the Western Hemisphere." *World Affairs* 135(Summer): 54–70.

Hatton, Timothy J., and Jeffrey G. Williamson. 1994. "International Migration 1850–1939: An Economic Survey." In *Migration and the International Labor Market, 1850–1939*, Timothy J. Hatton and Jeffrey G. Williamson, eds. London: Routledge, pp. 3–32.

Hausman, Jerry A., and William E. Taylor. 1981. "Panel Data and Unobservable Individual Effects." *Econometrica* 49(November): 1377–1398.

Higman, John. 1984. *Send These to Me: Immigrants in Urban America*. Baltimore: Johns Hopkins University Press.

Hill, Peter J. 1975. *The Economic Impact of Immigration into the United States*. New York: Arno Press.

Houstoun, Marion F., Roger G. Kramer, and Joan Mackin Barrett. 1984. "Female Predominance in Immigration to the United States since 1930: A First Look." *International Migration Review* 18(Winter): 908–963.

Huang, Wei-Chiao. 1987. "A Pooled Cross-Section and Time-Series Study of Professional Indirect Immigration to the United States." *Southern Economic Journal* 54(July): 95–109.

International Monetary Fund. Various years. *International Financial Statistics Yearbook.* Washington, D.C.: IMF Publication Services.

Jasso, Guillermina, and Mark R. Rosenzweig. 1982. "Estimating the Emigration Rates of Legal Immigrants Using Administrative and Survey Data: The 1971 Cohort of Immigrants to the United States." *Demography* 19(August): 279–290.

_____. 1990. *The Chosen People: Immigration in the United States.* New York: Russell Sage Foundation.

Jerome, Harry. 1926. *Migration and Business Cycles.* New York: National Bureau of Economic Research.

John S. Swift Co., Inc. (no date). *Air Traffic*, Worldwide Book I, New York.

Johnson, George E. 1979. "The Labor Market Effects of Immigration into the United States: A Summary of the Conceptual Issues." In *Interagency Task Force on Immigration Policy*, Staff Report Companion Papers, Departments of Justice, Labor, and State (August), pp. 109–162.

_____. 1980. "The Labor Market Effects of Immigration." *Industrial and Labor Relations Review* 33(April): 331–341.

Kimenyi, Mwangi S. 1989. "Immigration and Black-White Unemployment Rates in the United States." *Konjunkturpolitik*: 297–309.

King, Alan G., B. Lindsay Lowell, and Frank D. Bean. 1986. "The Effects of Hispanic Immigrants on the Earnings of Native Hispanic Americans." *Social Science Quarterly* 67(December): 673–689.

Kmenta, Jan. 1986. *Elements of Econometrics* (2nd ed.). New York: Macmillan.

Kuznets, Simon. 1958. "Long Swings in the Growth of the Population and Related Economic Variables." *Proceedings of the American Philosophical Society* 102(February): 25–52.

Kuznets, Simon, and Ernest Rubins. 1954. *Immigration and the Foreign Born*, Occasional Paper no. 46, National Bureau of Economic Research, New York, pp. 26–34.

LaLonde, Robert J., and Robert H. Topel. 1991a. "Labor Market Adjustments to Increased Migration." In *Immigration, Trade, and the Labor Market*, John M. Abowd and Richard B. Freeman, eds. Chicago: University of Chicago Press, pp. 167–199.

_____. 1991b. "Immigrants in the American Labor Market: Quality, Assimilation, and Distributional Effects." *American Economic Review, Papers and Proceedings* 81(May): 297–302.

Layard, Richard, Olivier Blanchard, Rudiger Dornbusch, and Paul Krugman. 1992. *East-West Migration: The Alternatives.* Cambridge, Massachusetts: MIT Press.

Leser, C.E.V. 1961. "Commodity Group Expenditure Functions for the United Kingdom, 1948–1957." *Econometrica* 29(January): 24–32.

Long, John E. 1980. "The Effect of Americanization on Earnings: Some Evidence from Women." *Journal of Political Economy* 88(June): 620–629.

Long, Stewart. 1987. "Undocumented Immigrants in the Los Angeles Garment Industry: Displacement or Dual Labor Market?" *Journal of Borderlands Studies* 2(Fall): 1–11.

Lucas, Robert E.B. 1976. "The Supply of Immigrants Function and Taxation of Immigrants Incomes." In *The Brain Drain and Taxation 2*, J.N. Bhagwati, ed. Amsterdam: North-Holland, pp. 63–82.

Maram, Sheldon L., and Jeanne C. King. 1983. *The Labor Market Impact of Hispanic Undocumented Immigrants: An Analysis of the Garment and Restaurant Industries in Los Angeles.* Study prepared for the Rockefeller Foundation.

Marshall, Ray. 1986. "Controlling Illegal Immigration," *Hearings before the Subcommittee on Economic Resources, Competitiveness and Security Economics of the Joint Economic Committee*, 99th U.S. Congress (May): 21–46.

Martin, Philip L. 1993. *Trade and Migration: NAFTA and Agriculture.* Washington, D.C.: Institute of International Economics.

Massey, Douglas S., Rafael Alarcon, Jorge Durand, and Huberto Gonzalez. 1987. *Return to Aztlan: The Social Process of International Migration from Western Mexico.* Berkeley: University of California Press.

Matta, Benjamin N., and Anthony V. Popp. 1988. "Immigration and the Earnings of Youth in the U.S." *International Migration Review* 22(Spring): 104–116.

McCarthy, Kevin F., and R. Burciaga Valdez. 1986. *Mexican Immigration in California: Dispelling the Myths about Migrants.* Santa Monica, California: RAND Corporation (May).

McDowell, John M., and Larry D. Singell, Jr. 1993. "An Assessment of the Human Capital Content of International Migrants: An Application to U.S. Immigrants." *Regional Studies* 27(4): 351–363.

McManus, Walter S., William Gould, and Finis Welch. 1983. "Earnings of Hispanic Men: The Role of English Language Proficiency." *Journal of Labor Economics* 1(April): 101–130.

McNamara, Regina. 1982. "Demographic Transition Theory." In *International Encyclopedia of Population*, Volume 1, John A. Ross, ed. New York: Free Press, pp. 146–147.

Mincer, Jacob. 1978. "Family Migration Decisions." *Journal of Political Economy* 86(October): 749–773.

Mines, Richard, and Philip L. Martin. 1984. "Immigrant Workers and the California Citrus Industry." *Industrial Relations* 23(Winter): 139–149.

Mokyr, Joel. 1983. *Why Ireland Starved: A Quantitative and Analytical History of the Irish Economy, 1800–1850.* London: George Allen & Unwin.

Muller, Thomas, and Thomas J. Espenshade. 1985. *The Fourth Wave: Californias New Immigrants.* Washington, D.C.: Urban Institute Press.

National Research Council. 1997. *The New Americans: Economic, Demographic, and Fiscal Effects of Immigration.* Washington, D.C.: National Academy Press.

Parks, Richard W. 1969. "Systems of Demand Equations: An Empirical Comparison of Alternative Functional Forms." *Econometrica* 37(October): 629–650.

Piore, Michael J. 1979. *Birds of Passage: Migrant Labor and Industrial Societies.* New York: Cambridge University Press.

Pollak, Robert A., and Terence J. Wales. 1969. "Estimation of the Linear Expenditure System." *Econometrica* 37(October): 611–628.

Quigley, John Michael. 1972. "An Economic Model of Swedish Emigration." *Quarterly Journal of Economics* 87(February): 111–126.

Ravenstein, E.G. 1885. "The Laws of Migration." *Journal of the Statistical Society* 48(June): 167–227.

Reports of the Immigration Commission, 61st Congress (1911), *Statistical Review of Immigration 1820–1910—Distribution of Immigrants 1850–1900,* Vol. 20, Washington, D.C.: U.S. Government Printing Office.

Rolph, Elizabeth S. 1992. *Immigration Policies: Legacy from the 1980s and Issues for the 1990s.* RAND report R-4184-FF, Santa Monica, California: RAND Corp.

Scott, Franklin D. 1972. *The Peopling of America: Perspectives on Immigration.* American Historical Association pamphlet 241, Washington, D.C.: American Historical Association.

Select Commission on Immigration and Refugee Policy. 1981. *U.S. Immigration Policy and the National Interest.* Staff report, Washington, D.C., April.

Simon, Julian L. 1984. "Immigration, Taxes and Welfare in the United States." *Population Development Review* 10(March): 55–69.

Simon, Julian L., Stephen Moore, and Richard Sullivan. 1993. "The Effect of Immigration on Aggregate Native Unemployment: An Across-City Estimation." *Journal of Labor Research* 14(Summer): 299–316.

Smith, Barton, and Robert Newman. 1977. "Depressed Wages along the U.S.-Mexico Border: An Empirical Analysis." *Economic Inquiry* 15(January): 51–66.

Smith, James P. 1991. "Hispanics and the American Dream: An Analysis of Hispanic Male Labor Market Wages 1940–1980." Photocopy, RAND Corp., Santa Monica, California.

Sorensen, Elaine, Frank D. Bean, Leighton Ku, and Wendy Zimmermann. 1992. *Immigration Categories and the U.S. Job Market: Do They Make a Difference?* Urban Institute report 92–1, Washington, D.C.: The Urban Institute Press.

Spengler, Joseph J. 1956. "Some Economic Aspects of Immigration into the United States." *Law and Contemporary Problems* 21(Spring): 277–296.

_____. 1958. "The Economic Effects of Migration." In *Selected Studies of Migration since World War II.* New York: Milbank Memorial Fund, pp. 172–192.

Stewart, James B., and Thomas J. Hyclak. 1986. "The Effects of Immigrants, Women, and Teenagers on the Relative Earnings of Black Males." *The Review of Black Political Economy* 15(Summer): 93–101.

Taylor, Philip. 1971. *The Distant Magnet: European Emigration to the U.S.A.* New York: Harper & Row.

Thomas, Brinley. 1973. *Migration and Economic Growth: A Study of Great Britain and the Atlantic Economy.* Cambridge, Massachusetts: Cambridge University Press.

Thomas, Dorothy Swain. 1941. *Social and Economic Aspects of Swedish Population Movements.* New York: Macmillan.

Topel, Robert H. 1994. "Regional Labor Markets and the Determinants of Wage Inequality." *American Economic Review, Papers and Proceedings* 84(May): 17–22.

Tyree, Andrea, and Katherine M. Donato. 1985. "The Sex Composition of Legal Immigrants to the United States." *Sociology and Social Research* 69(July): 577–589.

_____. 1986. "A Demographic Overview of the International Migration of Women." In *International Migration: The Female Experience,* Rita J. Simon and Caroline B. Brettel, eds. New York: Rowman and Allanheld, pp. 21–41.

UNESCO. Various years. *Statistical Yearbook.* Paris: United Nations Educational, Scientific and Cultural Organization.

United Nations. 1979. *Trends and Characteristics of International Migration Since 1950.* Department of Economic and Social Affairs, Demographic Studies No. 64, New York.

_____. 1995. *The Worlds Women: 1995 Trends and Statistics.* New York: United Nations.

_____. Various years. *Demographic Yearbook.* New York: United Nations.

U.S. Bureau of the Census. 1975. *Historical Statistics of the United States, Colonial Times to 1970.* Washington, D.C.: U.S. Government Printing Office.

U.S. Commission on Immigration Reform. 1995. *Legal Immigration: Setting Priorities.* Washington, D.C.

U.S. Department of Defense. Various years. *Selected Manpower Studies.* Washington, D.C.

U.S. Department of State, Bureau of Consular Affairs. 1987. *Report of the Visa Office 1986.* Washington, D.C.: Department of State Publications.

_____. 1997. *Visa Bulletin* 7(April), Washington, D.C.

U.S. General Accounting Office. 1986. *Illegal Aliens: Limited Research Suggests Illegal Aliens May Displace Native Workers.* GAO/PEMD-86-9BR, April.

_____. 1988. *Illegal Aliens: Influence of Illegal Workers on Wages and Working Conditions of Legal Workers.* GAO/PEMD-88-13BR, March.

U.S. Immigration and Naturalization Service. 1972. *Annual Report of the Immigration and Naturalization Service, 1972.* Washington, D.C.: U.S. Government Printing Office.

_____. 1989. *1988 Statistical Yearbook of the Immigration and Naturalization Service.* Washington, D.C.: U.S. Government Printing Office.

_____. 1991. *1990 Statistical Yearbook of the Immigration and Naturalizaton Service.* Washington, D.C.: U.S. Government Printing Office.

_____. 1992. *1991 Statistical Yearbook of the Immigration and Naturalization Service.* Washington, D.C.: U.S. Government Printing Office.

_____. 1996. *1994 Statistical Yearbook of the Immigration and Naturalization Service.* Washington, D.C.: U.S. Government Printing Office.

_____. 1997. *1995 Statistical Yearbook of the Immigration and Naturalization Service.* Washington, D.C.: U.S. Government Printing Office.

U.S. Social Security Administration Office of Research, Evaluation and Statistics. Various years. *Social Security Programs throughout the World.* Washington, D.C.: U.S. Government Printing Office.

Vialet, Joyce. 1980. *A Brief History of U.S. Immigration Policy.* Report no. 80-223 EPW, Congressional Research Service, The Library of Congress.

Waldinger, Roger. 1985. "Immigration and Industrial Change in the New York City Apparel Industry." In *Hispanics in the U.S. Economy,* George J. Borjas and Marta Tienda, eds. Orlando, Florida: Academic Press, Inc., pp. 323–349.

Warren, Robert, and Ellen Percy Kraly. 1985. *The Elusive Exodus: Emigration from the United States.* Occasional Paper no. 8, Population Trends and Public Policy, Washington, D.C.: Population Reference Bureau, Inc.

Weintraub, Sidney, Francisco Alba, Rafael Fernåndez de Castro, and Manuel Garcia y Griego. 1998. "Responses to Migration Issues." In *Migration between Mexico and the United States*, Binational Study, Volume 1. U.S. Commission on Immigration Reform and Mexican Ministry of Foreign Affairs. Austin, Texas: Morgan Printing.

Wilkinson, Maurice. 1967. "Evidence of Long Swings in the Growth of Swedish Population and Related Economic Variables." *Journal of Economic History* 27(March): 17–38.

_____. 1970. "European Migration to the United States: An Econometric Analysis of Aggregate Labor Supply and Demand." *The Review of Economics and Statistics* 52(August): 272–279.

Williamson, Jeffrey. 1982. "Immigrant-Inequality Trade-Offs in the Promised Land: Income Distribution and Absortive Capacity Prior to the Quotas." In *The Gateway: U.S. Immigration Issues and Policies*, Barry R. Chiswick, ed. Washington, D.C.: American Enterprise Institute, pp. 251–288.

Winegarden, C.R., and Lay Boon Khor. 1991. "Undocumented Immigration and Unemployment of U.S. Youth and Minority Workers: Econometric Evidence." *Review of Economics and Statistics* 73(1): 105–112.

World Almanac Books. 1996. *World Almanac*. Mahwah, New Jersey: Funk and Wagnalls.

World Bank. Various years. *World Tables*. Baltimore: Johns Hopkins University Press.

Author Index

Subject Index

About the Institute

The W.E. Upjohn Institute for Employment Research is a nonprofit research organization devoted to finding and promoting solutions to employment-related problems at the national, state, and local levels. It is an activity of the W.E. Upjohn Unemployment Trustee Corporation, which was established in 1932 to administer a fund set aside by the late Dr. W.E. Upjohn, founder of The Upjohn Company, to seek ways to counteract the loss of employment income during economic downturns.

The Institute is funded largely by income from the W.E. Upjohn Unemployment Trust, supplemented by outside grants, contracts, and sales of publications. Activities of the Institute comprise the following elements: 1) a research program conducted by a resident staff of professional social scientists; 2) a competitive grant program, which expands and complements the internal research program by providing financial support to researchers outside the Institute; 3) a publications program, which provides the major vehicle for disseminating the research of staff and grantees, as well as other selected works in the field; and 4) an Employment Management Services division, which manages most of the publicly funded employment and training programs in the local area.

The broad objectives of the Institute's research, grant, and publication programs are to 1) promote scholarship and experimentation on issues of public and private employment and unemployment policy, and 2) make knowledge and scholarship relevant and useful to policymakers in their pursuit of solutions to employment and unemployment problems.

Current areas of concentration for these programs include causes, consequences, and measures to alleviate unemployment; social insurance and income maintenance programs; compensation; workforce quality; work arrangements; family labor issues; labor-management relations; and regional economic development and local labor markets.